Bigfoot Casebook
Updated

Bigfoot Casebook Updated

Sightings and Encounters from 1818 to 2004

Janet & Colin Bord

Foreword by Loren Coleman

Pine Winds Press

Pine Winds Press
An imprint of Idyll Arbor, Inc.

Cover Design: Judy Ness
Pine Winds Press Editor: Thomas M. Blaschko

Revised and updated version of *The Bigfoor Casebook*, first published in 1982.

ISBN 0-937663-10-7

Library of Congress Cataloging-in-Publication Data

Bord, Janet, 1945-
  Bigfoot casebook updated : sightings and encounters from 1818 to 2004 / Janet & Colin Bord.
    p. cm.
  Rev. ed. of: Bigfoot casebook. c1982.
  Includes bibliographical references and index.
  ISBN-13: 978-0-937663-10-3 (alk. paper)
  ISBN-10: 0-937663-10-7 (alk. paper)
  1. Sasquatch. I. Bord, Colin. II. Bord, Janet, 1945- Bigfoot casebook. III. Title.
  QL89.2.S2B67 2005
  001.944--dc22

                                                        2005019264

Contents

Part 1
Bigfoot Across North America

Part 2
Chronological List of Bigfoot Sightings 1818-1980

Acknowledgments

This book could not have been written but for the hard work carried out by Bigfoot investigators in the United States and Canada, and also by those who take the trouble to publish the data and thus make it available to researchers. Many of these people have been most helpful to us, supplying details of investigations and other useful information. We especially wish to thank Lucius Farish and Warren Thompson, both mines of information; and John Green, for allowing us to mention many cases collected by him and published in his own invaluable books on Bigfoot. Also helpful were Archie Buckley, Tim Church, Loren Coleman, Cliff Crook, René Dahinden, Dave Drake, George W. Earley, Henry Franzoni, John Fuhrmann, Mark A. Hall, Grace Gensman Hamby, Joan LaBord Jeffers, Norman O. Josephsen, Wayne W. King, Edward Loughran, Gary S. Mangiacopra, Christopher L. Murphy, Daniel Perez, Marion T. Place, Ron Schaffner, Mike and Linda Ward, R. Martin Wolf, and Don Worley.

For help with illustrations we wish to thank Loren Coleman, Cliff Crook, René Dahinden, Paul Freeman, Tony Healy, Peter Jordan, Wayne

W. King, *The Mobridge Tribune,* Christopher L. Murphy, Daniel Perez, Wesley Proppe, William M. Rebsamen, Ron Schaffner, Richard Svensson, Warren Thompson, and R. Martin Wolf. Most of the illustrations are held by the Fortean Picture Library, and sources are given after each illustration (RD=René Dahinden).

Grateful acknowledgment is made to the following for their kind permission to reprint copyright material:

The Editor, for material from the Vancouver, WA, *Columbian*; William P. Cheshire, Editor-in-Chief, for material from the Charleston, WV, *Daily Mail;* René Dahinden, for extracts from *Sasquatch* by Don Hunter with René Dahinden; excerpt from *Situation Red: The UFO Siege* by Leonard H. Stringfield, copyright 1977 by Leonard H. Stringfield. Reprinted by permission of Doubleday & Company, Inc. and Sphere Books Ltd.; Charles Edmonds, for an extract from his report on the 1962 sighting at Fort Bragg; Albert Fletcher, for his 1917 sighting report; John Green and Cheam Publishing Ltd., for extracts from Albert Ostman's abduction story; Jove Publications, Inc., for an extract from *Abominable Snowman: Legend Come to Life* by Ivan T. Sanderson, copyright 1961, 1968 by Ivan T. Sanderson; Mrs. Callie Lund, for an extract from her 1969 letter to John Green; Elliott Merrick, for an extract from his book *True North;* Ron Schaffner, for extracts from two sighting reports (Gallipolis 1912, Eaton 1977); Stewart Spencer, Editor, for material from the Charlotte, NC, *News,* reprinted by permission of *The Charlotte News;* C.P. Cheney, Managing Editor, for material from the Ogden, UT, *Standard-Examiner;* Mrs. Myrtle Walton, for William Roe's 1955 sighting report; R. Martin Wolf, for extracts from his report on the 1977 Wantage sightings; Mrs. Bruce Wright, for an extract from *Wildlife Sketches, Near and Far* by Bruce S. Wright; Burns Yeomans, for an extract from his 1939/40 sighting report.

We would like to add a further acknowledgment to this updated edition. Our thanks go to Tom Blaschko for his enthusiasm, to Loren Coleman for his generous help, and not least to the late great René Dahinden for his spirit and determination.

The Bigfoot Casebook: A Classic Renewed for the Ages

Foreword by Loren Coleman

You are reading a book that I feel changed the history of Bigfoot research. Let me explain.

One day, sometime in the 1960s, we all woke up and the world had grown decidedly weirder. Was it the anti-war, peace, and hippie movements? Or the cultural trends evidenced in the music revolution and new sexual freedoms? Could it have been the breakout from the Eisenhower doldrums and unreality of the shock from the JFK assassination? It seems like it was much more than the Beatles and Vietnam that changed us all. But something did happen, and it altered the landscape of Bigfoot studies too.

During the 1960s, Bigfoot began to bask in the glow of continental wonder, much differently than how "wildmen" and Sasquatch had experienced the calmer local outbreaks of interest before 1958. Certainly, the post-Patterson-Gimlin film days seemed, at first, to be a moment in Bigfoot history when the ultimate quest appeared nearly at an end. One of these animals would be captured and classified soon, it was assumed, and a new zoological discovery tale would be told. But then a detour down some side roads in Minnesota and Bossburg gave a hint of a bizarre new age ahead. The ensuing period became known as one of "high strangeness."

The impact of those times still influences the stories gathered, and the books produced today. It was an era in which the mixing of several threads of the inexplicable overlapped, danced about together, and merged. Bigfoot met Forteana, whether it was globes, cattle mutilations, electromagnetic effects, or other bizarre imports from the world of the so-called paranormal.

Ufologist Jerome Clark talks of the transformations of this period in his 1996 encyclopedia, *High Strangeness: UFOs from 1960 through 1979*. Clark noted that the "UFO controversy [changed] from a debate about aerial phenomena into one about experiences at ground level...[in which] the strangeness of the content of these claims seemed to escalate. No wonder many ufologists lost their bearings. The distinction between a hoaxer's tall tale and a frightened witness' sincere testimony blurs when the content of one is barely less outlandish than the other. Both shameless liars and earnest souls told of meetings, sometimes with extended communication, with alien humanoids." Clark also noted that other persons spoke "falsely or sincerely" of sightings of hairy creatures, which he has characterized as "Hairy Biped" sightings, some in conjunction, supposedly, with UFOs.

During the 1970s, individuals like California researcher Peter Guttilla began discussing what he saw as the overlapping nature of Bigfoot and UFO reports. Mostly unaccredited talks between Guttilla, Barbara Ann Slate, and Alan Berry would lead to writings by Slate and Berry highlighting the UFO link to Bigfoot sightings.

In Pennsylvania, UFO researcher Stan Gordon was promoting attention for the strange hairy creature reports that were coming his way. He was especially intrigued by a rash of reports beginning in 1973 that seemed to link sightings of Bigfoot and UFOs. Gordon told of sightings on October 25, 1973, near Uniontown and Greensburg, on November 2, 1974, again near Uniontown, and on February 6, 1974, in rural Fayette County, Pennsylvania, in which glowing objects would be seen near where Bigfoot were also being seen. Through police officers alerting Stan Gordon, he and Dr. Berthold Eric Schwarz did the primary investigations on these cases. Tracks found at a landing site, Bigfoot seen near a UFO site, and other tentative associations made the UFO/Bigfoot link for Gordon, and he was convinced of the interactions. "We have hundreds of unexplained cases that stand out," he said.

Other Ufologists were getting into the Bigfoot business too. Coral Lorenzen, Leonard Stringfield, Andrew Collins, Dr. Leo Sprinkle, John S. Derr, R. Martin Wolf, and Steven Mayne began looking into hairy creature sightings during the 1970s. These individuals' ufological philosophies caused them to think in terms of their frame of references and their literature now contains clear-cut Bigfoot accounts, which were collected by ufologists. There is no doubt a body of work that has Bigfoot-like creatures directly connected to UFO sightings has been deduced and chronicled by ufologists (not Forteans, not cryptozoologists) as worthy of their time. Other authors, such as Brad Steiger, Warren Smith, and their humorously combined single author, known under the pseudonym "Eric Norman," were also producing paperback books full of new stories of UFOs and apemen.

In New York, writer John A. Keel was pondering the material he gathered a few years earlier in a place called Point Pleasant, West Virginia, which lumped Bigfoot, dog killings, Mothman, Men-In-Black, and UFOs in the same vortex. The volume he wrote even before his famous *Mothman* book was published in 1975 was *Strange Creatures from Time and Space* (1970). It was typical of the new wave of paperback books that would capture the mood of the times. A year before *Strange Creatures* came out, Keel had introduced Jerome Clark to me and we carried on a lively exchange of stories and ideas. I found myself investigating the reports of glowing red-eyed creatures, such as those haunting the cornfields of Farmer City, Illinois in 1970, and the railways during the Enfield Horror of 1973. Clark, in the meantime was digging into airship reports and exploring fairy lore and ufology. By the mid-1970s, Clark and Coleman were actually coauthoring articles that merged our two fields of study, full of sociological and psychological assessments, including the now rejected Jungian hypothesis set forth in our *Creatures of the Outer Edge* (1978, reprinted 2006). Creatures spawned a wave of psychosocial thinking that lives on today in various pockets of theorizing still current in Europe.

Clark, with the distance of time, looked anew at Hairy Bipeds and UFOs in 1996, when he noted: "In the most extreme UFO stories — those that allege extensive communications with (usually benevolent) extraterrestrials — Hairy Bipeds make an occasional appearance." Clark, while intrigued by the reports in the 1970s, concluded that the evidence for direct contact between the Bigfoot and UFOs is anything but secure. He finishes with this observation: "These are huge suppositions tied to small evidence. At this stage, given the limitations of human knowledge, there is hardly anything about Hairy Bipeds, or their possible connections with the UFO phenomena, that can be stated with any degree of confidence."

It was into these times of high strangeness that Janet and Colin Bord stepped in, to write their book *The Bigfoot Casebook*, first published in 1982, and in the revised version, which you now are reading. The Bords sharply captured the mood of the times, and they must be congratulated for this classic work in the field of hominology, for it succeeded on a couple of essential fronts. First of all, their approach was different from other chroniclers. This collection has always been important because the Bords strictly documented "sightings" — without restrictions to location — in time and space — without getting sidetracked by debates about tracks, signs, and "Pacific-Northwest-only" groupings.

Furthermore, praise can be given to this early work, updated here in this new book, by speaking a moment about its unique Fortean point of view. Whereas other books on Bigfoot and Sasquatch may have looked at the data to support notions that certain-sized, specifically looking creatures might exist in special locations, the Bords broke that mold. Without being bogged down by excluding information because it just "didn't fit" into someone's theories, the Bords open-mindedly examined what data came their way. The Bords' use of a Fortean philosophy of inclusion combined with a restrictive exclusive look at eyewitness accounts gave this book a cutting edge, critical-thinking, open-minded, skeptical angle in times in which people were falling all over each other to push their own fossil candidates for Bigfoot or promoting their own theory about what Bigfoot *really* are. The Bords presented the data, without bias actually, stepped back, and allowed decades of researchers to make of it what they wanted.

For that reason, in many ways, the Bords' *The Bigfoot Casebook* with its straightforward sightings and chronology, put hominology back on track. Only through looking at all the sightings can we begin to see that several qualities and kinds of hairy hominoids appear to be in the mix. The Bords' singular book, coming out as it did, must be credited as a major milestone allowing a broader and more extensive examination of all the data. For that, the Bords must be appreciated, and the flow of hominology was forever extended to examining credible reports from throughout North America, and not in just a special little corner of the Pacific Northwest.

On another level, of course, the skeptics, debunkers, fast-money promoters, and fake artists are still out there. If nothing more, this book demonstrates that a mountain of good evidence exists for these creatures, these unknown animals we today call Bigfoot, Sasquatch, cryptids all, that may be finally discovered in your lifetime. The Bords have updated this classic, and you will not be disappointed. In the wake of the Ray Wallace fiasco, we must carve out the positive nature such things bring to us, including dismissing fake footprints that no longer deserve our attention and appreciating the need for this book. But the converse of bad footprints still in the record and being published as "good data" is the sightings, as shown here in this work, which still are occurring. It is obvious a thousand sightings cannot easily be explained away, whether it's Patterson-Gimlin's Bigfoot of 1967 or those recent sightings from Manitoba and the Yukon.

Enjoy a masterpiece that changed the direction of Bigfoot research, all for the good.

— Loren Coleman 12 July 2005
Author, *Bigfoot! The True Story of Apes in America* (2003),
The Field Guide to Bigfoot, Yeti, and Other Mystery Primates Worldwide (1999), and many other works in cryptozoology.

Preface

Unlike the Himalayan Yeti, or Abominable Snowman, the North American "Bigfoot" has only achieved worldwide notoriety in the last few decades. But sightings of this tall, hairy, manlike creature go back to at least the beginning of the nineteenth century and in quantity far exceed the number of sightings of similar creatures in the Himalayas. It was at first thought that Bigfoot dwelt only in the forested mountain ranges of the northwest United States and southwestern Canada, and hunters concentrated their searches on those areas. But research has shown that creatures of a similar kind have been seen all over the United States, one of the bigger concentrations of reports coming from faraway Florida in the southeast. The only American mainland states for which we at present have no reports on file are Delaware, Rhode Island, and South Carolina. But this does not mean that no Bigfeet have been seen there. Other researchers may have found cases, or Bigfoot-type footprints may have been found; we do not claim that our collection of cases is complete. Many reports, published in local newspapers, may never have been picked up by Bigfoot investigators, especially those reports published before the 1960s. And of course, not everyone who sees a Bigfoot reports it. Fearing ridicule, many people keep quiet about their sightings. But we feel confident that the 1,000 cases detailed in our "Chronological List of Sightings" give a representative picture of Bigfoot activity in the United States and Canada during the years the list covers: 1818-1980.

Many of the available reports simply describe huge footprints found in earth, sand, mud, or snow. The only sensible explanation for such prints, when experienced investigators have judged them to be genuine and not made by hoaxers, is that they were made by a Bigfoot-type creature. Often a Bigfoot is also seen in the area, and sometimes the creature is watched as it makes the prints. The last example is the only type of footprint case we include in this book. So many footprints have been found that we decided to concentrate on those reports that describe sightings of the creature itself. Plenty of data on footprints is available in the books listed in the Bibliography.

The cases are presented chronologically rather than geographically because, as far as we know, such a presentation has not been attempted before, and it may reveal patterns that will help researchers in determining the nature of the beast. John Green has already provided a useful geographical survey in his book *Sasquatch: The Apes Among Us*. Because the arrangement is chronological, those reports where no year was mentioned could not be included. This has meant excluding a few cases with intriguing details, but such cases can be found in other books.

Since the main aim of this book is to present a roundup of Bigfoot sightings from 1800 to the present day, and we have many hundreds of cases on file, it is not possible for every case to be described in detail. Therefore, although all the cases we have on record are included in the Chronological List of Sightings at the end of the book, only the most interesting have been fully described in the main body of the book. Nor do we have space to discuss the theories that have been put forward to explain the presence of a hairy giant in modern North America. Other writers have already done this, and their conclusions can be found in the books detailed in the Bibliography.

If before seeing this book you have read a Bigfoot report and thought, "It must be a hoax!", then read on, for in our *Bigfoot Casebook Updated* we present enough reports to convince the most determined skeptic that something strange and unexplained roams the wilderness in North America.

Part 1

Bigfoot Across North America

1
Wild Men of the Woods
Pre-1900

Today, apparently sane United States and Canadian citizens are, in the hundreds, reporting seeing creatures which do not, indeed cannot, exist in those countries. What they usually see is a tall, hairy, long-armed, heavy man-beast standing upright on its hind legs — an impossibility, according to most scientists. Are we then to believe either that hundreds, even thousands, of North American citizens are experiencing similar hallucinations (and have been for more than 190 years), or that all over the country 7-9-foot-tall people are bowing to an irresistible impulse to dress up in fur suits and frighten people? If that is the case, the hoaxers must really be mad, not to mention supernaturally protected against gunfire. In many instances, hunters have fired at Bigfoot, as the man-beast is often called, but it rarely seems unduly worried by the impact of the bullets, even when fired from point-blank range.

Figure 1: Bigfoot/Sasquatch: early human, giant ape, ghost, or figment of the imagination? *Picture: Richard Svensson/FPL*

Taking into consideration the different interpretation placed on "wild man" reports in the nineteenth century, the pattern of Bigfoot's behavior remains largely consistent throughout the 190 years for which there are records, which seems to suggest that, whatever Bigfoot is, it has been around for a long time. Was it the first human occupant of North America, a prehistoric survival whose territory is increasingly being encroached upon by the avaricious white man? Or is it some unknown kind of giant ape? Both theories have their proponents, as does the idea that it is non-physical, a phantom monster. As our story unfolds, some evidence will seem to support one theory, some will support another. The Bigfoot enigma remains unsolved, a tale full of contradiction, confusion, and conflict.

Our search for Bigfoot begins in New York State in 1818. This report from the *Exeter Watchman* of 22 September 1818 is the oldest North American newspaper report of a Bigfoot sighting yet discovered, and its content is startling. If we ignore the dated wording, this could be a report of a sighting nearly 200 years later.

Sacket's Harbor (N.Y.) Sept. 6
ANOTHER WONDER

Report says, that in the vicinity of Ellisburgh, was seen on the 30th Ult. by a gentleman of unquestionable veracity, an animal resembling the Wild Man of the Woods. It is stated that he came from the woods within a few rods of this gentleman — that he stood and looked at him and then took his flight in a direction which gave a perfect view of him for some time. He is described as bending forward when running — hairy, and the heel of the foot narrow, spreading at the toes. Hundreds of persons have been in pursuit for several days, but nothing further is heard or seen of him.

The frequent and positive manner in which this story comes, induces us to believe it. We wish not to impeach the veracity of

this highly favored gentleman — yet, it is proper that such naturally improbable accounts should be established by the mouth of
at least two direct eyewitnesses to entitle them to credit.

Twenty years later, in the late 1830s, there were reports of a "wild
child" around Fish Lake in Indiana. Four feet tall, and with a covering of
chestnut hair, it was often seen among the sand hills near the lake, as well
as swimming in the water. It ran very fast and could not be caught, and
made awful yelling and whining noises. Also in the 1830s, but farther
east, in Pennsylvania, child-size hairy creatures were seen on at least two
occasions, as this report, published afterwards in newspapers, describes:

STRANGE ANIMAL,
OR FOOD FOR THE MARVELLOUS

Something like a year ago, there was considerable talk about a
strange animal, said to have been seen in the southwestern part
of Bridgewater. Although the individual who described the animal persisted in declaring that he had seen it, and was at first
considerably frightened by it, the story was heard and looked
upon more as food for the marvellous, than as having any
foundation in fact.

He represented the animal as we have it through a third person, as having the appearance of a child seven or eight years old
though somewhat slimmer and covered entirely with hair. He
saw it, while picking berries, walking towards him erect and
whistling like a person. After recovering from his fright, he is
said to have pursued it, but it ran off with such speed, whistling
as it went, that he could not catch it. He said it ran like the
"devil," and continued to call it after that name.

The same or similar looking animal was seen in Silver Lake
township about two weeks since, by a boy some sixteen years
old. We had the story from the father of the boy, in his absence,

and afterward from the boy himself. The boy was sent to work in the backwoods near the New York state line. He took with him a gun, and was told by his father to shoot anything he might see except persons or cattle.

After working a while, he heard some person, a little brother as he supposed, coming toward him whistling quite merrily. It came within a few rods of him and stopped.

He said it looked like a human being, covered with black hair, about the size of his brother, who was six or seven years old. His gun was some little distance off, and he was very much frightened. He, however, got his gun and shot at the animal, but trembled so that he could not hold it still.

The strange animal, just as his gun "went off," stepped behind a tree, and then ran off, whistling as before. The father said the boy came home very much frightened, and that a number of times during the afternoon, when thinking about the animal he had seen he would, to use the man's own words, "burst out crying."

Apart from their small stature, these "wild boys" sound exactly like the huge Bigfeet seen today. Perhaps they were young Bigfeet, or a similar but smaller species? The "wild man" seen in Arkansas during the first half of the nineteenth century was "of gigantic stature." Known since at least 1834 in St. Francis, Greene, and Poinsett Counties, two hunters had a close encounter with it in Greene County in 1851. They saw a herd of cattle apparently being chased, and, watching, they found that the pursuer was "an animal bearing the unmistakable likeness of humanity. He was of gigantic stature, the body being covered with hair and the head with long locks that fairly enveloped the neck and shoulders. The 'wild man' after looking at them deliberately for a short time, turned and ran away with great speed, leaping twelve to fourteen feet at a time. His footprints measured thirteen inches each." The local explanation for this strange being, an explanation as far-fetched as some of today's, was that "he was a survivor of the earthquake disaster which desolated that region in 1811." A common factor of these early reports is that the creature is described as a "wild man" or "wild boy," with the implication that the creature was a human being who had taken to the woods and in doing so somehow developed a thick coat of body hair.

In the same decade, the 1850s, gold prospectors in California's Mount Shasta area were seeing Bigfeet. As John Weeks recalled in 1959 after reading an article on Bigfoot:

> My grandfather prospected for gold in the eighteen fifties throughout the region described as being the home of the Snow-man. Upon grandfather's return to the East he told stories of seeing hairy giants in the vicinity of Mount Shasta. These monsters had long arms but short legs. One of them picked up a 20-foot section of a sluiceway and smashed it to bits against a tree.
>
> When grandfather told us these stories, we didn't believe him at all. Now, after reading your article, it turns out he wasn't as big a liar as we youngsters thought he was.

The Bigfoot's habit of destroying equipment and belongings of any white men who have penetrated into his territory, almost as if it resented their presence and wished to frighten them away, is a feature which will reappear in later reports.

A story of forest giants told by a hunter named Bauman was recounted at length by Theodore Roosevelt in his book *Wilderness Hunter,* and the events he describes, dated roughly to the mid-nineteenth century, are evidence that Bigfoot (if indeed it was the culprit) can sometimes act violently towards humans. But since Bauman never actually saw a clearly identifiable Bigfoot, and this is a book of sighting reports, we will give only brief details of the case. Bauman and a fellow trapper were in the mountains near the Wisdom River on the Idaho-Montana border. While away from their camp something destroyed their lean-to and investigated their belongings. Footprints had been left, showing that the intruder walked on two legs. That night, Bauman awoke and glimpsed a great dark shape, which he fired at; he also smelled a strong odor. The next evening, on returning to camp, the men found their lean-to again destroyed, and they decided next morning to leave the area. They began to collect their traps, and later they split up, Bauman going to fetch the last three traps, his friend returning to their camp. When Bauman several hours later got back to the camp he found it strangely silent. His friend lay dead, his neck broken and four fang marks in his throat. "The footprints of the unknown beast-creature, printed deep in the soft soil, told the whole story."

If the following story is to be believed, a creature whose description resembled that of the Bigfeet reported today was actually captured in Arkansas in the second half of the nineteenth century. There is no well-authenticated capture on record, though we know of six cases where Bigfoot-like creatures of various sizes have allegedly been captured, all before 1920. It seems strange that, if Bigfeet really have been captured in the past, none has been captured today, in view of the intense interest in the creature, and the numbers of hunters roaming his territory, keen to be the first to bring in a Bigfoot, dead or alive. The creature's apparent ability to avoid this fate suggests either that the old-time capture stories are untrue, or that what was captured was not a Bigfoot as we know them today, or that Bigfeet have become wilier and more suspicious of man. But this last is not borne out by the number of instances where a Bigfoot curiously strolls over to investigate a forest camp and is seen by its occupants, who could theoretically (i.e. were they properly equipped and knowledgeable) capture the beast. Presumably the Bigfoot realizes that in such instances it has little to fear from humans. But the problem remains: Why is it apparently unaffected by gunfire? This question will be repeated throughout this book, as we record many instances of apparent invulnerability to gunfire, but meanwhile let us return to the subject of captured Bigfeet. The story of a nineteenth-century capture was told by Otto Ernest Rayburn in his 1941 book *Ozark Country*. According to Rayburn, the Giant of the Hills was often seen in the Arkansas Ouachita

Mountains. This 7-foot "wild man" was covered with thick hair and lived in caves or by the Saline River. Everyone was afraid of him, although he does not appear to have harmed anyone. The decision was made to capture him, and the story tells that the men actually succeeded in this. They lassoed him in his cave and took him away to Benton jail. They also dressed him in clothes, which he tore off before escaping from the small wooden building. He was recaptured, but there the story suddenly ends.

Around the same time (the late 1860s), but in Kansas, to the north-west of Arkansas, many of the inhabitants of the Arcadia Valley in Crawford County saw a "wild man or gorilla, or 'what is it?'" The description which follows could apply equally well to many sightings being made now, nearly 140 years later. Remember that this report of 1869 was made at a time when "Bigfoot" was unheard of, and so Mr. Trimble's description was unlikely to have been influenced by other sighting reports.

...Several times it has approached the cabins of the settlers much to the terror of the women and children, especially if the men happen to be absent working in the fields. In one instance it approached the house of one of our old citizens, but was driven away with clubs by one of the men.

It has so near a resemblance to the human form that the men are unwilling to shoot it. It is difficult to give a description of this wild man or animal. It has a stooping gait, very long arms with immense hands or claws; it has a hairy face and those who have been near it describe it as having a most ferocious expression of countenance; generally walks on its hind legs but sometimes on all fours. The beast or "what is it?" is as cowardly as it is ugly and it is next to impossible to get near enough to obtain a good view of it.

The settlers, not knowing what to call it, have christened it "Old Sheff." Since its appearance our fences are often found

down, allowing the stock free range in our corn fields. I suppose
Old Sheff is only following his inclination, as it may be easier
for him to pull them down than to climb over. However, as it is,
curses loud and deep are heaped upon its head by the settlers.
The settlers are divided in opinion as to whether it belongs to the
human family or not. Probably it will be found to be a gorilla or
large orangutan that has escaped from some menagerie in the settlements east of here.

At one time over sixty of the citizens turned out to hunt it
down, but it escaped; but probably owing to the fright that it
received it kept out of sight for several days, and just as the settlers were congratulating themselves that they were rid of an
intolerable nuisance, Old Sheff came back again, seemingly as
savage as ever.

If this meets the eye of any showman who has lost one of his
collection of beasts, he may know where to find it. At present it
is the terror of all women and children in the valley. It cannot be
caught and nobody is willing to shoot it.

While the inhabitants of the Arcadia Valley were having to put up
with the presence of Old Sheff around their homes, away to the west in
California a hunter witnessed some unusual Bigfoot behavior, which has
rarely been recorded. The hunter, from Grayson, California, wrote a long
letter to the Antioch *Ledger,* part of which we now quote:

…Last fall [i.e. 1869] I was hunting in the mountains about 20
miles south of here [i.e. in the vicinity of Orestimba Creek], and
camped five or six days in one place, as I have done every
season for the past fifteen years. Several times I returned to
camp, after a hunt, and saw that the ashes and charred sticks
from the fireplace had been scattered about. An old hunter
notices such things, and very soon gets curious to know the
cause. Although my bedding and traps and little stores were not

disturbed, as I could see, I was anxious to learn who or what it was that so regularly visited my camp, for clearly the half burnt sticks and cinders could not scatter themselves about.

I saw no tracks near the camp, as the hard ground covered with leaves would show none. So I started in a circle around the place, and three hundred yards off, in damp sand, I struck the track of a man's foot, as I supposed — bare and of immense size. Now I was curious, sure, and I resolved to lay for the barefooted visitor. I accordingly took a position on a hillside, about sixty or seventy feet from the fire, and, securely hid in the brush, I waited and watched. Two hours and more I sat there and wondered if the owner of the feet would come again, and whether he imagined what an interest he had created in my enquiring mind, and finally what possessed him to be prowling about there with no shoes on.

The fireplace was on my right, and the spot where I saw the track was on my left, hid by the bushes. It was in this direction that my attention was mostly directed, thinking the visitor would appear there, and besides, it was easier to sit and face that way. Suddenly I was surprised by a shrill whistle, such as boys produce with two fingers under their tongues, and turning quickly, I ejaculated, "Good God!" as I saw the object of my solicitude standing beside my fire, erect, and looking suspiciously around. It was the image of a man, but it could not have been human.

I was never so benumbed with astonishment before. The creature, whatever it was, stood fully five feet high, and disproportionately broad and square at the fore shoulders, with arms of great length. The legs were very short and the body long. The head was small compared with the rest of the creature, and appeared to be set upon his shoulders without a neck. The whole was covered with dark brown and cinnamon colored hair, quite long on some parts, that on the head standing in a shock and growing close down to the eyes, like a Digger Indian's.

As I looked he threw his head back and whistled again, and then stopped and grabbed a stick from the fire. This he swung round, until the fire on the end had gone out, when he repeated the maneuver. I was dumb, almost, and could only look. Fifteen minutes I sat and watched him as he whistled and scattered my fire about. I could easily have put a bullet through his head, but why should I kill him? Having amused himself, apparently, as he desired, with my fire, he started to go, and, having gone a short distance he returned, and was joined by another — a female, unmistakably — when both turned and walked past me, within twenty yards of where I sat, and disappeared in the brush.

I could not have had a better opportunity for observing them, as they were unconscious of my presence. Their only object in visiting my camp seemed to be to amuse themselves with swinging lighted sticks around. I have told this story many times since then, and it has often raised an incredulous smile; but I have met one person who has seen the mysterious creatures, and a dozen of whom have come across their tracks at various places between here and Pacheco Pass.

The "wild man" seen, and pursued, in the late 1860s in northern Nevada exhibited a feature rarely reported by Bigfoot witnesses — he carried a club. We have on record only three other instances of this, and all are relatively early cases: from Dover, New Jersey, in 1894; from Chesterfield, Idaho, in 1902; and from Labrador, Canada, around 1913, where the creature carried a club or stick. Such behavior suggests human rather than animal intelligence, but the rarity of such reports is puzzling. The Nevada "wild man" caused great excitement.

...A large party, armed and equipped, lately started in pursuit of "it," and one night a splendid view was obtained of the object which, it was concluded, had once been a white man, but was now covered with a coat of fine, long, hair, carried a huge club in the right hand, and in the left a rabbit. The moment it caught sight of the party, as the moon shone out, it dashed past the camp "with a scream like the roar of a lion," brandished the huge club and attacked the horses in a perfect frenzy of madness.

The savage bloodhounds which the party had brought along refused to pursue the object; and so the party hastily raised a log rampart for self-defense; but, instead of making attack, the object merely uttered the most terrible cries through the night, and in the morning had disappeared. It was evident, however, from the footprints, that the object would require a "pair of No. 9 shoes," and this is all we know. The party could have shot it on first see-ing it, but failed to do so.

Notice that the "savage bloodhounds" would not chase the "wild man." Such a reaction by animals, and especially dogs, towards Bigfoot is not unusual, and we shall report many similar cases. Conversely, there have been occasions when a dog has attacked a Bigfoot, but usually to find itself contemptuously brushed aside or, worse, torn to pieces.

If Bigfeet playing with fire and wielding clubs may seem unbeliev-able, then what are we to make of those reports, admittedly very rare, which tell of humans being abducted by Bigfeet and carried away to their living quarters? We shall come to the classic abduction, of Albert Ostman in 1924, in Chapter 3, but some fifty years earlier, in 1871, an Amerindian woman claimed she had been kidnapped by a Bigfoot and forced to live with it for a year. She was age 17 at the time and living in British Columbia. The creature forced her to swim the Harrison River and then carried her to a rock shelter where it lived with its parents. It kept her for a year but then took her home, because she "aggravated it so much." Her experiences have been exaggerated by some writers; she told a Bigfoot researcher who knew her well that the Bigfoot had treated her kindly.

A Bigfoot seen near Warner's Ranch, California, in February 1876 was described as having "rather fine features," which is a puzzling way to describe a face usually compared with that of an ape. In all other respects the report seems to describe a Bigfoot.

About ten days ago Mr. Turner Helm and myself were in the mountains about ten miles east of Warner's Ranch, on a prospecting tour, looking for the extension of a quartz lode which had been found by some parties sometime before. When we were separated, about half a mile apart — the wind blowing very hard at the time — Mr. Helm, who was walking along looking down at the ground, suddenly heard someone whistle.

Looking up he saw "something" sitting on a large boulder, about fifteen or twenty paces from him. He supposed it to be some kind of an animal, and immediately came down on it with his needle gun. The object instantly rose to its feet and proved to be a man. This man appeared to be covered all over with coarse black hair, seemingly two or three inches long, like the hair of a bear; his beard and the hair of his head were long and thick; he was a man of about medium size, and rather fine features — not at all like those of an Indian, but more like an American or Spaniard.

They stood gazing at each other for a few moments, when Mr. Helm spoke to the singular creature, first in English and then Spanish and then Indian, but the man remained silent. He then advanced towards Mr. Helm, who not knowing what his intentions might be, again came down on him with the gun to keep him at a distance. The man at once stopped, as though he knew there was danger.

Mr. Helm called to me, but the wind was blowing so hard that I did not hear him. The wild man then turned and went over the hill and was soon out of sight; before Mr. Helm could come to me he had made good his escape. We had frequently before seen this man's tracks in that part of the mountains, but had supposed them to be the tracks of an Indian. I did not see this strange inhabitant of the mountains myself; but Mr. Helm is known to be a man of unquestioned veracity, and I have no doubt of the entire truth of his statement.

L.T.H.

The Green Mountains of Vermont were traditionally said to be the haunt of a "strange animal … resembling a man in appearance," and the old stories were recalled when, in October 1879, two young men hunting in the mountains south of Williamstown saw a "wild man." They described it as being

> about five feet high, resembling a man in form and movement, but covered all over with bright red hair, and having a long strag-gling beard, and with very wild eyes. When first seen the crea-ture sprang from behind a rocky cliff, and started for the woods near by, when, mistaking it for a bear or other wild animal, one of the men fired, and, it is thought, wounded it, for with fierce cries of pain and rage, it turned on its assailants driving them before it at high speed. They lost their guns and ammunition in their flight and dared not return for fear of encountering the strange being.

The reader will already have noticed that a high proportion of Big-foot sightings were made in the old days by hunters and prospectors, that is people whose business took them into rarely visited wilderness areas. Today that is still the case, but with the gradual encroachment on such areas by human settlements, more sightings are made by ordinary people in their own back yards. The trend will gradually become apparent as this book progresses.

In the 1880s a young Bigfoot was allegedly captured in British Columbia. The story of "Jacko" has been widely discussed in other books on Bigfoot and so we will give only the basic details here, especially since some researchers tend to feel that the whole affair was a

Figure 2: One explanation for the creature known as Bigfoot is that he is an early hominid, neither ape nor man, and this painting interprets him as one such, a Gigantopithecus. *Picture: William M. Rebsamen/FPL*

hoax of some kind. It was reported that railway men had captured a
creature beside the track 20 miles from Yale in June or July 1884. It was
described as 4 feet 7 inches tall, weighing 127 pounds, and covered with
long black hair. The man appointed its keeper fed it on berries and milk,
and it was planned to take it across to London and to exhibit it there
(Why London? Why not New York, or some nearer center?), but no more
was heard, and it was supposed that Jacko had died on the journey.

A year after the purported capture of Jacko, hunters in the Cascade
Mountains near Lebanon, Oregon, saw a Bigfoot eating deer flesh. We
quote the whole newspaper report of this sighting, since it is a good
example of the tendency of the time to identify Bigfeet as once-normal
men who had gone wild. This must have seemed to the journalists and
reporters the only solution to a mystery which threatened to be insoluble
if they did not find a "logical" solution. Unfortunately their solution is no
more acceptable than any of the other solutions put forward during the
last hundred years to explain the inexplicable Bigfoot sightings.

WILD MAN IN THE MOUNTAINS

Much excitement has been created in the neighborhood of Lebanon, Oregon, recently over the discovery of a wild man in the
mountains above that place, who is supposed to be the long lost
John Mackentire. About four years ago Mackentire, of Lebanon,
while out hunting in the mountains east of Albany with another
man, mysteriously disappeared and no definite trace of him has
ever yet been found. A few days ago a Mr. Fitzgerald and others,
while hunting in the vicinity of the butte known as Bald Peter,
situated in the Cascades, several miles above any settlement saw
a man resembling the long-lost man, entirely destitute of clothing, who had grown as hairy as an animal, and was a complete
wild man.

He was eating the raw flesh of a deer when first seen, and
they approached within a few yards before he saw them and fled.

Isaac Banty saw this man in the same locality about two years ago. It is believed by many that the unfortunate man who was lost became deranged and has managed to find means of subsistence while wandering about in the mountains, probably finding shelter in some cave. A party of men is being organized to go in search of the man.

We doubt that they ever found him and returned him to civilization. The mind boggles at the idea of shaving a hairy Bigfoot all over and trying to convince it that it is really John Mackentire!

Our next story, from Michigan, is a warning to would-be Bigfoot hunters not to use dogs in any attack on the creature. The brief newspaper report dates the incident October 1891.

George W. Frost and W.W. Vivian, both reputable citizens, report having seen a wild man near the Tittabawassee River, in Gladwin County. The man was nude, covered with hair, and was a giant in proportions. According to their stories he must have been at least seven feet high, his arms reaching below his knees, and with hands twice the usual size. Mr. Vivian set his bull dog on the crazy man, and with one mighty stroke of his monstrous hand he felled the dog dead. His jumps were measured and found to be from 20 to 23 feet.

In 1894, a "wild man" was reported in New Jersey. He does not seem to have been hair-covered, but his behavior as described in the following newspaper report bears comparison with that given in later reports of hairy Bigfeet.

DOVER, N.J., Jan. 8, 1894. — There is a wild man in the woods near Mine Hill, and though the parties that have been hunting for him for several days have often felt cold in their heavy coats the object of the search seems to get along comfortably with no more protection from the winter chill than an abundant set of whiskers.

Though this place is in a ferment of excitement over the affair, there are some persons who cast doubt upon the genuineness of the wild man; but that there is such a person and that he is in a condition that invites a speedy death from cold is blushingly told by Bertha Hestig, Lizzie Guscott, and Katie Griffin.

They saw the wild man for a brief moment Saturday afternoon, and they shrieked so loud and long that the business of the mill and nearly the whole town came to a standstill. The wild man didn't, however. He gave an answering shriek of terror and took to the woods.

"He didn't have no shoes on," ingenuously said Bertha, in telling the story to-day, "and mutton suet on his chest wouldn't ha' done him a bit of harm."

The existence of the wild man doesn't rest on the testimony of the girls alone, and although many persons who claim to have seen the uncanny stranger differ in their descriptions of him, "Mike" and "Bill" Dean tell a straight story. They are woodchoppers, and they first saw him.

They were cutting wood on Friday last near the Indian Falls clearing, in one of the most lonely parts of the mountain. Suddenly their hounds began a violent barking at the base of a large rock.

"It's a bear or some varmint," said "Bill," seizing his axe more firmly and running over to the dogs. He was closely followed by "Mike." As they reached the spot a savage looking figure sprang from behind the rock. "Mike" Dean, who was almost upon him, sprang backward as though indeed faced by a bear. The stranger was apparently middle aged, nearly six feet tall, and about a hundred and eighty pounds in weight.

His face was thickly covered with a dark, unkempt beard. He looked savagely at the woodchoppers for an instant and then sprang to the rocks and began talking to an imaginary object.

As he was approached he darted from the rocks and began running up and down the clearing and at intervals yelling frantically, all the time working his arms as though rowing a boat. This leads to the belief that he is probably a crazy sailor. The Deans endeavored to seize him, but he picked up a club and brandished it. One of the dogs sprang at him and received a blow that nearly killed it.

The woodchoppers then fled and telephoned from the company store to this city for help. A scouting party was at once organized, and under the direction of City Marshal James Hagen and Policeman Tredenick started for the scene. The wild man had disappeared into the dense underbrush. The searchers found the imprint of his bare feet in the middle ground.

The party separated and kept up the search until late that night. Parties have left this city every day since. Fifty men scoured the mountains in every direction on Saturday, but without success. Sunday the woods were searched all day by numerous bands.

The man appeared on Saturday evening at the home of the Russels, about a half-mile from the scene of Friday's encounter. He tried to gain an entrance, but finding he was unable to do so began searching the premises as though looking for food. The family was greatly frightened. The man disappeared as mysteriously as he came.

William Mullen was returning from a walk on Sunday morning when the wild man suddenly made his appearance in the road in front of him. Both stopped and gazed at each other intently. Then the wild man gave a shriek and darted towards the woods in the direction of the Dickerson mine.

One of the searchers that went out on the mountain Saturday said the party found numerous imprints of the man's bare feet, and in one instance they had found a small sapling which had been gnawed, as though by a human being. It was on Saturday afternoon that the three girls who are employed at the Dover Silk Mill at the foot of the Dover Mountains saw the man. They were standing at their looms and looking out the windows.

They noticed the underbrush part and the next instant the man stepped into view. Their screams brought the other employees to the windows. The girls said the man's body was a mass of scratches and bruises.

The scouting party that has been out at various times will leave this place to-morrow morning under the leadership of Marshal James Hagen and prosecute a more rigorous search. Inquiry has been made at the Morris Plains Asylum, but none of the inmates are missing.

The Dover "wild man" was seen and unsuccessfully hunted in January 1894. Only four months later, in May 1894, a "classic" Bigfoot report came out of rural Kentucky. For months people around Deep Creek had noticed that something was stealing chickens, eggs, young pigs, lambs, and other items of food. Then the "man-beast" was seen, and described by Joseph Ewalt as having "great long white hair hanging down from his head and face that was as coarse as a horse's mane. His legs were covered with hair and the only article of clothing he wore was a piece of sheepskin over the lower portion of his body, reaching nearly for his knees. He said a light came from his eyes and mouth similar to fire."

It was decided to try and catch the creature, and so the men kept a lookout for it. One morning Eph Boston and his sons saw it making for their barn. They saw that the man-beast was about 6½ feet tall, had clawed feet and cat-like hands. Soon it came rushing from the barn grasping three chickens. Tom Boston shot at it, but it escaped, running very fast into a cave. When the men and their neighbors later examined the cave entrance they found evidence of occupation in the form of bones, feathers, and so on, but they were afraid to enter. When they did go in a short distance, an "unearthly yell" so scared them that they retreated quickly. All efforts to capture the man-beast, including smoking it out, failed.

In an 1897 sighting near Sailor, Indiana, one man shot at a Bigfoot and seemed to have wounded it, but as is always the case, no further trace of it was seen. This encounter took place in late April, when two farmers saw a hair-covered, man-sized "beast" walking on its hind legs. When it saw them approaching, it made for thick woods, but "afterwards dropped on its hands and disappeared with rabbit-like bounds." This feature, of a Bigfoot going down on all fours, will be seen again in later cases, but only rarely is it reported.

Also in late April 1897, a "wild man" was seen in woods near Stout, Ohio. Thirty armed men hunted it (presumably unsuccessfully, since we have no report of a capture) after it had attacked a boy. One witness said it was very tall, almost naked, and could run like a deer. Another said it wore a pair of tattered pants! Lest this last feature suggest that the "wild man" really was that rather than a Bigfoot, we note that we have details of six other sightings in which an apparent Bigfoot wore clothes, all relatively recent sightings (apart from the Deep Creek "man-beast" of 1894), and we shall give more details in the appropriate chapters. This feature is yet another puzzle to add to the many already facing Bigfoot investigators.

On 26 May 1897 a "wild man," described as "gorilla-like," and possibly the same creature as that seen near Stout during April, was seen near Rome in Ohio. Two men cutting timber saw a 6-foot-tall creature covered with long curly hair and drove it into a rocky area by the Ohio River, but there they lost it.

Our final report of the century shows Bigfoot in a more sympathetic role than that in which it is usually seen, and suggests it may have a kindly, human-loving side. The witness was an Indian who lived near Tulelake, California, in a cabin in the mountains. One summer evening in 1897 he saw what looked at first like a tall bush ahead of him on the trail. Then he caught a strong, musky scent, and realized the bush was alive: it was a creature covered in thick, coarse hair. He could see its brown eyes.

It made a noise, and moved; so the Indian laid down the string of fish he was carrying as a gesture of friendship. The creature took the fish and moved away into the trees, making a long, low call. A few weeks later the Indian heard a noise outside his cabin early one morning and went out to find a pile of fresh deerskins ready for tanning. Again he heard the strange Bigfoot call in the trees. Later other items were left, like wild fruits and berries, and wood for the fire. A few years later the same Indian had another important Bigfoot encounter, but we shall tell of that in the next chapter, as it took place early in the twentieth century.

2
The Pattern Emerges
1900-20

There are relatively few Bigfoot reports for the first four decades of this
century, compared with the large number of cases reported and publicized today. But that, of course, does not necessarily mean that the
creature was not being seen as much as it is today. These early descriptions of Bigfoot and its behavior parallel very closely the reports that are
coming in today, and it is likely that the principal reason there are fewer
reports for the early years is that people who saw Bigfoot, often people
living in isolated areas, simply did not know whom to report the sighting
to, and so did not tell anyone. Any that may have been reported would be
unknown to us now if they did not find their way into local newspapers,
which are almost our only source of information for these early reports.
Very few, if any, of the sightings were actually investigated at the time by
people knowledgeable about Bigfoot.

One early sighting, which was reported in a newspaper, took place some time in 1900 near Myrtle Point, Oregon. The creature's mode of locomotion earned it the nickname of "Kangaroo Man" and, surprisingly, it is reported as being "very good looking."

> The Sixes mining district in Curry County has for the past 30 years gloried in the exclusive possession of a "kangaroo man." Recently while Wm. Page and Johnnie McCulloch, who are mining there, went out hunting McCulloch saw the strange animal-man come down to a stream to drink. In calling Page's attention to the strange being it became frightened, and with cat-like agility, which has always been a leading characteristic, with a few bounds was out of sight.
>
> The appearance of this animal is almost enough to terrorize the rugged mountainsides themselves. He is described as having the appearance of a man — a very good looking man — is nine feet in height with low forehead, hair hanging down near his eyes, and his body covered with a prolific growth of hair which nature has provided for his protection. Its hands reach almost to the ground and when its tracks were measured its feet were found to be 18 inches in length with five well formed toes. Whether this is a devil, some strange animal or a wild man is what Messrs. Page and McCulloch would like to know.

Also in 1900, many miles farther north in Alaska, a group of hair-covered creatures ran at a prospector who had climbed a tree to get his bearings. They were, he said, "the most hideous creatures. I couldn't call them anything but devils, as they were neither men nor monkeys, yet looked like both. They were entirely sexless, their bodies covered with long coarse hair, except where scabs and running sores replaced it." The prospector ran for his canoe, the Bigfeet in hot pursuit, and somehow he managed to escape. This happened in a wild area east of Thomas Bay, where others too saw hairy creatures around the same time.

Figure 3: This photograph shows an unidentified animal shot by trappers at Lillooet in British Columbia early in the 20th century. *Photo: RD/FPL*

It was also in the early years of the century that the Indian whose first Bigfoot encounter we described at the end of the last chapter had another meeting with the creatures known by him as the "Matah Kagmi." Acting as a guide for gold prospectors, he was exploring alone at the foot of Mount Shasta in California when he was bitten by a snake. He fainted after killing it, and when he came to he found himself surrounded by three Bigfeet 8-10 feet tall which had treated his wound and were carrying him down a trail. They left him under a tree, and from there he was able to alert the prospectors.

In 1901, timber cruiser (one who searches for good timber) Mike King actually watched a Bigfoot washing roots. King was on Vancouver Island in British Columbia, in the Campbell River area, and he was alone because his Indian packers were afraid of the "monkey men" in the forest. He saw a "man-beast" washing roots in a pool of water and stacking them in two neat piles. When it realized it was being watched, it ran off with a cry; then it stopped and looked back. The witness described it as being "covered with reddish-brown hair, and his arms were peculiarly long and were used freely in climbing and in brush running." He also noted that its footprint was humanlike, "but with phenomenally long and spreading toes."

Early in the next year, 1902, an unusual sighting of a club-wielding Bigfoot was made in rural Idaho. Its behavior, as described in the following newspaper report, was unusual, too.

...the residents of the little town of Chesterfield, located in an isolated portion of Bannick County, Idaho, are greatly excited over the appearance in that vicinity of an eight-foot, hair-covered human monster. He was first seen on January 14, when he appeared among a party of young people, who were skating on the river near John Gooch's ranch. The creature showed fight, and, flourishing a large club and uttering a series of yells, started to attack the skaters, who managed to reach their wagons and get away in safety. Measurements of the tracks showed the creature's feet to be 22 inches long and 7 inches broad, with the imprint of only four toes. Stockmen report having seen his tracks along the range west of the river. The people of the neighborhood, feeling unsafe while the creature is at large, have sent 20 men on its track to effect its capture.

The unusual features of club-brandishing and Bigfoot's apparent possession of only four toes should not lead the reader to doubt this case. Although rare, such violent behavior has been reported on other occasions, as has the occurrence of less than five toes.

The man-beasts of the Myrtle Point area of Oregon were active during the early years of the century, as the following 1904 newspaper report indicates:

At repeated intervals during the past ten years thrilling stories have come from the rugged Sixes mining district in Coos County, Oregon, near Myrtle Point, regarding a wild man or a queer and terrible monster which walks erect and which has been seen by scores of miners and prospectors...

The appearance again of the "Wild Man" of the Sixes has thrown some of the miners into a state of excitement and fear. A report says the wild man has been seen three times since the 10th of last month. The first appearance occurred on "Thompson Flat." Wm. Ward and a young man by the name of Burlison were sitting by the fire of their cabin one night when they heard something walking around the cabin which resembled a man walking and when it came to the corner of the cabin it took hold of the corner and gave the building a vigorous shake and kept up a frightful noise all the time — the same that has so many times warned the venturesome miners of the approach of the hairy man and caused them to flee in abject fear.

Mr. Ward walked to the cabin door and could see the monster plainly as it walked away, and took a shot at it with his rifle,

but the bullet went wild of its mark. The last appearance of the
animal was at the Harrison cabin only a few days ago. Mr. Ward
was at the Harrison cabin this time and again figures in the
excitement. About five o'clock in the morning the wild man gave
the door of the cabin a vigorous shaking which aroused Ward
and one of the Harrison boys who took their guns and started in
to do the intruder. Ward fired at the man and he answered by
sending a four-pound rock at Ward's head but his aim was a little
too high. He then disappeared in the brush.

Many of the miners avow that the "wild man" is a reality.
They have seen him and know whereof they speak. They say he
is something after the fashion of a gorilla and unlike anything
else that has ever been known; and not only that but he can
throw rocks with wonderful force and accuracy. He is about
seven feet high, has broad hands and feet and his body is covered
by a prolific growth of hair. In short, he looks like the very devil.

The creatures' behavior in shaking the miners' cabins might suggest that
they were annoyed by the presence of the men, and wanted them to go
away and stay away!

Three years later, in March 1907, the Indians living in a small settlement at Bishop's Cove on Vancouver Island, British Columbia, were so
scared by the sight of a 5-foot, long-haired "monkey" which came out at
night to dig clams on the beach and howl, that when the steamer
Capilano sailed close to shore the Indians sought refuge on her.

The recent publicity given to Bigfoot sightings has meant that some
past witnesses are belatedly revealing their experiences. This can result
in researchers learning about some unusual and interesting stories, such
as that reported by an Oregon resident who wrote to *Argosy* magazine in
1976. She told of how, about 1910 when she was 10 years old, she saw a
large, fur-covered creature in the woods near her home at Mirrow Lake,
Wisconsin. It walked like a man and had a man's eyes, she said. It
followed her most of the way home but did not attack or frighten her. She

wondered if it needed help of some kind. Her father dismissed the creature as a friendly bear, but would not go out to see it. Next day the girl found its footprints in the snow, twice as long as her father's, but again no one would look at them!

Another early sighting was revealed in a letter written to researcher John Green in 1969 by Mrs. Callie Lund. The location of the events was a ranch near Oakville, in western Washington.

The spring of 1933 was a wet one and also as I remember we had a lot of snow. All the ranches in our area were on the river. We all farmed the bottom land but built our homes on the hillside. This area had been logged by the Balch Logging Company in the period of 1915-1923. By 1933 a lot of the hill area had second growth timber on it. I was attending High School in Oakville at

Figure 4: A comparison of the footprints made by a human (left), bear (center), and Bigfoot (right). *Photo: RD/FPL*

this time and this particular weekend I had been to a dance in Oakville with a group of other young girls. When I returned home I always walked around the house to the back door. All my life I had heard coyotes and cougars. Just as I started to open the back door I heard a very loud noise up on the hill. I had never heard a noise like it before and I was a little scared. I went in and woke up my mother and told her to come and listen as this was a noise I had never heard before. Also I could hear another one answer way over on another hill.

Mother got up and her reaction was so strange that I could hardly believe it was my mother. She kept saying, "It's that terrible Ape again." When I kept trying to ask her to explain she kept saying "I'll tell you tomorrow, and let's get inside as we are not safe out here." This is the story my mother told me the next day.

After my Grandfather died my Grandmother divided up the old ranch and gave the children a Stump Ranch. About 40 acres and most of my mother's land was the area where our house stood. The timber came down almost to the back of the house. She said in the fall of 1912 my father had gone to Aberdeen to sell potatoes he had raised on the 10 acres they had cleared. He had to stay all night so Mother was alone in the small house.

The house had a porch across the front and a large bay window. She said she had not slept very soundly because she was not used to being alone. She said about 1:00 a.m. she heard a terrible stomping noise on the front porch. She got up to see what it was. It was moonlight outside, and at first she thought it was a bear on the porch, but this animal was standing on its back legs and was so large it was bending over to look in the window. She said it appeared over 6 feet tall and it didn't look like a bear at all in the moonlight. She said in a few minutes it walked over and jumped off the front porch and started around the house. She went into the kitchen so she could get a good look and she said it looked just like an ape. She said the strange thing that had scared her most was the noise it made as it walked around the house.

She said as soon as it was daylight she went over to my Grandmother's place and told them what she had seen. Her brothers all made fun of her and told her she had had a nightmare. When my Father returned home he wouldn't believe her either. She said that they made her feel so ridiculous she said she would never mention it again. This was the first time I heard her tell the story.

Also around 1912, a very strange Bigfoot encounter took place about 10 miles from Gallipolis in Ohio. This foreshadows later occurrences in which UFOs have apparently been involved. The witnesses, Mr. J.M. and his mother, were berry picking on their farm when they saw a strange dark cloud which first hovered above them, and then followed as they made their way along a path through a wood. Mr. J.M. tells what happened next:

My mother started off at a pretty good pace and she got somewhat, maybe 30 to 50 feet, ahead of me.

Well, in the meantime, this monster was standing just a little bit to our right, when we first saw it. It was walking parallel to me. Now, it was over a roll in the land, and I couldn't see it from the knees down. I don't remember about the arms. It had a bulky head and appeared to have no neck. Monstrous wide shoulders, that were probably twice the width of a man's. The color was dark.

When my mother turned at me, she screamed, "Let's GO!" The monster walked a bit to the left and it stopped and seemed to turn its body around and gaze at me. It made some sort of noise, like growling or maybe a barking sound.

By the time they had gone a further hundred yards, both creature and cloud had disappeared.

Another remote area where early Bigfoot activity occurred that is strongly reminiscent of that reported today is the small rural community of Traverspine near Goose Bay in Labrador. The events of 1913 were first published years later by Elliott Merrick, in his book *True North,* and although he seems to have regarded the tales he heard while living in the community in the 1930s as "ghost stories," the description he gives in his book suggests that a very real creature was seen, a Bigfoot.

Ghost stories are very real in this land of scattered lonely homes and primitive fears. The Traverspine "gorilla" is one of the creepiest. About twenty years ago one of the little girls was play-ing in an open grassy clearing one autumn afternoon when she saw come out of the woods a huge hairy thing with low-hanging arms. It was about seven feet tall when it stood erect, but some-times it dropped to all fours. Across the top of its head was a white mane.

She said it grinned at her and she could see its white teeth. When it beckoned to her she ran screaming to the house. Its tracks were everywhere in the mud and sand, and later in the snow. They measured the tracks and cut out paper patterns of them which they still keep. It is a strange-looking foot, about twelve inches long, narrow at the heel, and forking at the front into two broad, round-ended toes. Sometimes its print was so deep it looked to weigh 500 pounds. At other times the beast's mark looked no deeper than a man's track. They set bear traps for it but it would never go near them. It ripped the bark off trees and rooted up huge rotten logs as though it were looking for grubs.

They organized hunts for it and the lumbermen who were then at Mud Lake came with their rifles and lay out all night by the paths watching, but with no success. A dozen people have told me they saw its track with their own eyes and it was unlike anything ever seen or heard of. One afternoon one of the children saw it peeping in the window. She yelled and old Mrs. Michelin grabbed a gun and ran for the door. She just saw the top of its head disappearing into a clump of willows. She fired where she saw the bushes moving and thinks she wounded it. She says too that it had a ruff of white across the top of its head. At night they used to bar the door with a stout birch beam and all sleep upstairs, taking guns and axes with them.

The dogs knew it was there too, for the family would hear them growl and snarl when it approached. Often it must have driven them into the river for they would be soaking wet in the morning. One night the dogs faced the thing, and it lashed at them with a stick or club, which hit a corner of the house with such force it made the beams tremble. The old man and boys carried guns wherever they went, but never got a shot at it. For the two winters it was there.

Note that the "gorilla" is thought to have carried a club, like the Idaho Bigfoot seen about 11 years before. The white ruff on top of its head, though unusual, is not unique: a Bigfoot seen near Cobalt, Ontario, in 1923 and 1946 had a light mane, and so was called "Yellow Top," and one seen around Lancaster, Pennsylvania, in 1973 was gray with a white mane. The footprint described is certainly strange. Although a high proportion of apparent Bigfoot tracks are five-toed, with some four-toed found and a surprising number of three-toed, we do not have many other two-toed tracks on record.

Another report on the Traverspine "gorilla" was written by Professor Bruce Wright who visited the community to investigate the story. In his book *Wildlife Sketches Near and Far* he described two of the creatures, and his account in this way differs from the Merrick account, though in other respects the reports tally.

About 1913 the little settlement of Traverspine at the head of Lake Melville was visited in winter by two strange animals that drove the dogs to a frenzy and badly frightened the people. They left deep tracks about twelve inches long indicating great weight and they rooted up rotten logs with great strength and tore them apart as if searching for grubs.

They sometimes stood erect on their hind legs (at which time they looked like great hairy men seven feet tall, and no doubt from this description Merrick got his title of the Traverspine Gorilla), but they also ran on all fours. They cleaned up some seal bones "too big for the dogs," and what is too big for a husky is really big, and many dogs followed them and did not return when they came around the settlement at night. This was a serious loss as dogs were the people's sole means of transportation.

These two strange animals, which the inhabitants called the man and the woman because one was larger than the other, stayed about the settlement despite attempts to trap them or drive them away. One day Mrs. Michelin was alone in her house with her young daughter playing in the edge of the bush behind. Suddenly the child rushed in crying, "It's following me, Mummy, it's following me!"

Mrs. Michelin reached for a shotgun loaded with buckshot which she always had near when her husband was away, and stepped out the back door.

"All I could see was the moving bush and the shape of a great animal standing seven feet tall in the alders. It seemed to have a sort of white ruff across the top of its head, I could not make out the rest. I fired into the bushes and I heard the shot hit. I went back into the house and bolted the door. It never came back and there was blood where it had stood when the men from the sawmill came back."

The sawmill closed down and the men turned out in force to look, but they never found it. Similar animals have been reported since and their tracks have been found at intervals, the latest being about 1940.

I asked Mrs. Michelin point blank if this could have been a bear. "It was no bear, Mr. Wright. I have killed 12 bears on my husband's trapline and I know their tracks well. I saw enough of this thing to be sure of that. I fired a shotgun at it and I heard the shot hit."

Although a creature seen in Maryland in 1914 was hair-covered, and was presumably a Bigfoot, it also had a definite nose and a sharp chin, neither of them familiar Bigfoot facial features. The witness was eight years old at the time and lived in Churchville, Maryland. He was looking for his cap behind his home, using a lantern as it was evening, and he saw the creature sitting on a log. His lantern held high was level with the Bigfoot's eyes, and although the creature could have attacked him, it just watched.

Around 1915, Crum King, a young man returning one night from a dance to his home near Wann, Oklahoma, saw a 5-6-foot-tall, hairy, manlike creature standing by the gate to his house. It had a wide chest (about 4 feet, said King) and "stood with its arms stretched out." He did not wait to discover the Bigfoot's intentions.

In Washington, lumber-camp worker Albert M. Fletcher was one of several people to see a Bigfoot around the camp in 1917. In 1969 he wrote an account of the incident, which was obviously still fresh in his memory over 50 years later:

In the fall of 1917 when I was seventeen years old I was working for a lumber camp on the Cowlitz River in the state of Washington. One moonlit evening I was walking down a logging road en route to a dance when I had the uneasy feeling that something was following close behind me. I kept looking over my shoulder but could not see anything. When I came to a bend in the road I ducked behind a tree and waited to see what it was. Almost immediately a very large manlike creature about six and a half or seven feet tall came into view. It was walking on its hind legs, was covered with dark hair, had a bearded face and large chest and so far as I could see was not wearing clothes of any kind. Startled, I let out a yell of alarm and the creature instantly turned and ran off into the woods, still on its hind legs. I told some of my co-workers about it and some laughed but others said they, too, had seen it. No one had an explanation for it and no name was given to it but all agreed that it was a large ape-like something and that it also resembled a very large man.

3
Attacks and Kidnappings
1921-40

During the 1920s two "major" Bigfoot encounters took place, both in 1924 — an attack on a hut in the Cascade Mountains of Washington, and the kidnapping of Albert Ostman in British Columbia. In the previous year one of a series of occasional sightings of "Yellow Top" was made by prospectors in Ontario, as reported in the North Bay *Nugget* at the time.

COBALT — July 27, 1923 — Mr. J.A. MacAuley and Mr. Lorne Wilson claim they have seen the Precambrian Shield Man while working on their mining claims North and East of the Wettlaufer Mine near Cobalt. This is the second time in seventeen years that a hairy apelike creature nicknamed "Yellow Top" because of a light-colored "mane" has been seen in the district.

    The two prospectors said they were taking test samples from

their … property when they saw what looked like a bear picking
at a blueberry patch. Mr. Wilson said he threw a stone at the
creature.

"It kind of stood up and growled at us. Then it ran away. It
sure was like no bear that I have ever seen. Its head was kind of
yellow and the rest of it was black like a bear, all covered with
hair." The first report of the creature was made in September,
1906, by a group of men building the headframe at the Violet
Mine, east of Cobalt. It has not been seen since that time.

Exactly a year later, in July 1924, Fred Beck and his prospecting
colleagues came up against several Bigfeet in a canyon near Kelso,

**Figure 5: In 1968, Fred Beck (right) showed Bigfoot researcher René
Dahinden the gun with which he claimed to have shot at a Bigfoot in
1924 at Ape Canyon, Washington.** *Photo: RD/FPL*

Washington, afterwards known as Ape Canyon. The basic story is told in a report in the Portland *Oregonian*:

> The strangest story to come from the Cascade Mountains was brought to Kelso today by Marion Smith, his son Roy Smith, Fred Beck, Gabe Lefever and John Peterson, who encountered the fabled "mountain devils" or mountain gorillas of Mount St. Helens this week, shooting one of them and being attacked throughout the night by rock bombardments of the beasts.
>
> The men had been prospecting a claim on the Muddy, a branch of the Lewis River about eight miles from Spirit Lake, 46 miles from Castle Rock. They declared that they saw four of the huge animals, which were about 400 pounds and walked erect. Smith and his companions declared that they had seen the tracks of the animals several times in the last six years and Indians have told of the "mountain devils" for 60 years, but none of the animals ever has been seen before.
>
> Smith met with one of the animals and fired at it with a revolver, he said. Thursday, Fred Beck, it is said, shot one, the body falling over a precipice. That night the animals bombarded the cabin where the men were stopping with showers of rocks, many of them large ones, knocking chunks out of the log cabin, according to the prospectors...

Roger Patterson, the man who in 1967 filmed a Bigfoot in California, interviewed Fred Beck in 1966 and obtained fuller details of the prospectors' hair-raising experiences. A transcript of the interview is given in John Green's *Sasquatch: The Apes Among Us*; it conveys the excitement of the encounters, even though Beck was describing them 42 years later. The events had obviously remained fresh in his memory. Of the attack on the hut he said: "Well! I wanta tell you, pretty near all night long they were on that house, trying to get in, you know. We kept a shootin'. Get up on the house we'd shoot up through the ceiling at them.

Couldn't see them up there, you could hear them up there. My God, they made a noise. Sounded like a bunch of horses were running around there."

One interesting point to emerge is that Marion Smith claims to have fired three shots into a Bigfoot's head, plus two more into its body, and still it kept running. At the interview Fred Beck also described the creatures: "Well, they was tall... they looked to me like they was eight foot tall, maybe taller, and they was built like a man, little in the waist, and big shoulders on, and chest, and their necks was kinda what they call bull necks..." Their ears were covered by hair, they had hairy faces, and "a kind of pug nose, flat nose, kind of flat." Their arms were long and big, and the creatures weighed 600-800 pounds, he estimated.

It is hardly surprising that the Ape Canyon creatures were not particularly friendly towards the prospectors, and attacked their hut after the men had shot at them. The Bigfoot that kidnapped Albert Ostman did not injure him, but gave him an unforgettable experience. Ostman, perhaps not surprisingly in view of its unbelievability, did not reveal the details until 1957, at a time when Bigfoot was in the news. He wrote out an account of the events as he remembered them, and this account has often been quoted in full. Here we will tell the story using extracts.

In 1924 Ostman had been doing construction work and needed a holiday, so he decided to look for gold around the head of Toba Inlet in British Columbia. He made camp in the mountains and did some prospecting. Over several days he kept finding his belongings disturbed, so one night decided to stay dressed in his sleeping bag, with his rifle handy, and keep awake to await the intruder. But he fell asleep, and was woken by something picking him up.

My first thought was — it must be a snow slide, but there was no snow around my camp. Then it felt like I was tossed on horseback, but I could feel whoever it was, was walking.

I tried to reason out what kind of animal this could be. I tried to get at my sheath knife, and cut my way out, but I was in an almost sitting position, and the knife was under me. I could not get hold of it, but the rifle was in front of me, I had a good hold of that, and had no intention to let go of it. At times I could feel my packsack touching me, and could feel the cans in the sack touching my back.

After what seemed like an hour, I could feel we were going up a steep hill. I could feel myself rise for every step. What was carrying me was breathing hard and sometimes gave a slight cough. Now, I knew this must be one of the mountain Sasquatch giants the Indian told me about.

I was in a very uncomfortable position — unable to move. I was sitting on my feet, and one of the boots in the bottom of the bag was crossways with the hobnail sole up across my foot. It hurt me terribly, but I could not move.

It was very hot inside. It was lucky for me this fellow's hand was not big enough to close up the whole bag when he picked me up — there was a small opening at the top, otherwise I would have choked to death.

Now he was going downhill. I could feel myself touching the ground at times and at one time he dragged me behind him and I could feel he was below me. Then he seemed to get on level ground and was going at a trot for a long time. By this time, I had cramps in my legs, the pain was terrible. I was wishing he would get to his destination soon. I could not stand this type of transportation much longer.

Now he was going uphill again. It did not hurt me so bad. I tried to estimate distance and directions. As near as I could guess we were about three hours traveling. I had no idea when he started as I was asleep when he picked me up.

Finally he stopped and let me down. Then he dropped my packsack, I could hear the cans rattle. Then I heard chatter — some kind of talk I did not understand. The ground was sloping so when he let go of my sleeping bag, I rolled downhill. I got my head out, and got some air. I tried to straighten my legs and crawl out, but my legs were numb.

As it was dark, Ostman could not immediately see his kidnappers. Nor could he see any way of escape. Gradually it grew lighter, and he saw four hairy creatures, two big and two small, presumably a mother and father and two children, a boy and a girl. He checked over his possessions (he had a compass, some food, rifle shells, a few matches, and a knife) and found a place to camp until he could work out how to escape. The "old man" was sitting by the opening to the valley they were in, which was surrounded by high mountains. A day or two later, when Ostman tried to leave, the "old man" blocked the way. So Ostman had to survive until an opportunity for escape presented itself. He found a water supply and made coffee, and ate some cold food, and got to know the young male Bigfoot, and studied the family's way of life. They slept beneath an overhanging rock on dry moss, using moss-filled "blankets," and went out in the daytime to gather food: grass, twigs, shoots, nuts, and roots. He never saw them eat meat. Ostman had time to observe the creatures minutely, and described them thus:

> The young fellow might have been between 11-18 years old and about seven feet tall and might weigh about 300 lbs. His chest would be 50-55 inches, his waist about 36-38 inches. He had wide jaws, narrow forehead, that slanted upward round at the back about four or five inches higher than the forehead. The hair on their heads was about six inches long. The hair on the rest of their body was short and thick in places. The women's hair on the forehead had an upward turn like some women have — they call it bangs, among women's hair-do's. Nowadays the old lady could have been anything between 40-70 years old. She was over seven feet tall. She would be about 500-600 pounds.
>
> She had very wide hips, and a goose-like walk. She was not built for beauty or speed. Some of those lovable brassieres and

uplifts would have been a great improvement on her looks and her figure. The man's eyeteeth were longer than the rest of the teeth, but not long enough to be called tusks. The old man must have been near eight feet tall. Big barrel chest and big hump on his back — powerful shoulders, his biceps on upper arm were enormous and tapered down to his elbows. His forearms were longer than common people have, but well proportioned. His hands were wide, the palm was long and broad, and hollow like a scoop. His fingers were short in proportion to the rest of his hand. His fingernails were like chisels. The only place they had no hair was inside their hands and the soles of their feet and upper part of the nose and eyelids. I never did see their ears, they were covered with hair hanging over them.

If the old man were to wear a collar it would have to be at least 30 inches. I have no idea what size shoes they would need. I was watching the young fellow's foot one day when he was sitting down. The soles of his feet seemed to be padded like a dog's foot, and the big toe was longer than the rest and very strong. In mountain climbing all he needed was footing for his big toe. They were very agile.

Ostman hoped to use his supply of snuff to help him escape. By gaining the "old man's" interest he planned to feed him enough snuff to make him ill. His patience was rewarded when one day the "old man" grabbed a whole box and gulped it down. Soon he became sick and rushed off to get water, whereupon Ostman grabbed his belongings and made for the valley opening. He fired his rifle to scare off the rest of the family and ran down the hillside. "I was in a canyon, and good traveling and I made fast time. Must have made three miles in some world record time." He was not followed and eventually found his way back to civilization.

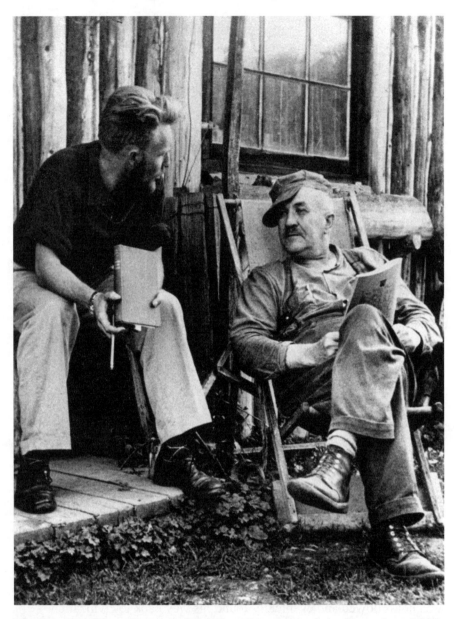

Figure 6: Albert Ostman (right), who claimed to have been kid-napped by a Bigfoot in British Columbia in 1924, is interviewed by René Dahinden. *Photo: RD/FPL*

Although Ostman is now dead, John Green, an experienced Bigfoot investigator, knew him for over 12 years and had no reason to consider him a liar. Also, none of those who questioned him, such as a magistrate, zoologist, and primate specialists, could catch him out; and we therefore have no logical option but to assume that his story, fantastic though it may sound, was true.

There was a third Bigfoot sighting in 1924, near Flagstaff, Arizona. Two women saw one in their ranch garden, pulling up turnips. The 7-foot creature, covered with light-colored hair, also carried some corn. It ran off with its spoils, jumping a fence on the way to the forest.

In 1926 a Bigfoot showed its dislike for dogs, a trait which often reveals itself in Bigfoot reports. A number of times they are reported as fighting with or killing dogs. On this occasion, on the Mountain Fork River in Oklahoma, two hunters accompanied by a dog spotted a big, black, hairy "ape man" in a clearing. They shouted and it ran away. One of the hunters set his dog after it, and about an hour later they found the dog's corpse. It had "been just almost tore in two," presumably by the Bigfoot.

A New Jersey taxi-driver had an alarming experience around 1927 on his way to Salem one night. In wooded country he had a flat tire and stopped to change the wheel. He had just finished when the car began to shake. Looking up he saw "something that stood upright like a man but without clothing and covered with hair." He drove off so fast he left his flat tire and jack behind. In Salem he told his story and two men drove back to investigate. They found the tire and jack, but no Bigfoot.

Only four years after Albert Ostman's adventure, another kidnapping allegedly took place in British Columbia. The victim was an Indian, Muchalat Harry of the Nootka Tribe. A fearless trapper, he was in the woods on Vancouver Island, having reached his camp by canoe. One night, dressed only in his underwear and wrapped in blankets, he was picked up and carried a few miles into the hills by a tall Bigfoot. In daylight he saw he was among a community of around twenty hairy creatures which studied him with interest, especially his "loose skin" (woolen underwear) which they pulled at. Later in the day, when they began to lose interest in him and he was sitting alone and cold, he saw his chance to escape, and ran off. He kept going for twelve miles until he reached his canoe, and then paddled the 45 miles home on a winter's night dressed only in his underwear. His friends managed to nurse him back to health, but Muchalat Harry refused to go back to fetch his camp equipment and rifle.

A number of travelers in the Oregon wilds reported seeing a Bigfoot in 1933, and a newspaper report dated 19 August gives some details:

> A "wild man" was hunted by a party of veteran woodsmen in the scrub pine and manzanita of Tillamook Head today. Three persons who saw the wild man said he was a "shaggy-appearing human," with an animal-like face, who bounded away when observed. At last report the creature, whether lunatic, hermit or figment of imagination, had eluded his pursuers and left no trace. Searching parties sent out recently to find lost vacationists in the wild region which overlooks the sea reported the wild man. Irving C. Allen, city attorney of Seaside, said: "I happened to lag behind the searching party on Bald Mountain. I glanced behind me, and there it was. It looked like a shaggy beast, yet human. It was growing dark, and I couldn't see it plainly. As I stood watching, it turned and fled into the darkness." Clement Klink, member of another search party a few days later, said: "We were hunting near the 'death trap.' I looked up a cliff and saw an animal-like human peering down at me. I watched the creature, which was at a considerable distance, and it bounded away." William Laighton, who knows every animal trail and crag on Tillamook Head, was reported to have seen the wild man. "Well I saw something queer," Laighton said when questioned. He refused to say more.

Another British Columbia Indian had encounters with Bigfoot in this period, in 1934 and 1936. On the first occasion, Frank Dan, living on the Chehalis Reserve near the Harrison River, heard his dog barking and, on going to investigate, "came face to face with a hairy giant. The creature, according to his report, was nude, covered with a fluff of black hair from head to foot, except for a small space around the eyes. He is described as tall, muscular, and of ferocious aspect. After one look Frank ran into the house and secured the door. The giant, undisturbed, strode leisurely into the nearby bush and disappeared." In 1936, while canoeing along Morris Creek, a tributary of the Harrison River, Frank Dan was alarmed when a rock apparently fell from the slope above, landing in the water close by. Looking up, he saw a hairy creature with a great stone under its arm, which it then hurled out towards the canoe. Not being very keen on the Bigfoot's attitude, the Indian paddled away to safety.

Again in British Columbia, Mrs. Jane Patterson had an unusual encounter with a Bigfoot in an abandoned ranch garden near Bridesville, probably in 1937. She went there to gather rhubarb, and came across a hairy creature sitting only a few feet away. She spoke to it, and it just blinked, probably as surprised as she was at the meeting. She described it as taller than herself, a light brown in color, and looking like a big monkey. She backed away and hurried home, and her description of her husband's attitude must be given in her classic words.

> I wanted to go back, and I told my husband about it, and he said he hadn't lost no monkey, he wasn't going up there. I talked him into it about three days later... he said he hadn't lost no monkey and he didn't want to see no monkey, but anyway he did it. That was three days after, of course.

A prospector camping in the desert near Borrego, California, in 1939 was approached by several hairy creatures. They had light-colored hair and glowing red eyes, a feature we shall meet with increasing frequency. The man had a campfire, and felt it was only that which prevented them from attacking him. In the same year, or it may have been in 1940, another prospector, Burns Yeomans, watched an unusual Bigfoot gathering near Silver Creek, up Harrison Lake, British Columbia. John Green interviewed him in 1965, and the transcript in his book *Sasquatch: The Apes Among Us* reveals the full details of the sighting. Apparently two men saw the creatures, from a distance of three-quarters of a mile, and they were able to observe them for about half an hour. They were dark in color, standing on two legs, but they did not look like bears. They were about 7 feet tall, and weighed around 400 pounds. There were four or five of them, and they were "wrestling just like men, down in this valley... One would throw the other down, he would jump right up on his hind legs again."

4
Bigfoot Can't Be Killed
1941-60

Bigfoot continued to put in enigmatic appearances in the fifth and sixth decades of the twentieth century. In 1941-2 many people near Mount Vernon, Illinois, saw "a large baboon," and although it was hunted, it eluded capture. A report in *Hoosier Folklore* details some sightings, beginning with one in the Gum Creek bottom near Mount Vernon.

> …During the summer of 1941, a preacher was hunting squirrels in the woods along the creek when a large animal that looked something like a baboon jumped out of a tree near him. The preacher struck at the beast with his gun barrel when it walked toward him in an upright position. He finally frightened it away by firing a couple of shots into the air.
>
> Later the beast began to alarm rural people by uttering terror-

izing screams mostly at night in the wooded bottom lands along the creeks. School children in the rural districts sometimes heard it, too, and hunters saw its tracks … By early spring of 1942, the animal had local people aroused to a fighting pitch. About that time, a farmer near Bonnie reported that the beast had killed his dog. A call went out for volunteers to join a mass hunt to round up the animal.

The beast must have got news of the big hunt, for reports started coming in of its appearance in other creek bottoms, some as much as 40 or 50 miles from the original site. A man driving near the Big Muddy River, in Jackson County, one night saw the beast bound across the road. Some hunters saw evidence of its presence away over in Okaw. Its rapid changing from place to place must have been aided considerably by its ability to jump, for, by this time, reports had it jumping along at from 20 to 40 feet per leap.

During the time that this "baboon" was being seen in Illinois, Mrs. Jeannie Chapman lived through a terrifying afternoon 1,800 miles to the northwest in British Columbia. It was a fine day in September 1941, and she was at home with her three children aged nine, seven, and five in a small and isolated house near Ruby Creek, beside the Fraser River. Her eldest son reported seeing a "cow" coming out of the woods, but when she went to look, she thought the creature was a bear. As it came nearer, she could see that it was a huge, hairy man about 7½ feet tall, wide-shouldered and with long arms. The hair was pale yellow-brown, about 4 inches long. As the creature seemed to be making for their house, Mrs. Chapman grabbed the frightened children and, shielding them from the creature's view, shepherded them away to the safety of the village. Later that day, George Chapman returned home from work and found the house deserted. He was rather alarmed to find huge, 16-inch-long human-like footprints everywhere, and a broken woodshed door, but then he saw his family's tracks beside the river, not followed by the huge

Figure 7: The cabin at Ruby Creek, British Columbia, abandoned by Mrs. Jeannie Chapman and her family in 1941 following a visit by a Bigfoot. Photographed in 1957. *Photo: RD/FPL*

ones. It seemed that after the Chapmans had fled, the Bigfoot had looked around and broken open a 55-gallon tub of salt fish which it had scattered around. In the days that followed, the Bigfoot returned to the house every night for a week, and although it did no harm to people or property, the experience was too much for the family and they left the house for good.

One of the rare known cases of murder by Bigfoot is said to have occurred in 1943, at Dewilde's camp, near Ruby, Alaska. The victim was John Mire or McQuire, also called "The Dutchman" by the local Indians. He lived alone with his dogs in a cabin at the isolated camp, and one day in 1943 he is reported to have gone by boat to the nearest village and told how he had been attacked by "the Bushman" but his dogs had chased it away. However "The Dutchman" died not long afterwards of internal bleeding caused by the attack.

A Bigfoot whose witnessed activity sounds like that of an athlete in training was briefly seen by Alex Oakes on Vancouver Island, British Columbia, in the early 1940s. The 7-foot, brown-hair-covered creature crossed the road in front of Oakes as he drove near his home at Coombes. It crossed at high speed, hurdling the fences on both sides, and Oakes particularly noticed its 6-inch-long shoulder hair streaming out behind. Another highway sighting was made in the spring of 1947 by a man and wife traveling on old Highway 99 south of Shasta, California. They saw what they at first took to be a post beside the road and, thinking it indicated a "washout," they stopped to see if the road ahead was clear. Then the "post" began to cross the road, and they realized it was in fact an 8- or 9-foot creature covered with long reddish-brown hair. It came up to the car and looked in at them, then went across the road to look at the bank, before finally returning to its first location, where another similar creature was waiting. This, according to the witnesses, was clearly a female, and the male helped it across the road and up the bank. They walked into the trees with their arms around each other. Such behavior, of apparent affection between two Bigfeet, is rarely witnessed. The two seemed to have no fear of the onlookers, who said that the female never even looked their way. Was she blind, perhaps? This would explain the excessive care on the part of the male. It would also suggest that the Bigfeet are rather more human than animal, insofar as only humans, generally speaking, take care of their sick fellows. However, this is speculative thinking.

Yet another roadway sighting, indicating what a high proportion of Bigfoot sightings do take place on roads, was made in 1947, this time only a short distance from Vancouver, British Columbia. Mr. and Mrs. Werner were in a jeep traveling along a logging road when they came upon two naked creatures which, they felt, were not quite human. The description they gave contains several non-Bigfoot-like features: the creatures had "a skin wrapped around them" (reports of clothed Bigfeet are rare); both had bare feet and long shoulder-length hair, but there was no mention of hair-covered bodies; one carried a stick over one shoulder with a kind of bag tied to the end and appeared to be leading the smaller creature, whose hands may have been tied. But lest the reader wonder if these may merely have been humans, maybe somewhat demented, or merely play-acting, the Werners also reported that the creatures had "huge" feet, that the leader was about 8 feet tall, and the smaller one 6 feet. Facially, they had flat, wide noses, small eyes, and bushy eyebrows. The Werners had not heard of Bigfoot, and could only think they had seen some kind of wild man. In view of the uncharacteristic features of this sighting, we cannot be sure that they did see Bigfeet. But if they did, then it seems there are aspects to this creature which suggest it is rather more than an unknown ape.

A grizzly bear seen briefly and at a distance by an inexperienced witness might be mistaken for a "Bigfoot," but this would not explain all the detailed descriptions of creatures clearly not grizzlies, while many witnesses are well able to tell a grizzly from a Bigfoot. One such was Clayton Mack, a Bella Coola, British Columbia, Indian who was a well-respected grizzly bear hunter and big-game guide. He saw a Bigfoot in the 1940s while he was in a boat heading for Quatna to do some fishing, and in 1967 he described to Bigfoot hunters John Green and René Dahinden what he had seen.

> I saw this thing walking on the beach; a light brown color, stand-ing about eight to nine feet tall. I thought it was a big bear — but he didn't go down on his four legs. I was nosing right towards him but I was about four hundred yards away so I didn't get a good look at his face. I kept wondering because he didn't go down on his four legs. He was right on the edge of the water; he stood up straight and looked at me, then turned and walked up to the timber. Then halfway up to the driftwood logs he stopped and turned and looked at me, twisting his head round. I never seen a grizzly bear on its hind feet stand and twist round with just its

head; they always turn the whole body, and they go down on four feet to do it. Then he went on and got to the logs and walked on top of them. He got to the timber — it's second-growth and it looked as though he just reached out and spread the trees apart as he walked through them, young spruce and hemlock trees.

Not long after the 1947 report of possible Bigfeet wearing rudimentary clothes already quoted, comes another such sighting, from around 1950. The witness was a 10-year-old girl who later wrote her story in a letter to biologist and author Ivan T. Sanderson after reading something he had written concerning Bigfoot. The relevant part of her letter follows.

When: About 9 years ago, at about 10 o'clock in the morning. Where: Near the Eel River above Eureka, California. At the edge of a meadow near the river's edge. Under what circumstances: My family and I were fishing on the Eel River. We had been camped in the vicinity for about two weeks and had had poor luck when it came to fishing. I used to go for a short walk before breakfast because there was a very pretty meadow about a mile or two from our camp and I used to love to see the mist rise off the grass. I was only about 10 years old at the time and the world of nature was something which both fascinated and enthralled me. I entered the meadow and proceeded to cross it in order to reach a small knoll at the other side. When I approached the foot of the knoll I heard a sound. It was the sound of someone walking and I thought perhaps my little brother had followed me and was going to jump out and try to scare me. I hollered, "All right, stinker, I know you're there." Needless to say it was not my brother that appeared. Instead it was a creature that I will never forget as long as I live. He stepped out of the bushes and I froze like a statue. He or "it" was about 7½ to 8 feet tall. He was covered with brown stuff that looked more like a soft down than fur. He had small eyes set close together and had a red look about them. His nose was very large and flat against his face. He had a large mouth with the strangest looking fangs that I have ever seen… His form was that of a human and he had hands and feet of enormous size, but very human looking. However, there was one thing that I have not mentioned, the strangest and most frightening thing of all. He had on clothes! Yes, that's right. They were tattered and torn and barely covered him but they were still there. He made a horrible growling sound that I don't think could be imitated by any living thing. Believe me I turned and ran as fast as I could. I reached camp winded and stayed scared all while we were there.

If Bigfoot — and the creature in this report really does sound like a Bigfoot — is as well adapted to living in the wild as most reports suggest, why does he need to don tattered clothes? The only explanation that occurs to us is that this was a "freak" sighting: that the Bigfoot had found the old clothes somewhere and, having seen humans dressed in clothes, decided to copy them. The fact that the clothes "barely covered him" does suggest that they once had a smaller, human, owner.

The clothed Bigfoot was so close to the young girl it could easily have injured her had it wished to. But despite giving a horrible growl, it kept its distance. A Bigfoot seen near Orleans, California, one terrifying night in 1952 definitely acted in a menacing way, but again did not attack, even though it was at one point face to face with the witness. Indeed, when the witness raised his fist, the Bigfoot backed off. If the creature did not really intend to attack the witness, why behave in the frightening way it did? Was it all a game? Was the Bigfoot trying to convey something to the witness? Or did it intend to kidnap him? That seems unlikely, for it had the chance but did not take it. The witness's account was sent in a letter to Bigfoot hunter Roger Patterson, and the man was later seen by John Green, who said he appeared to be serious about his story.

Figure 8: Cryptozoologist Ivan T. Sanderson, who wrote an early classic book on man-beasts worldwide — *Abominable Snowmen: Legend Come to Life* **(1961) — made this drawing of the North American Sasquatch/Bigfoot in 1970.**

I had been reading a story written by Ivan T. Sanderson about a Bigfoot monster that people had seen in Northern California. As I was reading the story I suddenly had the eerie realization that I, too, had had a similar experience. As the story came snaking its way out of my subconscious, I began to remember more and more of what happened. I had me a bad case of the jitters as the memory uncoiled.

The first part of the story took me back to 1952, when I had gone down to Orleans to start preliminary work on a logging operation with two men by the names of Lee Vlery and Josh Russel.

One evening Josh told me Lee had gone up to Happy Camp, but not having transportation back, wanted me to take the Mercury and go up and get him. I had driven the extremely crooked and dangerous road up there, but not being able to find him started back alone to Orleans.

It had been raining very heavily and after going back a few miles I found there had been a slide across the road. There was a man with a flashlight there who told me I could still get back to Orleans by way of a detour across the river. He said it was a dirt road that went through Bear Valley and would come out at the mouth of Bluff Creek a few miles below Orleans.

I had been driving slowly down this road for about twenty miles, I guess, sort of daydreaming, when I saw it … dimly in the headlights and the rain was the shaggy orangutang-like apparition of a human. For an instant I had the impression the shaggy hair of the creature was a hoary blue gray in the headlights. An ogre! I remember thinking, but the thing swiftly backpedalled off the road and behind a tree. I automatically passed it off as imagination and drove on by the spot.

Suddenly, without warning, the car went into a violent and unreasonable skid. I brought the car back under control, but for some reason glanced into the rear view mirror. In the dim light of the tail lights and license-display bulb, I thought I could see a savage looking face looking through the rear glass. I continued on, and when I looked again there was no face, so again concluded it was imagination.

I had gone another quarter mile, I guess, when across the road was a small six-inch sapling — I stopped the car and got out, intending to drag it aside if possible. Suddenly I heard the swift thud of flying feet of something coming down the road. Reality was upon me and I remember cursing myself for not paying attention to what I had previously seen. It was the shaggy human-like monster I had seen in the headlights.

It at once started circling around me, snarling and acting very menacing. It kept this circling up for some time and once came up quite close, and I could see its face reflected by the headlights much better. The eyes were round, and rather luminous, the hair on top of its rather low and rounded head pretty short. Its eye teeth were far longer than a human's, also the chest and upper part of the torso was rather bare of hair, and also leathery looking. It wasn't too tall — not much more than my own 5 feet 9 inches — although it had a stooped, long-armed posture.

Then it suddenly changed tactics — it would stalk off down the road but would come charging back, like a bat out of hell, when I started toward the car. The hour was late, the thing was becoming more and more menacing, and I was almost paralyzed by this time, paralyzed by fear.

Suddenly a plan of escape, born out of desperation, popped into my mind. Since the monster seemed to think I couldn't get away, why not, when it went down the road again, playing cat and mouse, try and get in the car and smash through the sapling. This I did, and sprang for the door of the car a dozen feet away. No sooner was I inside when there it was, trying to claw through the window. I jerked the car into gear, floored the accelerator, and can vividly remember the wet sapling glistening whitely in the headlights as the car slashed it aside.

I remember then the scream of rage and frustration it then gave. It was a curious trumpeting sound like the scream of a stallion and the roar of a mad grizzly. The car then felt as though it were being held back by something half riding and attempting to stop it, but the powerful Mercury proved too much for it, and after a couple of hundred yards I felt no more resistance.

To top this unbelievable experience off, believe it or not, I promptly forgot the whole experience. Then and there it went out of my mind. Not even the next day when Lee asked me if I had seen anything unusual on that road last night did I remember. (He had come later from Happy Camp with another man he hired to take him to Orleans.)

A few days later an incident happened that should have brought the experience back but didn't. Lee noticed a big dent in the grill of the car and asked me how it got there. I told him I didn't know. Incidentally, Lee told me that something had tried to push them off the road, when they came through on the detour. He said there's something strange going on around here and let the matter drop.

A Bigfoot seen in Georgia on 1 August 1955 really did act violently towards the witnesses, but it may have done so in self-defense, or at least revenge. Twenty-year-old Joseph Whaley was alone on the Bronwood-Smithville highway near the community of Kinchafoonee Creek, cutting grass and undergrowth with a scythe. He heard a strange noise and, going into the woods to investigate, saw a creature at least 6 feet tall and covered with "shaggy gray hair." It had "tusk-like teeth and pointed ears" and reminded him of a gorilla, though it was also manlike. It was "grunting like a wild pig" as it kept walking towards him. Whaley, not surprisingly frightened, swung his scythe at it and hit it on the chest and arms. But it kept coming and Whaley retreated to his jeep, intending to call for help on his radio. But he could not get through, and before he could start the engine and drive away, the creature was "upon him" and had scratched his arm and shoulder and torn his shirt. He jumped out of the jeep and kept it between him and the beast. Then, with the creature following him, moving in a "lumbering and slow-moving" manner, he ran into the woods and then doubled back to his jeep, getting it started and managing to drive off before the creature could return. When we remember the athletic Bigfoot described earlier, and indeed many other reports of fast-moving creatures, this report of a "lumbering and slow-moving" beast sounds unlike Bigfoot. Yet the physical description fits Bigfoot. As the reader will have noted, the Bigfoot phenomenon abounds in contradictions.

This book deals specifically with *sightings* of Bigfoot and so the many cases where evidence of Bigfoot (usually footprints) has been found but no actual creature seen have been omitted. However, there is one case which we felt we had to include, even though no Bigfoot was seen. The witness, Mrs. Darwin Johnson, had a most frightening experience while swimming in the Ohio River near Dogtown, Indiana, on 14 or 21 August 1955, and all the evidence we have suggests that a Bigfoot was to blame for her understandable terror. When she was about 15 feet from the shore, a large furry hand with claws grabbed her knee and pulled her under the water. She screamed and struggled, grabbing at her friend's innertube, and the hand released its grip. Back on shore, Mrs. Johnson found scratches on her leg, and a green stain with a palm outline could be seen for several days. After the incident was reported in the newspaper, several people came forward to say they had seen "a shiny oval" in the sky above the river at about the same time. This is one of around thirty incidents we have on file linking Bigfoot and UFO activity. Such a small number of reports can hardly be considered as positive evidence that UFOs and Bigfeet are linked, but perhaps some types of Bigfoot have UFO links, though not all of them.

Perhaps the best-known Bigfoot sighting of the 1950s is that of William Roe on Mica Mountain in British Columbia. At John Green's request he wrote out the details, and also made a statutory declaration as to the truth of the story. Roe's was an interesting encounter because he was very close to the creature, and, being hidden, had time to examine it at leisure.

Ever since I was a small boy back in the forest of Michigan, I have studied the lives and habits of wild animals. Later, when I supported my family in Northern Alberta by hunting and trapping, I spent many hours just observing the wild things. They fascinated me. But the most incredible experience I ever had with a wild creature occurred near a little town called Tete Jaune Cache, British Columbia, about eighty miles west of Jasper, Alberta.

I had been working on the highway near Tete Jaune Cache for about two years. In October, 1955, I decided to climb five miles up Mica Mountain to an old deserted mine, just for something to do. I came in sight of the mine about three o'clock in the afternoon after an easy climb. I had just come out of a patch of low brush into a clearing when I saw what I thought was a grizzly bear, in the bush on the other side. I had shot a grizzly near that spot the year before. This one was only about 75 yards away, but I didn't want to shoot it, for I had no way of getting it out. So I sat down on a small rock and watched, my rifle in my hands.

I could see part of the animal's head and the top of one shoulder. A moment later it raised up and stepped out into the opening. Then I saw it was not a bear.

This, to the best of my recollection, is what the creature looked like and how it acted as it came across the clearing directly toward me. My first impression was of a huge man, about six feet tall, almost three feet wide, and probably weighing somewhere near three hundred pounds. It was covered from head to foot with dark brown silver-tipped hair. But as it came closer I saw by its breasts that it was female.

And yet, its torso was not curved like a female's. Its broad frame was straight from shoulder to hip. Its arms were much thicker than a man's arms, and longer, reaching almost to its knees. Its feet were broader proportionately than a man's, about five inches wide at the front and tapering to much thinner heels. When it walked it placed the heel of its foot down first, and I could see the gray-brown skin or hide on the soles of its feet.

It came to the edge of the bush I was hiding in, within twenty feet of me, and squatted down on its haunches. Reaching out its hands, it pulled the branches of bushes toward it and stripped the leaves with its teeth. Its lips curled flexibly around the leaves as it ate. I was close enough to see that its teeth were white and even.

The shape of this creature's head somewhat resembled a Negro's. The head was higher at the back than at the front. The nose was broad and flat. The lips and chin protruded farther than its nose. But the hair that covered it, leaving bare only the parts of its face around the mouth, nose and ears, made it resemble an animal as much as a human. None of this hair, even on the back of its head, was longer than an inch, and that on its face was much shorter. Its ears were shaped like a human's ears. But its eyes were small and black like a bear's. And its neck also was unhuman. Thicker and shorter than any man's I had ever seen.

As I watched this creature, I wondered if some movie company was making a film at this place and that what I saw was an actor, made up to look partly human and partly animal. But as I observed it more, I decided it would be impossible to fake such a specimen. Anyway, I learned later that there was no such company near that area. Nor, in fact, did anyone live up Mica Mountain, according to the people who lived in Tete Jaune Cache.

Finally the wild thing must have got my scent, for it looked directly at me through an opening in the brush. A look of amazement crossed its face. It looked so comical at the moment I had to grin. Still in a crouched position, it backed up three or four short steps, then straightened up to its full height and started to walk rapidly back the way it had come. For a moment it watched me over its shoulder as it went, not exactly afraid, but as though it wanted no contact with anything strange.

The thought came to me that if I shot it, I would possibly have a specimen of great interest to scientists the world over. I had heard stories of the Sasquatch, the giant hairy Indians that live in the legends of British Columbia Indians, and also many claim, are still in fact alive today. Maybe this was a Sasquatch, I told myself.

I levelled my rifle. The creature was still walking rapidly away, again turning its head to look in my direction. I lowered the rifle. Although I have called the creature "it," I felt now that it was a human being and I knew I would never forgive myself if I killed it.

Just as it came to the other patch of brush it threw its head back and made a peculiar noise that seemed to be half laugh and half language, and which I can only describe as a kind of a whinny. Then it walked from the small brush into a stand of lodgepole pine.

I stepped out into the opening and looked across a small ridge just beyond the pine to see if I could see it again. It came out on the ridge a couple of hundred yards away from me, tipped its head back again, and again emitted the only sound I had heard it make, but what this half-laugh, half-language was meant to convey, I do not know. It disappeared then, and I never saw it again.

I wanted to find out if it lived on vegetation entirely or ate meat as well, so I went down and looked for signs. I found it in five different places, and although I examined it thoroughly, could find no hair or shells of bugs or insects. So I believe it was strictly a vegetarian.

I found one place where it had slept for a couple of nights

under a tree. Now, the nights were cool up the mountain, at this time of year especially, and yet it had not used a fire. I found no sign that it possessed even the simplest of tools. Nor a single companion while in this place.

Whether this was a Sasquatch I do not know. It will always remain a mystery to me, unless another one is found.

I hereby declare the above statement to be in every part true, to the best of my powers of observation and recollection.

William Roe

This Bigfoot was obviously not interested in abducting the human who had taken it so much by surprise. But not so the Bigfoot seen near Marshall, Michigan, in May 1956. According to Otto Collins and Philip Williams, the huge, hair-covered creature, with green eyes "as big as light bulbs" and smelling "like something rotten," picked them up and held each under an arm, until their colleague Herman Williams grabbed his gun. Maybe the Bigfoot knew what a gun was for, since it dropped the two men and made its escape.

Whether it really did intend to abduct the two men is not clear. The Bigfoot may only have wanted to frighten them. But the motives of a Bigfoot seen at Wanoga Butte near Bend, Oregon, in the autumn of 1957 are more apparent. Gary Joanis and Jim Newall were hunting, and Joanis had just shot a deer. Before he could go over to it, a 9-foot, hairy creature came into the clearing, picked the deer up, and carried it off under its arm. Very annoyed at such behavior, Joanis fired his .30-06 repeatedly into the beast's back as it departed, but it gave no sign that it had been injured, unless its "strange whistling scream" was a cry of pain. It kept on walking, and Joanis let it go, since he obviously had no choice.

Another unsuccessful shooting attempt was made in October 1959. This was at Ten Mile, west of Roseburg, Oregon, and the witnesses were two boys, one 12 and one 17, named Wayne Johnson and Walter Stork. After the 12-year-old had seen the Bigfoot near an abandoned sawmill, the two went back there together, with guns, to look for it. It obliged them by showing up, but began to chase them, and they both shot at it. The 17-year-old, reputed to be a good shot, was able to get some good shots in with his .30-06, but the creature kept coming, though it did fall forward a couple of times onto its knuckles. The boys wondered later if it had merely been trying to shoo them from its territory. It had its arms outstretched as if herding them, and it did not actually catch up with them, though it could have done, being, they reckoned, 14 feet tall! (An overestimate by the terrified young witnesses?) Suddenly it was no longer following them, but they did not see where it went. Bob Titmus, Bigfoot investigator, was on the scene within two days and found some strange tracks. They were only 11½ inches long, but 8 inches wide at the toes, of which there were five, and with no apparent claws. In wet ground the prints sank in as deep as 14 inches, but Titmus could make only a 2- or 3-inch impression with his heel in similar ground.

If territory-possessiveness was the explanation for the Ten Mile Bigfoot's behavior, it may equally well have been the motive behind the behavior of a Bigfoot briefly seen at Hidden Lake in the Okanagan Valley of British Columbia in the autumn of 1959. Mr. and Mrs. Bellvue were camping there, and one evening at dusk, while gathering firewood, Mrs. Bellvue felt she was being watched. Looking around, she saw a humanlike figure over 6 feet tall standing partly hidden by a tree about 50 feet away. It was covered with rust-colored hair, except for parts of its face, and had a slit-like mouth, "a flat area with two holes" for a nose, and a forehead which sloped back. It continued to watch as Mrs. Bellvue returned to camp, and she said later, "I felt that it didn't want me to know it was there." She did not immediately tell her husband, but that night suddenly felt that they had to leave. So she then told him, and he announced that he had got the same feeling the day before! As they packed their gear next day, they heard the sound of running feet which gradually faded away.

Figure 9: Mr. and Mrs. Bellvue, who saw a Bigfoot at Hidden Lake in 1959 (photographed in 1966). *Photo: RD/FPL*

As the next chapters will show, Bigfoot activity seemed to increase in the 1960s and 1970s. This apparent build-up may be due in part to an increasing human interest in the creature. This has meant that more sightings are reported in the press, and researchers are now unlikely to miss such newspaper reports. Before the 1960s, many reports must have gone unnoticed, and there is probably much important data hidden away in old newspaper files. Researchers have already located some such reports, and there are likely to be many more. So although from 1960 onwards we have details of more Bigfoot sightings, this does not necessarily mean that Bigfoot is being seen more often.

The first notable report we have from 1960 describes a weird and frightening encounter which took place in woods near Davis, West Virginia. During the summer a group of young men were camping out, and one had gone out at night to cut firewood. The others must have been close at hand, judging by the main witness's report of what happened. Feeling someone poking him in the ribs, he naturally thought it was one of his friends — until he turned and found himself face to face with a "horrible monster." "It had two huge eyes that shone like big balls of fire and we had no light at all. It stood every bit of eight feet tall and had shaggy long hair all over its body. It just stood and stared at us. Its eyes were very far apart." Leaving giant footprints as proof of its existence, it finally wandered off without harming them, but the boys nevertheless felt no inclination to stay, and next day they left their campsite.

Another intriguing sighting, maybe of the same creature, took place in West Virginia in 1960. This was in October, in the Monongahela National Forest near Marlington. W.C. "Doc" Priestley was driving through the forest, following a bus in which were some friends of his. The car had been behaving normally, but suddenly it sputtered and stopped. Then Priestley saw a "monster with long hair pointing straight up toward the sky" standing beside the road. "I don't know how long I sat there, until the boys missed me and backed the bus back to where I was. It seemed this monster was very much afraid of the bus and dropped his hair (which had been standing on end) and to my surprise as soon as he did this, my car started to run again. I didn't tell the boys what I had seen. The thing took off when the bus stopped." Priestley followed the bus as before, but soon his car again began to misbehave. "I could see the sparks flying from under the hood of my car as if it had a very bad short. And sure enough, there beside the road stood the monster again. The points were completely burned out of my car." Again the bus returned, and the Bigfoot left, this time for good. This apparent ability of some Bigfeet to affect the working of electromagnetic devices may be linked to the question of whether they are physical or non-physical creatures, a question that became even more relevant as the 1960s progressed.

5
Monster Mania Develops
1961-65

The decade of the sixties started quietly so far as reported sightings went, although an interesting case has been recorded from some time in 1961. Larry Martin went with friends one evening to pick up a deer one of them had killed near Alpine, Oregon. They found that the carcass had been dragged away, and they heard thrashing noises in the brush. Not sure what was making the noise, they cautiously looked around. Suddenly Martin's light illuminated a tall, hair-covered Bigfoot only a few feet away: "I knew it wasn't a bear 'cause it had human-like features, you know, it looked like an ape or gorilla or something like that, and it was coming at me." Martin, 5 feet 10 inches tall, had to shine the light up into the Bigfoot's face. Shocked, the man turned and ran, as did his friends. They got back to their car, but it would not start. Martin could see the Bigfoot in the rearview mirror: it was close behind the car.

Fortunately the car then started and "we got out of there." A question that immediately arises is: Why did the Bigfoot not catch the men? A big, 400-500-pound beast such as Martin described could easily have overtaken the frightened men before they reached the car, if it had wanted to. Perhaps it only wished to scare them off, so that it could deal with the dead deer in peace. Further evidence that Bigfeet don't intend to catch the people they chase seems to be provided by an incident that took place in October 1968, near Estacada, Oregon, when a fisherman was chased back to his truck by a Bigfoot waving its arms. In his haste, he fell — and the Bigfoot waited for him to get up before continuing the chase!

In June 1962 Robert Hatfield was woken by his barking dogs and went outside his house near Fort Bragg, California, to see what was disturbing them. He saw a dark form looking at his dogs over a 6-foot fence, so he returned to the house to wake his brother-in-law Bud Jenkins and show him the largest bear he had ever seen. Outside the two men could see nothing of the animal so Jenkins returned to the house to fetch a light and a gun. Meanwhile Hatfield thought he would take a look around the back of the house and as he rounded the corner he came face to chest with an 8-foot hairy creature that stood on two legs. Jenkins says that Hatfield

> let out a scream and stepped backwards and as he stepped back-wards he fell, so he came into the house on his hands and knees going like mad.
>
> My wife was at this time holding the screen door open for him to come in. I heard the commotion and I ran to the inside door which we have here before you step onto the porch, and as he came through the door I saw this large creature going by the window, but I could see neither its lower body nor its head, all I could see was the upper part of its body through the window there.
>
> When he came in my wife tried to close the door and they

got it within about two to four inches of closing and they couldn't close it. Something was holding it open. My wife hollered at me and said, "Hurry and get the gun, it's coming through the door!"

Of course by that time I was standing right behind her here in this door leading onto the porch, and I said, "Well, let it through and I'll get it."

At that time the pressure went off the door and she pushed the door to and threw the lock on it, and I walked to the window and put my hand up to the window and looked out, so that I could see out into the yard, because it was still dark, and it was raining, and this creature was standing upright, and I would judge it to be about eight feet tall and it walked away from the house, back out to this little fence we have, and stepped over the little fence and walked past my car and out towards the main road.

Jenkins judged that the creature would weigh about 400 pounds, and said that it always walked upright, never went down on all fours, and had a very bad smell, which lingered on the air after it had gone. In daylight the yard was searched and 16-inch-long footprints with only four toes were found. On the wall by the house door was found a handprint 11½ inches long. The two men later said that, although they had been very frightened at the time, the attitude of the creature was one of curiosity rather than aggression.

In this same month of June 1962 something strange was also appearing in Trimble County, Kentucky. We are not too sure whether the reports belong in this book or not, because although some witnesses described a creature that was 6 feet tall, covered in black hair, walked on its hind legs, and had arms which reached to its knees, others had seen a creature which was "not quite a dog, a panther, or a bear." At the same time dogs were mauled and elsewhere a calf was killed by a blow on the head, and there were other animal deaths and disappearances in the area. Claw marks and black hairs were found on the barn where the dead calf was found. These violent acts are not typical of most Bigfoot cases, but are similar to some of the big cat reports which have in recent years been published in both the United States and Britain. Possibly there was more than one type of mysterious visitor on the prowl during this time. This is not impossible. See, for example, the Minerva, Ohio, case of 1978 reported in Chapter 8, where the witnesses saw two puma-type creatures along with a Bigfoot.

A month later, in July 1962, two young couples were in a parked car near Mount Vernon, Rockcastle County, Kentucky, when a Bigfoot hunched up on all fours hopped up to the car. They said it was covered in hair and about the size of a man, and growled at them. The number of cases in which Bigfeet take an interest in courting couples in cars suggests that this is more than chance or coincidence. Such couples parked in unfrequented "lovers' lane" areas also seem to attract more than their normal share of attention from UFOs and associated phenomena. Whether this characteristic behavior will eventually help in solving the puzzle presented by Bigfoot and UFOs remains to be seen.

In August a lady named Mrs. Calhoun who was on a prospecting and fishing holiday had an unsettling experience. She was just off the Cariboo Highway between Quesnel and Prince George, British Columbia, and was in a small creek waiting for her daughter to return with their lunch. She heard a noise which she thought was her daughter and, turning to speak to her, met the half-human, half-animal eyes of a creature that was observing her. She was carrying a hunting rifle which she immediately swung up for self-protection. She told René Dahinden, veteran Bigfoot researcher:

My first, fleeting impression was that it was a human with very long arms. But it took me weeks to get out of my mind the look it was giving me from its small, black eyes as it stood there. It was like an ape but like a human as well. It had blond-brown hair on its chest and long, loose, matted hair on its head. It had high

Figure 10: Mrs. Calhoun, who saw a Bigfoot in British Columbia in 1962; photographed in 1966. *Photo: RD/FPL*

cheek bones, a wide, flat nose, a forehead that sloped back, and a mouth that stuck out. It opened its mouth, but didn't make a sound; just stood there looking at me. I started moving away and the thing jumped into the bush and disappeared. All the time as I was backing off down the creek, I knew I was being watched.

The next Bigfoot witness chose to remain anonymous when he phoned the Tuolumne County Sheriff's Department on the afternoon of 27 January 1963. He said he had been cutting firewood near Cold Springs off the Sonora Highway, northern California, when he had seen a hairy, manlike creature that stood 9-10 feet tall moving through the brushwood that surrounded the gravel pit where he was working. Deputy Sheriff Bill Huntley met up with Elbert Miller who lived near Cold Springs and together they took a ride out to the area. Both men expected to find nothing. They guessed that the caller had been more than a little drunk and had encountered a bear. When they arrived at the gravel pit it was dark, and after looking around for a few minutes they were just about to leave when an unearthly sound rang through the frosty air. They described the noise as like the scream of a person in horrible agony. But the creature that made it did not remain stationary; it circled their car, remaining hidden in the heavy undergrowth. It seemed to answer their shouts as it moved from one position to another with incredible speed and absolute silence, except for the hair-raising cries. Eventually the cries faded into the distance and Huntley and Miller left the scene. Later Huntley made a public appeal for the anonymous caller who had first alerted the police to come forward and give a fuller description, but he never did.

Bigfeet often seem curious about people camping in the wilds. In 1963 Harry Squiness was preparing for bed when his tent flap was opened and a hairy monkey face with human eyes peered in at him. Squiness was camped at Goose Point near Anahim Lake in British Columbia. He snatched up a light, which failed to work, so he ran outside and flung some petrol onto his dying campfire. In the light from the roaring flames he could see four creatures both man- and ape-like about 14 feet away, lying down as though trying to hide. When the light from the flames revealed them they jumped up and walked off into the darkness. The witness called out: "Hey, what are you doing out there? Hey, come back!" But the hairy creatures made no response and silently blended into the shadows of the night. The grassy ground revealed no footprints, but Squiness did note a huge handprint on a tree trunk which he showed to Clayton Mack, a respected Indian bear hunter and big-game guide from Anahim Lake.

In May 1964 a troop of boy scouts were camping at Brown's Gulch some 15 miles from Butte, Montana. At 4:00 o'clock one morning one of the boys heard something moving outside the tent. When he looked outside he was confronted by a manlike figure which was covered all over in brown hair, silver at the tips; the creature also had a thick beard. When the scout let out a scream it ran off and could be heard a little later splashing about in the nearby creek and making humanlike giggling noises. In the daylight a trail of human-shaped footprints was found running for 150 yards until they came to rocky ground and could no longer be found. Each footprint measured 20 inches long and 6 inches wide, and the creature had a 7-foot stride. Something with tracks nearly as big (18 inches by 5 inches), described as a 9-foot tall monster, covered with black hair, and with eyes that glowed with reflected light, was reported in May 1964 to be causing terrified fruit pickers to leave their jobs in the fields of Sister Lakes, Michigan. Since 1962 there had been various odd reports of something huge that lurked in the adjoining swamps, but it was not until the spring of 1964 that the reports escalated and then dominated the local newspaper headlines. On 9 June Gordon Brown, a fruit picker from Georgia, was driving with his brother when they saw the creature in their headlights. When it moved away into the woods, they followed the tracks, and when they caught up with it they saw a monster which seemed to be a cross between a gorilla and a bear, standing as straight as a tree and 9 feet tall. The two men sensibly decided to retreat to their car and get away quickly. Brown had also seen the Bigfoot the year before, but had then kept quiet to avoid ridicule.

The land on which the two men had tracked the monster was part of a farm owned by Evelyn Utrup and her husband John, and they too had a number of encounters with the creature when it frequently prowled about their property. Utrup had seen it standing in his yard with its "big, bright shining eyes" reflecting his headlights, and Mrs. Utrup told how the 500-pound creature had chased her back into the house on "great thundering feet" which caused the ground to tremble. She also reported that one of their Alsatian dogs had chased the creature one night and had returned with one eye changed to pale blue. After some weeks it reverted to its usual color.

The day following Gordon Brown's experience, more locals saw it and heard its typical "baby crying" noise, and on 11 June three 13-year-old girls out walking in daylight were confronted by the creature on a lonely road in Silver Creek Township. Joyce Smith fainted, and Patsy and Gail Clayton were rooted to the spot with fear. Apparently satisfied with the impression it had made, the monster lumbered off into the bushes. Overnight Sister Lakes changed from a rural community of 500 inhabitants into a teeming tourist center. Hundreds of "hunters" and sensation-seekers flocked into the area, every shop ran a Monster Sale, cafés sold Monster Burgers, the local radio station played Monster Music interrupted by the latest monster reports, and a double-bill horror show played at the movie house. One shopkeeper advertised a special monster-hunting kit. For $7.95 the keen hunter could buy a light, a net, a baseball bat, and, to clinch matters, a mallet and a stake. Teenagers were prone to dress in old fur coats and goof around in public places, but surprisingly no one was hurt, though Sheriff Robert Dool said: "I had to order hunters away because it's getting mighty dangerous; three thousand strangers prowling about at night with guns …" Such circumstances are not likely to produce high-quality reports, since people are keyed up and expect to see Bigfoot. In this state of mind they are very likely to see something which they interpret as Bigfoot but which someone unaffected by the atmosphere realizes is nothing of the sort.

An odd characteristic of some Bigfeet is their habit of shaking cars and caravans or trailers. This happened to Benjamin Wilder on 13 September 1964 when he was asleep in his car in an uninhabited area near Blue Lake in northwest California. At one in the morning Wilder was woken up by his car moving. He first thought it was an earth tremor, but when it happened again and he could hear no rocks falling, he switched on a light to take a look. He was more than surprised to see a large creature with shaggy, 3-inch-long hair on its chest standing outside the driver's door with its two arms on top of his car. He shouted at it but it only made pig-like noises back, so he sounded the horn. This scared it off and it walked away on its hind legs over the hill. He did not get a chance to see its face.

Our last report from 1964 is one of those incredible stories which surface every so often in Bigfoot research. It should be remembered that the people who report these strange incidents are not publicity-seeking crackpots, but are normal citizens of reasonable education who hold responsible jobs and have stable family lives. The following experience was related to Leonard Stringfield some ten years after it happened. Stringfield was a mature and responsible UFO researcher and was generally acknowledged to be a reliable, trustworthy, and receptive reporter. At the time of the incident Mrs. Lister was 18 years old and was dating her future husband. One night about 11:00 p.m. they were sitting in a car parked about a mile from the family farm, with no lights on. They both saw a figure moving across a field. When Lew Lister turned on the headlights, the creature came towards the car taking large hops or leaps. As it came towards them it passed through a three-strand barbed-wire fence as though it were as insubstantial as mist. The girl screamed and the creature lunged at Lister and tried to grab him as the couple desperately tried to wind up the windows. Mrs. Lister felt hypnotized by the glowing eyes and felt that she had "had a time lapse or like I was living in another time … I just remembered its eyes focused on mine." She could see that the creature was 6 feet tall, with wide shoulders, and covered with a yellowish fuzz. "The head was horrible. It was pointed at the top and narrow at the chin and the brow was wrinkled — I'm sure of this — and its ears were large like pigs' and the nose was also like a pig's. I'm sure the eyes glowed orange, and the teeth were like fangs." Then, as she watched, she saw it change into another form. Its hands became paws and it went on all fours. It happened like a slow-motion movie, she said, and then suddenly it was gone. It had vanished into thin air.

Another strange experience, without the horrific overtones, was that of two brothers working as prospectors for mining companies. Their job was to travel the remote areas of Canada and report to their employers what minerals could be found there. On 28 June 1965 they were in the wild, mountainous area near Pitt Lake, about 25-30 miles northeast of the city of Vancouver. They were at an elevation of about 4,000 feet and deep snow lay everywhere although the weather was clear and sunny. Here is their firsthand report of what they saw:

> We were hiking into a valley about noon when we ran into these tremendous footprints that went down to a small stream that was frozen over. The ice had been broken and then the footprints led back up again, away from it. We spent some time studying the prints because of their size. They were twice the length of my boot, which would make them twenty-four inches long, and the width across the base of the toes was twelve inches. The distance between the footprints was twice my stride, and their depth in the snow was about two inches. You could tell the right foot from the left because of the bulbous big toes. We went on up the valley — and then, looking across a small frozen pond we could see this creature. We both figured the thing was between ten and twelve feet tall. It was covered in auburn hair, the head was close to the shoulders and seemed to have fairly long and very much darker hair than the rest of it. The arms were longer than a human's, seeming to come below the knee. When we saw it, it was within a city-block length of us, at about the same height as us on the

opposite side of the valley.

The hands were huge — they reminded me of our canoe paddle and they were open; they appeared to be a yellowish color. We spent some time watching the creature; in fact we both had a chocolate bar and a cigarette while we watched. It just stood, transferring its weight from one foot to the other, which gave it a kind of rocking motion, and its hands seemed to go back and forth as it moved.

It didn't seem to be ferocious or anything so we just stayed and watched it for a while, then we carried on up the valley. We were in the valley approximately four and a half hours. When we came down again it had gone and we returned to our base camp.

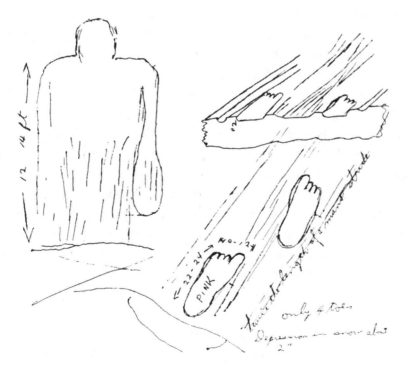

Figure 11: Sketches made by two prospectors following their Bigfoot sighting near Pitt Lake, British Columbia, on 28 June 1965.

An additional puzzle, besides the giant tracks these witnesses found, was the presence of parallel grooves in the snow, a wide shallow one between the footprints and a narrower and deeper one on each side of them. One of the men made a sketch of this in his notebook, and later made a sketch as they watched the creature. They also noted that the snow inside the footprints had a pink tint. The next day they saw similar footprints but smaller than those they had first seen, and these prints led to a hole broken in the ice in the middle of a small pond.

Three days later one of the brothers was back at the lake again, this time in a helicopter he had rented, and he was accompanied by a reporter from the Vancouver *Sun*. They took photographs of the tracks and found others which climbed over a cliff edge onto a ledge below. The brothers at that time would not allow publication of their names in order to protect their professional reputations, and so the full story was not published.

It is thought that Bigfeet have no fear of the water, and they appear to be strong swimmers. One incident which suggests this occurred in July 1965 near Princess Royal Island, not far from Butedale, British Columbia. The witness, a shore worker from Butedale, was out for an afternoon's fishing when he noticed on an islet some 75 yards away two gigantic bipedal creatures standing in the shadows. He could see they were covered in dark hair and were heavily built. He also saw something moving powerfully through the water but it did not seem to be using its arms to swim with. It was, he decided, another of the huge creatures and as it seemed to be heading directly towards him he started up his outboard motor and rapidly left. As he did so he had an impression that there were yet two more of the creatures standing on the mainland beach. His concentration, and it would not be unfair to say panic, on leaving the area, was such that he appeared not to notice a friend whom he passed and who was on his way out to join him.

Most of the reports indicate that Bigfoot, huge though it is, does not have an aggressive attitude towards humans; but the following case might be one of the exceptions. From the various sources we have consulted, it is difficult to be sure precisely what happened at the crucial moment. The injuries sustained by Christine van Acker could have been deliberate or the result of a clumsy movement. On 13 August 1965 Christine, aged 17, was driving through a wooded area near Monroe, Michigan, with her mother sitting beside her. The car windows were wound down and as they rounded a bend a huge, dark, hairy creature stepped out of the trees onto the road. In her haste to accelerate past it, Christine trod on the brake pedal and the car stalled. As she tried to restart the car the Bigfoot reached through the window and put a "huge hairy hand on top of her head." Both mother and daughter were now screaming, and as the Bigfoot left Christine's head was banged against the inside of the car. Nearby workmen heard the screams and the sound of the car horn and came running as the creature merged into the shadow of the woods. Christine, who suffered a black eye, said the Bigfoot was about 7 feet tall and would have weighed 300 to 400 pounds. She also remarked on the creature's strong smell.

The strength of Bigfoot, and the speed with which it can move across country, are illustrated by the following experience which Jimmy Nelson of Bella Coola, British Columbia, related to John Green. In November 1965 he was hunting at Green Bay a few miles from Bella Coola and was several thousand feet up a mountainside, crossing an area where all the timber had been cut ready to be taken by the loggers. He caught sight of a manlike black form walking up the mountainside. Nelson got the impression that the creature was large from the speed with which it covered the log-strewn ground. He watched it for ten minutes, during which time it crossed the swath of felled timber at an angle, simply walking over the trunks. The same "slashed" area took Nelson about two hours to cross as he had either to climb over or crawl under the fallen trunks. Moreover he took the shortest route and crossed at right angles to the strip of felled timber, whereas the Bigfoot crossed at a considerable slant, appearing on his left side and re-entering the trees far to his right.

Figure 12: Bigfoot investigator René Dahinden standing beside a life-size 8-foot-tall sculpture of Bigfoot at Willow Creek, California, made by Jim McClarin. *Photo: RD/FPL*

That Bigfoot seems impervious to gunfire is well known to investigators, for there are many cases on record where a Bigfoot has been shot at with no apparent effect. Occasionally blood has been found, but never a corpse, and usually the Bigfoot walks off without taking any more notice of his assailant. This happened when 14-year-old James Lynn Crabtree met one when he was squirrel hunting near his home in Fouke, Arkansas, some time in 1965. He was alerted to something unusual when he heard some galloping horses running into a nearby lake. Next he heard a dog howling with pain. Running towards the noise, he came up behind an 8-foot-tall creature covered all over its body with 4-inch-long reddish-brown hair. It had very long arms and was standing like a man. It turned to face the boy and he could see no features except for a flat brown nose. The rest of the face was covered with hair. The Bigfoot walked towards young Crabtree who, being thoroughly scared at this monstrosity, shot it in the face three times with a shotgun. But as it showed no signs of hesitating, the boy left as quickly as he could. During the following years there were many similar sightings in the area, and giant-sized footprints were found. A movie called *The Legend of Boggy Creek,* which told the story of the monster with many fictional additions, was shot on location there.

6
Red-Eyed Monsters in the Night
1966-70

Another aggressive move by a Bigfoot, similar to that reported by Christine Van Acker in the previous chapter, occurred just outside Fontana, California, on 27 August 1966. Earlier, in July, some boys had reported seeing an ape-like creature and one boy said he had been scratched and had his clothes torn by it, but nobody paid much attention to him. A couple of teenage girls drove around the area on 27 August looking for the monster; they found it, too. Sixteen-year-old Jerri Mendenhall was backing the car down a rough track when the Bigfoot stepped out of the bushes and grabbed her through the open window. She screamed and accelerated the car, and the Bigfoot walked back into the bushes. She described it as having very matted and slimy hair and smelling "like a dead animal." Later an officer from the sheriff's department found a two-toed footprint that measured 17 inches long by 6 inches wide. Later, when re-experiencing the encounter under regressive hypnosis, Jerri exhibited extreme terror and had to be brought out of the hypnotic state.

In Washington during the summer and autumn of 1966 there were a number of sightings of white or gray Bigfeet — maybe the same animal? In the area of Richland, the Bigfoot seen during the summer was described as being whitish-gray, 8 feet tall with red eyes, weighing at least 600 pounds, and walking like a human. It was seen by a group of young men on several occasions; in fact they used to drive around at night looking for it, and often found it in an old gravel pit. One of the witnesses, Greg Pointer, offered to take a lie detector test at any time. Another, Roger True, had from a range of only 20 feet hit it at least three times with bullets from a .270 caliber rifle, but didn't even knock it down; and Tom Thompson fired a 12-gauge shotgun from 10 yards. He said: "It screamed, a sort of high-pitched squeal, but the shots didn't stop it from running away." One group of teenagers had thrown rocks at it, then tried to ram it with their car, and as the car passed it, the Bigfoot scraped its hand down the side of the vehicle. This was the only action on its part that could be described as aggressive. Such a wild story naturally captured the interest of the investigators, who got the witnesses to go over the details repeatedly without finding any discrepancies. The young people insisted that they were not lying or exaggerating and had in fact reported incidents in the past to both parents and police, but were not taken seriously at any time.

If ever someone had sufficient nerve to act in a calm and friendly manner when meeting a Bigfoot, they might find that they could establish a fruitful relationship. It sounds as though this almost happened in the following case, but aggressive male instincts came to the fore and spoiled the situation. It was in the autumn of 1966 near Lower Bank, New Jersey, when a couple first found 17-inch, five-toed tracks outside their house after having seen a face peering in through a window that was over 7 feet high. They started to leave scraps of vegetables outside, which were eaten. The only delicacy Bigfoot rejected was a peanut butter and jelly (jam) sandwich. On the night they failed to leave the scraps out they heard a loud banging outside the house. When the husband went outside he found a gray-haired Bigfoot throwing a dustbin against the house wall. He fired a shot into the air, but Bigfoot did not budge, so he then shot at it and the creature ran off and did not return.

1967 was a memorable year for Bigfoot hunters. Not only was this the year Roger Patterson allegedly filmed a Bigfoot in California, but also during 1967 there were some other amazing encounters, some of which we shall now recount.

A report from May 1967 came from The Dalles in Oregon, where a group of teenagers several times saw Bigfeet, and gathered friends together to organize Bigfoot hunts. On the first occasion they were chased into a field by a creature that was 8-9 feet tall, which burst through a fence and then stopped to watch them. As they moved off quickly to get to the road, the creature moved away too and stopped when they did. They got onto the nearby road and saw in a car's headlights that the creature was crossing the road. They got a lift to a nearby café and rounded up some friends. Armed with sticks and rocks they returned to the area of the sighting. They saw a creature halfway up a hillside, but when they started to chase it, it easily outdistanced them. They returned the next night armed with guns, but saw only one Bigfoot at a distance. The third night the group numbered some twelve teenagers variously armed with heavy caliber guns. Dennis Taylor and Dave Churchill separated from the others and conducted their own search. They passed a tree on the hillside whose branches hung down to the ground. Pulling aside the branches, they peered into the gloom and saw, 8-10 feet away, a large figure that was still 7 feet tall in the crouched position. Dave Churchill blasted it twice in the chest with his 12-gauge shotgun. This knocked the creature down and it rolled over twice before it stood up and smashed its way through a fence, snapping off three fence posts at the ground. They returned next day to follow the tracks and claim their victim, but after 80-100 yards they lost the tracks and there were no bloodstains left to follow. Bigfeet were still seen in the area after that and they continued to watch the marauding parties with fearless curiosity. On one occasion there were five youngsters, in two groups of two and three, and, while the pair watched, they saw a Bigfoot standing 8 feet behind the other three boys and watching them. When it turned to leave and made a noise with a stone, the three became aware of it, but as it was going they refrained from firing at it. By that time they were, perhaps, becoming aware of the futility of shooting at these creatures.

Another area which featured multiple sightings was the Nooksack River, Washington. In the autumn of 1967 there were more than a dozen sightings, and some researchers equated this activity with the abundant run of salmon in the river that was reported at the time. In September Mr. and Mrs. Joseph Brudevold were fishing in the river when they saw an 8-foot Bigfoot standing with the water up to its knees. It bent down and slipped under the surface and they did not see it again. Later, footprints were found in the riverside mud, 13½ inches long and 2 inches deep. Their own, tested in the same mud, were half an inch deep. The creature's stride was 45 inches long. On 21 September, prints again measuring 13½ inches long were found after Mrs. Brudevold, who was fishing at night, saw a Bigfoot suddenly stand up in the water about 4 feet from the side of her boat.

Perhaps the most dramatic of these incidents occurred when an Indian, John Green (not the same person as the Bigfoot investigator of that name), was drifting with his fishing net out at night and the net seemed to catch on a snag. He shone his light across the water and saw a 7-foot-tall Bigfoot trying to get at the fish in his net. His shouts alerted two nearby fishermen who came over, training their lights on the creature as it waded ashore to an island and walked off into the trees. In the daylight Green, his fishing companions, and a law officer visited the site and found 16½-inch-long footprints. Green, who was quite sure he had not seen a bear, later passed a lie detector test.

One of the most momentous events in the annals of Bigfoot hunting occurred on 20 October 1967, when Roger Patterson shot 30 feet of 16-mm color film of a female Bigfoot at Bluff Creek in northern California. Patterson and his friend Bob Gimlin (who had both been searching for Bigfoot for several years and had on a number of occasions made plaster casts of very large footprints) were on horseback, riding through very wild country some 25 miles from the nearest made-up roadway. Bigfoot was known to inhabit this area and they were alert for whatever might appear. As they rounded a bend they saw a Bigfoot squatting beside the creek. At that moment their horses saw it too and reared in fright. Patterson's horse fell and he scrambled clear, wrenching his movie camera out of the saddlebag. The creature watched them for a moment and then walked unhurriedly away. Patterson ran after it trying to get closer and filming at the same time, stumbling and losing his footing as he crossed the creek. He was 80 feet away when he stopped and obtained reasonably clear pictures as the creature took nine paces before becoming partially hidden by trees. Just before this point, and without pausing, it turned to look at the photographer, and large, pendulous, hair-covered breasts are discernible on the movie image, identifying the Bigfoot as a female. Beyond the trees it was much farther away and in his excitement Patterson was not holding the camera rock-steady, so there is a certain amount of blur on all the film. Later the two men took casts of the footprints which the creature had made and they were found to measure 14½ inches long by 5½ inches wide.

In the decades since the film was shot, it has continued to puzzle and to infuriate in equal measure. It has its staunch supporters and its equally staunch opponents — and there are also a few people who claim to have actually *been* the Bigfoot (wearing an ape suit, of course). Many thousands of words have been devoted to this enduring mystery, but the skeptics have not yet been able to prove it a hoax, despite their deep longing to do so. The fact that the controversy has rumbled on for nearly 40 years demonstrates that if the film was a hoax, it was a good one. In 2004 hominologists Dmitri Bayanov and Igor Bourtsev made an announcement which they hope will bring an end to the controversy:

they offered $100,000 to anyone who can "successfully demonstrate to a panel of hominologists and anthropologists that the Patterson-Gimlin film shows a human being in a special suit."

For many years the rumor was that the ape suit used in the film was created by Academy-Award winning special effects man John Chambers — but when questioned in 1997, by which time he was in his seventies, Chambers explicitly said that he had had nothing to do with designing such a suit. In 1999 Bigfoot hunter Cliff Crook claimed to have seen a metal fastener on an enlarged still from the film, thus proving that the "creature" was a man in an ape suit, but others felt that it was impossible to enlarge the film to the extent necessary to pick out such a fastener and that what could be seen was merely a fastener-shaped blob. In 2004 Greg Long's book *The Making of Bigfoot: The Inside Story* was published, claiming to prove that Roger Patterson's Bigfoot footage was a hoax; but as Loren Coleman commented in his discussion of the book, "so many large holes exist in Long's case against Patterson that, had there ever been any reality to the hoax story, it would be very hard for anyone to see it now." In Long's book, it was claimed that Bob Hieronimus from Yakima, Washington, had worn the ape-suit (made by North Carolina gorilla-suit specialist Philip Morris) for Patterson's film, a claim hotly denied by Bob Gimlin who was with Patterson at the time the film was shot. Gimlin has always steadfastly maintained that no one wore an ape-suit, and in fact that no hoaxing took place. The most accessible and straightforward account of what occurred on that fateful day in 1967 can be found in Loren Coleman's book *Bigfoot! The True Story of Apes in America;* see also Christopher L. Murphy's book *Meet the Sasquatch* which contains more information on the numerous hoax claims, as well as many relevant photographs.

Figure 13: A scale model of the Bluff Creek film site (the scale is 1 inch = 9 feet) constructed by Christopher L. Murphy based on his visits to the site. Detailed site measurements can be found in his book *Meet the Sasquatch.* **Note especially the large distance between the fallen tree in the foreground and the location of the Bigfoot. The distance appears to be much less in the films because of Patterson's camera location.** *Photo: Christopher L. Murphy/FPL*

Figure 14: Frames from the cine film of Bigfoot taken by Roger Patterson on 20 October 1967 at Bluff Creek, northern California. *Photo: RD/FPL*

Figure 15: A still from the Patterson/Gimlin film showing clearly the terrain through which the Bigfoot was striding. *Photo: RD/FPL*

Figure 16: An enlargement of a still from the Patterson/Gimlin film showing a close-up of the Bigfoot turning back toward the camera. *Photo: RD/FPL*

Figure 17: Working from an enlargement of frame 352 of the Patterson/Gimlin film, Christopher L. Murphy enhanced the Bigfoot head with pastels on a laser color copy. *Photo: Christopher L. Murphy/FPL*

Figure 18: Roger Patterson photographed at Bluff Creek only hours after filming a Bigfoot there. He holds casts made from its footprints. *Photo: RD/FPL*

Figure 19: Bob Gimlin, who was with Roger Patterson when he filmed a Bigfoot at Bluff Creek, holds casts from tracks made by that Bigfoot. *Photo: RD/FPL*

Figure 20: US Forest Service worker Lyle Laverty took this photograph of a footprint the day after Roger Patterson captured a Bigfoot on film at Bluff Creek. *Photo: RD/FPL*

Figure 21: The mountainous and thickly wooded terrain around Bluff Creek, northern California, where Bigfeet could easily live — and spend most of their time out of sight of humans. *Photo: RD/FPL*

Figure 22: René Dahinden (left) holds the cast of a footprint left by the Bigfoot filmed at Bluff Creek, California, by Roger Patterson in October 1967, while Roger Patterson holds the cast of another footprint found earlier at Bluff Creek, in 1964. *Photo: RD/FPL*

The last significant case we have for 1967 was another detailed sighting of creatures that could be called Bigfeet, although they have some different characteristics from other reports already given. It was near the end of October and Glenn Thomas had been operating a power saw 6,000 feet up on the mountainside near Estacada, Oregon. He had taken a break from his work and was walking along a track through the woods. He came to a clearing where he saw three hairy humanlike creatures digging among the rocks. He took them to be a family group of male, female, and youngster. They appeared to be sniffing the rocks and when the male found what he was looking for he started to dig furiously, throwing up into the air rocks which weighed anything up to 100 pounds. Then he brought out a grass nest and from that extracted some hibernating rodents, marmots, or rock rabbits, Thomas thought. These were eaten as a human would eat a banana but with skin and all. For some fifteen minutes Thomas stood and watched the group until they became aware of him, when they moved off quietly and swiftly into the forest. He described their faces as more catlike than human, and also observed that they did not appear to use their thumbs very much when moving the rocks.

On 6 January 1968 two men had a sighting of a Bigfoot from an unusual vantage point. Robert James was piloting a light plane over Confidence Ridge, a desolate area north of Yosemite National Park, California, when 50 feet below he and his passenger Leroy Larwick saw a brown, fuzzy-haired creature about 10 to 12 feet tall standing erect.

Figure 23: Glenn Thomas (right) and René Dahinden standing on a pile of rocks thrown up near Estacada, Oregon, in October 1967 by a group of Bigfeet hunting for food. *Photo: RD/FPL*

They were quite sure it was not a bear and as they made another pass over it Leroy Larwick took a photograph. They landed the plane and returned to the area of the sighting, where they found 20-inch-long footprints which were also photographed. Photographs of Bigfeet are very rare and, as we have never seen this air-to-ground picture reproduced anywhere, we can only conclude that it was unsuccessful.

In the spring of 1968 Glenn Thomas had another Bigfoot encounter not many miles away from the first. He was 100 feet from the Bigfoot when he spotted it eating willow leaves. He climbed a roadside bank for a better view and could see that the creature had female breasts positioned low on the chest. It was covered in short, dark-brown hair and was between 5 and 6 feet tall. As with the rodent-eaters he had watched, he noticed its thumbs were farther back on the hand than a human's, and were not used. After a short while the Bigfoot noticed him and then ran away.

The reader will recall that reports earlier in this book suggest that some creatures of Bigfoot appearance behave in a manner that can only be called paranormal, and the following report is one of these. About 10:00 o'clock one autumn evening in 1968, the Abbott family, whose farmhouse was in the Point Isabel area of Ohio, heard a noise like metal being hit. Fifteen-year-old Larry Abbott, his father, and a relative, Arnold Hubbard, went outdoors to look around. They heard a rustling in the brush and by their flashlights saw a massive creature rise from the brush about 50 feet away and start walking towards them. It was about 10 feet tall and its massive shoulders were about 4 feet across. It was covered in light brown hair and had very long arms which swung at its sides. The teeth were prominent, the ears pointed, and its eyes were glowing. Larry said: "The thing put me into a sort of trance, I couldn't talk. Maybe it was just fright, but I couldn't open my mouth. And nobody else talked either. Maybe we were all in a trance." The creature dropped to the ground and they lost sight of it. A short time later they could hear it again near the garage. Hubbard borrowed a .22 rifle from Abbott and the men began a search of the property. As they crossed an open field the Bigfoot stood up about 50 feet away. Larry put his flashlight on it and Hubbard made a direct hit with his first shot. The creature uttered a horrible scream as two more shots were fired at it. And then as they watched a white mist enveloped it. A minute later the mist had cleared and there was nothing left but darkness. They made a search of the area but there was no blood or any other trace of the creature they had seen. The following day a thorough search of the whole farm was made but nothing was found that gave any help in solving the mystery.

Somewhat less weird, but still strange enough, is the report from Deltox Marsh, near Fremont, Wisconsin. During November 1968 a powerfully built, manlike creature covered with short dark-brown hair and with a hairless face and palms was seen several times in the area. On 30 November twelve men were on the Marsh, strung out in line on a deer drive. The men at the extreme left saw it first and passed the word down to the rest. The creature was not aggressive but was evidently interested in watching the men, keeping a certain distance from them, and moving forward if they backed away. After a while it moved away and was lost to sight in some woods. A few weeks later biologist Ivan Sanderson and Dr. Bernard Heuvelmans interviewed the witnesses and made a detailed record of the case. Although all the men were armed, no one had shot at the creature. They all said that it had looked too manlike.

In November 1968 Glenn Thomas, whose earlier sightings in October 1967 and spring 1968 we have already described, again saw some Bigfeet. First he found two pairs of 16-inch-long tracks in the snow, which he followed for several miles but lost the trail where the snow ended. Returning the next day, he cast around the area and spotted a dark object on the snow. Through his binoculars he could see two creatures asleep, resting on their knees and elbows with their backs to the sky. Thomas sat down nearby to watch. After an hour the creatures got up and went to a nearby creek to pull up water plants which they ate. Their pendulous breasts showed that they were females and one appeared to be in heat as its genital area was swollen and it gave an occasional loud call "like a scream in an echo chamber." They fed for about half an hour, and during this time Thomas saw one defecate into the water. They rested again for an hour and then climbed off into the woods. Glenn Thomas said that the creatures were heavily built and about 6 feet tall, covered with dark brown "shaggy" hair. He had another encounter a month later when he was out tracking elk. Looking back, he saw a scruffy dark-brown Bigfoot about 9 feet tall and standing 10 feet away. Both its arms were raised in what looked like a threatening gesture. As Thomas tried to get at a revolver he had beneath his waterproof clothing, the creature ran off and ducked down behind a fallen tree. So Thomas did not fire at it, as it was leaving and was no longer a danger.

We end the reports for 1968 with another from that group which seem to belong not to the rational everyday world but to that shadowy area inhabited by half-suggested terrors, the "Outer Edge" of Jerome Clark's and Loren Coleman's book title, or Dr. John Napier's "Goblin Universe." This particular series of weird events occurred in Salem, Ohio, near Youngstown, and the principal witnesses were the Allison family. In the spring of the year they were aware that in the nearby woods a large, shadowy, manlike creature would stand and watch the house. Once when it was disturbed near their driveway it ran off rapidly into the woods. Bruce, the son, remarked that it ran so fast it did not even seem to touch the ground, whereas a large person running at such a speed would inevitably stumble and trip over roots and rocks. He also found the place in the woods where it had been lying. But this creature was not the only weird visitor to the Allisons' property. They were also haunted by a large cat-like animal, some 3½ feet long and 3 feet high. It was often seen sitting out on the drive and left 3-inch-wide pug marks in damp ground and 6-inch-long claw marks on nearby trees. Neighbors as well as the family heard it growling and panting at night, and it left a line of huge muddy prints across the top of a neighbor's car. Naturally the nearest zoo at Cleveland, 70 miles away, was checked for escapees, but all their big cats were accounted for, and there are no wild animals of this description in Ohio, the cougar or mountain lion having been extinct for more than a century.

Whether there was any connection with these strange animals or not, it should also be recorded that about the same time Mrs. Allison had a UFO experience. A black, unlit object that sounded like a helicopter and looked like an airplane without wings or rotors hovered over a tree as she watched from a window. The top half was a Perspex-type dome within which she could see an occupant who had an olive skin and slanted eyes and who wore a khaki shirt. For 20 minutes the craft rocked about making sputtering noises before it eventually moved slowly away.

Some time in June 1969 at about 8:30 p.m. Bob Kelley and family in the Wildwood Inn area of Trinity County, California, heard a lot of noise outside and found a 6-foot-tall, brown-haired Bigfoot fighting with some of the local dogs. It was throwing the dogs four or five feet up into the air, and one dog was covered in saliva but had no tooth marks on its body. When several people arrived on the scene, the Bigfoot retreated by running up a steep embankment. Usually dogs and Bigfeet show an extreme antipathy to one another, and if the dogs do not cower away in terror they attack the Bigfoot wildly. However, there are exceptions to these behavior patterns, and the next case includes a dog which was neither scared nor aggressive.

During the summer of 1969 several Bigfeet were much in evidence in and around a sawmill which was situated some 20 miles north of Orofino, Idaho. Mr. Moore, the night watchman, and other employees had seen at least three different sizes of bare footprints in the sawdust, ranging from very large to a childlike size. Moore had also heard the creatures jabbering and throwing timber about. On one occasion he watched a black-haired, 6-foot creature with large red eyes for five minutes. He thought it may have been nursing a baby for it had large breasts. The nipple area, hands, and face were not covered by hair and the skin showed pink. It also had the unpleasant smell so often associated with Bigfoot, but it walked upright and could move quickly and gracefully. He had also seen an enormous dog with the Bigfeet. (This is an interesting and relatively rare case of two types of strange animal being seen together. The dog is unlikely to have been an ordinary dog, because, as we have already remarked, dogs and Bigfeet do not seem to mix.)

About 9:30 on the evening of 12 July 1969 Charles Jackson was in the backyard of his house on the Cherokee Road a mile or two outside Oroville, California. He was burning rabbit entrails and with him was his six-year-old son Kevin. As they watched the flames they heard a noise behind them and, turning, saw a Bigfoot standing 15 feet away. It was 7-8 feet tall, covered with 3-inch-long gray hair, but not on its face or palms, and had large breasts. Jackson said later it was not alarmed, but looked puzzled as if wondering what they were doing. His immediate reaction was to get himself and his son inside the house as quickly as possible, where his three usually fierce dogs were cowering beneath the furniture. When they thought it safe to venture out, the family ran to the car and drove to the police at Oroville. The police were not eager to go out to the house that night, so the family returned in the early hours and the police came to have a look round the next day, but there were no prints to be found on the hard ground. Homer Stickley lived on the same road as Jackson but nearer to Oroville, and later in the same month he too saw a Bigfoot moving about his property at a distance. He and his family also heard loud screams at night, and one night he had four to five bushels of apples taken from his trees, though his normally alert Alsatian watchdogs gave no hint of an interloper. During the following months frequent sightings were reported in the area and the Bigfoot hunters converged upon the town, interviewing witnesses and competing for a sight of tracks and other evidence.

Often the police tend to disregard apparently crazy reports made to them in the middle of the night. And who can blame them? But one witness who was taken seriously by the police was 30-year-old Verlin Herrington, who saw his Bigfoot at 2:35 a.m. on Sunday 26 July 1969. He was himself a deputy sheriff for Grays Harbor County, Washington State, and at the time was driving home on the Deekay Road in the direction of Copalis Beach. As he rounded a bend he found a large creature standing in the middle of the road which he first took for a bear.

Figure 24: Charles Jackson and his son at Oroville, California, showing where they saw a Bigfoot on 12 July 1969. *Photo: RD/FPL*

He braked hard and then coasted towards it. As he came nearer he noticed that it did not have a bear's snout and he could see fingers and toes on its hands and feet. From a distance of 70-80 feet he put his spotlight on it as it walked towards the edge of the road, not going down on all fours as would a bear, but remaining upright. He pulled out his revolver with the intention of shooting it in the leg and returning in daylight to follow the trail. But as he cocked his pistol the creature faded into the trees at the roadside and was lost to view. Herrington estimated that he had had about two minutes in which to study the creature, and he said it was 7-8 feet tall, weighed more than 300 pounds, and was covered in dark-brown hair about 3-4 inches long on the head, but shorter elsewhere. He also observed hair-covered breasts, with nipples which were black, as was its face.

Herrington did not intend to publicize his sighting, but he made the mistake of telling two incredulous colleagues when he met them in a café, where he was overheard, and the next day his story was the property of the news agencies. The two colleagues, who really did hold Herrington in respect, returned to the site with him the next morning, where they photographed an imperfect footprint 18 inches long by 7 inches wide. The reaction that the news story produced was such that the sheriff felt it necessary to issue a denial of the story by saying that Verlin Herrington had now decided that he had seen a bear, and that any future information would come from the sheriff's office and not from Herrington, and this announcement successfully took the pressure off the department. The sheriff was not, however, antagonistic to the idea of Bigfoot or that one of his deputies might see one, and helped such accredited researchers as John Green and René Dahinden (whose published reports we have used in compiling the above retelling) to interview Herrington some days after the press embargo. Herrington did, of course, maintain his original report that it was not a bear he had seen. Dahinden noted that the position of a deputy sheriff is on an annual basis and in the following year Herrington was not rehired by the sheriff's department but found a job in the parks service.

Figure 25: Verlin Herrington, a deputy sheriff of Grays Harbor County, Washington State, who saw a Bigfoot near Copalis Beach on 27 July 1969. *Photo: RD/FPL*

Bigfoot hunters found 1969 to be a very active year. Another significant sighting occurred on 24 August on the construction site of the Big Horn Dam on the North Saskatchewan River in Alberta. About 9:30 a.m. 19-year-old Guy L'Heureuse and 17-year-old Harley Peterson were building the foundations for a pumphouse down near the river when Peterson noticed a tall, dark figure standing on top of a 300-foot-high bank about half a mile away and apparently watching them. For nearly an hour they could see it and during that time they were joined by Harley's father Stan and Floyd Engen, both aged 46 years, and Dale Boddy, a 21-year-old student, all of whom were also working at the site. Although they were on the same bank as the figure they could not easily approach it because of a loop in the river. For half an hour it stood and watched; then it sat for ten minutes and then stood for another fifteen. It then walked along the bank of the river and was lost to sight among the trees. Having neither camera nor binoculars, the men could not record the sighting nor see the creature in detail, but they were sure it was quite tall. When two of them went over to where it had been standing while the others stayed below, they were able to make an estimate of its height. To their amazement they saw that a man in the same place was only a third the height of the creature, which made its height at least 15 feet! It had left no footprints on the grassy bank. When the sighting was publicized, hordes of Bigfoot hunters and curiosity seekers descended on the site, but nothing more was seen. The publicity also encouraged others to tell of their sightings. The local Indians were well aware of the creatures' presence, but preferred to say nothing, taking them for granted.

As we have already indicated, some of the reports of Bigfeet suggest that they have an affinity with or an ability to affect electrical gear or motors. This is again suggested by the following incident which took place about 3:00 o'clock one September afternoon in 1969 near Lost Trail Pass in Montana. A man cutting poles with a power saw felt he was being watched and, switching off his motor, turned and saw a 7-foot-tall, black-haired "ape man" weighing about 300 pounds and standing 25 feet behind him. Thinking he might be attacked, he turned his saw motor on again. The "ape man" did not move, but the hair on its neck stood up. When he turned off the saw, the hair lay down flat. Keeping its eyes fixed on the man, the big creature gracefully moved off.

The Bigfoot of Lake Worth, Texas, was seen repeatedly during 1969, and on some nights in July the road through the nature reserve was packed with cars as the locals watched the famous beast cavort up and down a bluff. At one time some of them apparently annoyed it and it picked up a spare wheel and hurled it some 500 feet towards the onlookers, who hastily leapt into their cars. The creature was said to be 7 feet tall, weighing 300 pounds, white and hairy, and to walk like a man. Allen Plaster, the owner of a local dress shop, had a fuzzy black and white photograph of the back of something white and hairy which he said was the Bigfoot, and author Sallie Ann Clarke saw it break down a barbed-wire fence instead of walking round it. On 7 November Charles Buchanan was camping at the lakeside when he was woken at 2:00 in the morning by being pulled off his pickup truck and onto the ground, still in his sleeping bag. The smell from the beast was overpowering, so in order to be rid of it Buchanan quickly picked up a bag of leftover chicken and pushed it into the Bigfoot's face. It fastened its teeth into the bag, mumbled incoherently and shuffled off into the water, then swam powerfully towards Greer Island.

In January 1970 four young men were driving near Whitewater, New Mexico, when something hairy and about 5 feet 7 inches tall joined them and ran on two legs alongside their car as they drove at 45 m.p.h. They wound up the windows and locked the doors, and the driver, Clifford Heronemus, increased his speed to 60 m.p.h., which was the maximum he could maintain on the curved road. The creature did not fall behind, so a gun was pulled out and one of them shot at it. It fell down but there was no sign of blood as it got up again and ran off.

The following is another case of Bigfoot curiosity about cars and their owners. Mrs. Louise Baxter had once before seen a Bigfoot cross the road in front of her, when she was driving in November 1969. And in

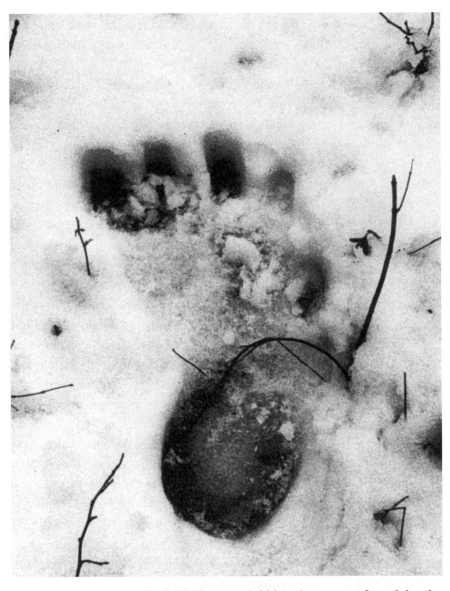

Figure 26: At the end of 1969, over 1,000 prints were found in the snow at Bossburg, Washington State. 16½ inches long, they had been made by a creature with one deformed foot, which became known as the "Bossburg cripple." *Photo: RD/FPL*

**Figure 27: Ivan Marx (left) and a Washington State wildlife agent hold casts made from footprints left by the "Bossburg cripple";
November 1969.** *Photo: RD/FPL*

August 1970 she had a longer look at one. Driving near North Bonneville, Washington, and hearing an odd noise, she stopped the car to see if
she had a flat tire. None of the tires was soft, so she bent down to see if
something had lodged beneath the car and was causing the noise. Then,
she reported later,

> I suddenly felt as if I was being watched and without straighten-
> ing up I looked towards the wooded area beside the road and
> looked straight into the face of the biggest creature I have ever
> seen except the one the time nearly a year before.
>
> The creature was coconut brown and shaggy and dirty look-
> ing. It had one huge fist up to its mouth. The mouth was partly
> open and I saw a row of large square white teeth. The head was
> big and seemed to set right onto the shoulders. The ears were not
> visible due to the long hair about the head. It seemed the hair
> was about two inches long on its head.
>
> It had a jutted chin and receding forehead. The nose and
> upper lip were less hairy and the nose was wide with big nostrils.
>
> The eyes were the most outstanding as they were amber
> color and seemed to glow like an animal's eyes at night when car
> lights catch them.
>
> It seemed contented there and seemed to be eating as the left
> fist was up toward the mouth as though it had something in it.
>
> I screamed or hollered but whether I made any noise I can't
> tell I was so terrified. I know it didn't move while I looked. I
> don't remember how I got back in the car or how I started it. As I
> pulled out I could see it still standing there, all 10 or 12 feet of
> him.

The next two reports suggest that if some of these creatures are
approached in a non-aggressive, calm manner, a basic level of
communication can be established. First Archie Buckley's encounter.
This took place on 18 June 1970 in Trinity National Forest, California,

where Buckley, a Bigfoot researcher since 1937, was camping out in the hope of seeing a Bigfoot. Having hung a large fish in a tree as "bait," he sat by his campfire and sent out friendly thoughts. Believing that Bigfoot can sense when man has hostile or fearful thoughts, Buckley never carries a gun. Three a.m. came and no Bigfoot had been seen, so Buckley climbed into his Volkswagen. The moon went down soon afterwards, and then suddenly Buckley knew there was something in the campsite. He shone a light on the fish, which was untouched; he swung the beam round and caught two glowing eyes 100 feet away. For three minutes Buckley watched a 7½-foot-tall, dark, hairy Bigfoot weighing about 450 pounds, but lost sight of it when he momentarily took his eyes away while changing to a more comfortable position. Next morning he found many footprints 15½ inches long by 6½ inches wide, some close to the Volkswagen as if the Bigfoot had crept up and peeked in at him.

On 11 August three people, Ben E. Foster Jr., Sharon Gorden, and Richard Foster, were camped at Basin Gulch in Trinity National Forest. Although they were on a fishing trip they had left out a bait of fish, raw chicken, and vegetables, in the hope of attracting a Bigfoot. Just after 8:00 p.m., at dusk, Sharon saw a Bigfoot watching them from a hilltop some 150 feet away. Ben walked towards it and stopped when about 75 feet away. They faced each other for a few moments, then, when Ben took another few steps forward, the Bigfoot tossed a five-pound rock towards him, which landed about 7 feet to his left. Ben walked quickly back to camp and they all got into the car. The Bigfoot had also retreated, up a ravine. About half an hour later Ben and Richard walked up the track hoping to see the creature again but without success. While they were gone, Sharon, who had stayed in the car, saw a Bigfoot about 30 feet away. She tried to start the engine, and the creature fled into the woods. That evening while they sat around a large fire, they could see the forms of several creatures in nearby timber and at least four pairs of glowing red eyes were seen in the darkness. Sharon spent the night in the car while Ben and Richard laid their sleeping bags near the fire. At 4:30 in the morning Sharon was woken by some loud footfalls and saw a dark form standing by the car. It reached across the wide car hood and flipped the radio aerial, which had Ben's shirt hanging on it. Then it walked off into the darkness. The next day many footprints were found around the camp, and four good plaster casts were made. That evening, 12 August, the creatures were seen again, and Ben walked up to within 75 feet of one. The creature gestured by moving its right hand from its hips outwards several times and Ben repeated the movement. They exchanged gestures three or four times. Then the creature walked a few steps away, turned, made one last gesture, as did Ben, and then went on its way. Ben returned to the camp. In response to a phone call other researchers joined the group, but no more Bigfeet were seen on this occasion.

Ben, Sharon, and Richard described the Bigfeet as being 8-10 feet tall and weighing 500-800 pounds. They were heavily built and dark in color, except the one Sharon had seen, which was a light color. The heads were egg-shaped, the faces had no hair on them and were a dark chocolate color, and the eyes were small, round, and deep beneath a heavy brow ridge. At night the eyes glowed red in the light from the campfire. Pictures from their descriptions are shown in Figure 28. It is especially important to notice that the faces in the picture seem to show a lot of hair while the description said there was no hair on the faces. We suspect the descriptions are more accurate, although there is no way to be sure. This mismatch points out a problem with Bigfoot research, long known to psychologists who study eyewitness reports: researchers and witnesses bring their expectations with them and the expectations can affect what the observers remember and what the researchers report.

In contrast to the previous cases, the witness in the following report was not only unprepared to meet a Bigfoot, but was taken completely by surprise. On 29 August 1970 at about 5:00 p.m. a young woman at Wilsonville, Oregon, heard someone shooting in some woods on her farm and went out to find the trespassers. She put her shotgun down in order to get through a barbed-wire fence on the edge of the woods. When she had climbed through the fence, but before she had time to straighten up, something grabbed her and threw her back over the fence. She was

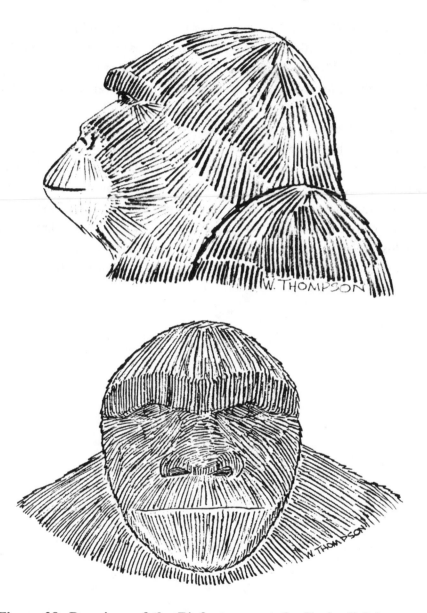

Figure 28: Drawings of the Bigfoot seen at the Basin Gulch campground in the Trinity National Forest, California, on 11 August 1970, based on descriptions given by witnesses Ben E. Foster, Jr. and Sharon Gorden. *Picture: Warren Thompson*

just able to register the fact that it was big and hairy and had a terrible smell. She landed 10 to 15 yards from the fence in a patch of thistles which scratched her but cushioned the impact, and she was not seriously hurt. By the time she had picked herself up, the Bigfoot had left the scene.

We end the year 1970 by relating another incident when a Bigfoot was seen in the water. This was at a small lake near Priest Lake in northern Idaho, some time during 1970. Two fishermen saw a Bigfoot swimming across the lake. They could not see just how it used its limbs in swimming, as the arms did not appear above the surface of the water. When it reached the shore it stood up, shook the water from its arms, and was lost to sight among the lakeside grasses. As in so many cases, a Bigfoot goes purposefully about its business and human witnesses can only stand and stare.

7
Phantom Bigfeet and UFOs
1971-75

The town of Fouke, Arkansas, has been the location of many sighting reports of Bigfoot since the early 1950s, and the movie based on the sightings, *The Legend of Boggy Creek,* has already been mentioned. It was part fiction, part fact; but there was no doubt about the reality of the creature that peeked through the window at Mrs. Ford on the night of 1-2 May 1971 as she lay sleeping on a living-room couch in their new house in the Jonesville area of Fouke. It had gleaming red eyes and a large, clawed, hairy hand which it stuck through a hole in the window screen. Mrs. Ford naturally screamed and her 25-year-old husband Bobby and his brother Douglas ran outside to look for the intruder. In the woods near the house they saw a massively built, 6-foot-tall creature covered with hair. Douglas fired at it as it moved away into the trees. They called out Constable Ernest Walraven from Fouke who searched and found some tracks. An hour later the creature was back kicking on the door. It was fired at again, whereupon it "vanished." (In the Bigfoot context this is a deceptive word to use: does the writer of the report mean that the creature slipped away among the trees, or that it "dematerialized" before his view? These creatures have been seen to do both!) In the early hours of 2 May Bobby took a walk outside and was grabbed and pulled to the ground but managed to break away. He was taken to a local hospital and treated for extensive scratches. During the next day officers from the sheriff's department found the large footprints typical of Bigfoot. The apparently aggressive behavior of this Bigfoot was not typical of the Fouke "monster" and in fact the locals tended to have an affectionate regard for the beast, which they displayed by wearing T-shirts inscribed with the message "Save the Fouke Monster" and organizing a "draw the monster" contest for the school children.

Just a month after the Fouke sighting a Bigfoot made a number of appearances at Pinewood Mobile Manor, a trailer court near The Dalles, Oregon. 1 June 1971 was a day of bright sunshine and the three owners of the trailer court, Dick Ball, Jim Forkan, and Frank Verlander, were having a business meeting at the office there. Looking through the window, they could see a meadow and beyond that a cliff. Moving among the small oak trees and rocks which had over the years fallen from the cliffs above, the men saw a 7½-8-foot-tall creature which appeared to be very large and dark gray. It was about 260 yards away. They watched for approximately 20 seconds as it moved hesitantly among the rocks before being eventually lost from sight.

On the evening of the following day, Richard Brown, a high-school music teacher who lived on the site, was returning home with his wife after choir practice. They saw a large creature standing in a nearby field. Brown fetched a rifle with an 8x telescopic sight from his trailer and for five minutes watched the creature which was only 150 yards away. He described a 10-foot-tall, muscular, hairy creature weighing 600-800 pounds. Brown, who had done a lot of hunting, was sure it was neither an ape nor a bear. As he lined it up in the scope sight he started to squeeze the trigger but found he could not shoot it. He said: "It seemed more human than animal." On another two occasions the Bigfoot was seen by Joe Mederios who worked on maintenance at the trailer court, and the investigators who interviewed all the witnesses were convinced of their sincerity.

When Joan Mills and Mary Ryan stopped their Volkswagen on Highway 79, a backwoods road near Louisiana, Missouri, they were looking for a quiet spot to picnic. This was in July 1971. They had set out their lunch and started to eat when they were assailed by a stupefying smell. Miss Ryan said: "I never smelled anything so bad in my life." Joan Mills likened it to a whole family of skunks. It was then that she saw the figure that was standing behind them in the bushes and waist-high weeds. Mary described it as half ape and half man: "the face was definitely human … like a hairy human."

Figure 29: Richard Brown standing where he stood when watching the Bigfoot. *Photo: RD/FPL*

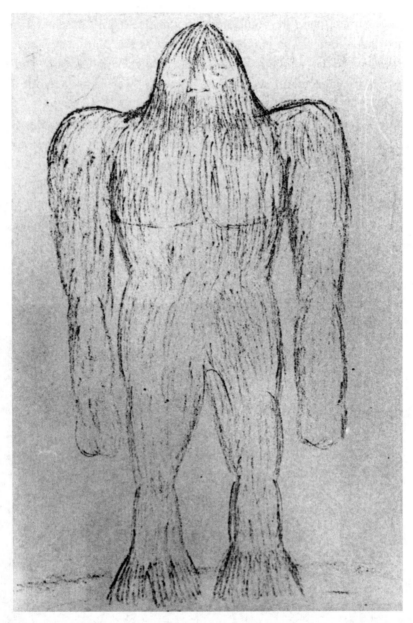

Figure 30: Drawing by music teacher Richard Brown of a Bigfoot that he saw walking across a field near The Dalles, Oregon on 2 June 1971. *Photo: RD/FPL*

With a gurgling sound the Bigfoot started to walk towards the two women, who leapt into their car and locked the doors. The creature, still making a noise, came up to the car and rubbed it with its hands and then tried to open the doors. They could not escape because the car keys had been left outside with the picnic, so they could only sit tight and wait for the Bigfoot to lose interest. When Joan Mills sounded the horn, the Bigfoot leapt backwards and kept at a distance from the car. Then it examined their picnic table and, after smelling a peanut butter sandwich, ate it in one gulp. It picked up Joan's purse in which was the car key, took a few steps towards the woods, and then dropped the purse and continued its amble until it was out of sight among the trees. Then Joan sprinted out to pick up her purse and key and they made good their escape at high speed.

One night in June or July 1971 a farmer, identified in the report only by the initials DK, went into his yard near Sharpsville, Indiana, to see what his dog Zipper was attacking. There he found the dog snapping and snarling at a great hairy creature that had an ape-like body but a head that was neither ape-like nor human. It looked, he said, more like a furry helmet. The Bigfoot was about 9 feet tall and covered in dirty, stringy hair, and it had a rank and sickening odor something like decaying meat and vegetables. It swung its long arms at the dog in a "slow motion" manner, not actually hitting it, and as it did so it growled in a "deep rumbling" voice. Although the dog was lunging with bared teeth, it did not appear to be actually connecting with the creature, so although there was much sound and fury very little damage was done to either party. DK said that the creature appeared confused and uncertain, as though it was in a situation in which it was unsure how to act. DK ran indoors for his shotgun and when he came out the creature had made off towards the creek. Although it was too far away, he fired a couple of shots after it. When he reported the incident to the sheriff he was laughed at, so although there were subsequent visitations he never again notified any authorities. DK told investigators Don Worley and Fritz Clemm that the creature came to his house five more times, always during darkness. And although he followed it back to the creek, he was never able to get a clear view of it for a shot. It was cunning, he said, and always positioned itself so that there was an obstruction between it and himself. On one occasion when he tracked it into thick woods it doubled back, and was seen, by his mother from the house, to be trailing DK. During the winter of that year DK found that a small pond had inexplicably dried up and beside it was a circular area of grass and weeds between 30 and 40 feet across which had been swirled and flattened with a counter-clockwise motion. This type of "nest" has been found in various parts of the world and is usually considered to be connected with UFO landings, as sometimes are dried-up ponds. Although UFOs quite often take an interest in ponds and other bodies of water, there is no really positive evidence that they are the cause of either "nests" or evaporated ponds. But as a matter of interest it must be noted in conjunction with the Bigfoot sightings.

The creature continued to haunt DK's property. By the spring of 1972 he and his brother were both married and living in the house. One evening they were both out and when they returned together they found their wives in a hysterical state. The women said that the Bigfoot had been trying to prize open an aluminum window. Outside was the usual strong Bigfoot smell, but strangely the damaged window frame showed no marks of claws or damage to the surrounding wood. The Bigfoot returned on two more occasions in the autumn. The first time DK saw it from the house and left it alone, and on the second visit he followed, carrying his gun, but he had no more success in apprehending the creature than on earlier occasions.

A creature which exhibited some very strange characteristics appeared during August 1972 at Roachdale, Indiana. Early in the month Randy and Lou Rogers became aware of an unsettling presence that seemed to be centered on their farmhouse outside the town. There was a great amount of banging on the walls and windows, and it seemed to be increasing in intensity each night. When Rogers ran outside, shotgun in hand, he would catch a fleeting glimpse of a heavily built, 6-foot-tall Bigfoot loping away into a nearby cornfield. For two to three weeks, regularly between 10:00 and 11:30 p.m., the Rogerses waited for the creature to arrive, and with it came a smell of dead animal or rotting garbage. Alongside her natural fear Mrs. Rogers had a good deal of curiosity, reasoning that if it had meant to harm them physically the Bigfoot could have done so before on a number of occasions. She left waste food out for it, which was taken, and sometimes it bobbed about outside, watching her through her kitchen window. Although it stood on two legs it ran using all fours, and in that position it still reached as high as Mr. Rogers — 5 feet 9 inches. Even more unnerving was the fact that it left no tracks, even when running through mud. It seemed to have a most tenuous relationship to the physical world, hardly touching the ground as it ran and making no noise as it went through the undergrowth. In fact sometimes the Rogerses thought that they could see through it when they looked at it.

The Rogerses were not the only people in the community to see the creature, and by the third week of August some three dozen people had made reports of an interloper wandering about at night. Also an incident which might have been connected had been noted by a number of locals, including Mrs. Rogers' brothers. They had seen a luminous object hovering over the cornfield into which the creature would retreat after visiting the Rogerses' house. It had exploded as though an aircraft had blown up, but no debris had been found. This had occurred only an hour or two before Mrs. Rogers' very first sighting of the strange creature. A group of friends made up a posse with Rogers to try and capture it. One young man who wished to remain anonymous met the Bigfoot when it stepped out onto the road in front of him. He challenged it but when it did not stop he fired at it. This had no apparent effect and the Bigfoot got away.

On 22 August Carter Burdine and Bill "Junior" Burdine, his uncle, found 60 chickens dead on Carter's farm at Roachdale. The corpses were dismembered but had not been eaten, and were strewn for 200 yards from the chicken house to the front yard of the farmhouse. Later that evening as the men searched the area with a local marshal, something big and heavy rushed across the road 6 feet from Bill Burdine. It was too fast for him to see what it was, but it was very heavy and it smashed a fence down and left a trail of trampled weeds. Later, in the early hours of the following day, the two Burdine men were returning again to the farm, having taken Carter's wife to stay in town with relatives. As they drove into the yard, they saw a massive Bigfoot standing in the 6-by-8-foot doorway of the chicken house. It completely filled the entrance, blocking out the lights from inside and with its head higher than the top edge of the door. This time the two men were joined by Carter's father, Herman, when they cornered the creature in the hay barn, but it broke loose and, followed by a hail of shot, ran off into the darkness. The Burdines found that another 110 chickens of their original 200-strong flock had been destroyed. Once again they had been pulled apart, drained of blood, but not eaten. The whole matter was investigated by Conservation Officer William Woodall. He said eventually: "I never could find any concrete physical evidence. All I ever had to go on were a lot of people's stories of what they saw. I think I couldn't find any tracks because the ground was hard and the vegetation high."

The frequency with which Bigfoot was reported seen beside or crossing a road suggested that sooner or later one would be involved in a traffic accident. There are, in fact, a few known cases, and one of them occurred in mid-January 1973. It happened to an unnamed truck driver who was taking a load of logs from Grants Pass, Oregon, to Eureka at about 7:30 in the evening. As he took a curve at 40-45 m.p.h., a creature with reddish-brown hair standing on two legs and about 6½-7 feet tall stepped out into the path of the truck. It did not appear to be aware of the truck, which hit it, causing the creature to hurtle off to the left shoulder of the road. The driver could hear nothing above the noise of his engine and, being well acquainted with the appearance of bears, was sure that it had not been a bear. Five or six miles down the road he stopped to inspect his vehicle. The front was badly smashed and would require extensive repairs, but there was no trace of hair or blood. He had noted that the creature had had no neck and that the shape of its head was rounded and humanlike, not like an ape's head, but that its arms had been very long with hands reaching nearly to the knees. His story received little credence, for when he reported it to his supervisor he was asked what he had been drinking.

Another highway encounter took place in April 1973. Don Stratton was driving 12 miles to the east of Estacada, Oregon, at 6:00 p.m. when an object was thrown from the woods and landed on the road in front of him. Stopping his truck, he got out to examine it. A lump of wood from a rotted stump lay on the road, and 25 feet beyond the roadside fence he could see a creature with brown hair tipped with silver. It was digging at the bottom of a rotted stump and had evidently thrown out the lump which had landed on the roadway. As it stood up Stratton could see that it was about 5 feet tall with broad shoulders and no neck. He could see the muscular bronzed skin of the throat and chest, which were hairless, but the rest of the body, arms, and legs were thickly covered with hair. A branch hung in front of its face, only revealing the mouth, which had teeth but no fangs. The lower part of the face was flat. Before he had more time for closer observations, the creature stepped sideways into the trees and was lost to view.

Do some Bigfeet have an affinity with certain humans and appear to them several times in succession? Some Bigfoot researchers think this may be so, and some cases seem to support this theory. Such a case comprises the series of incidents that happened to four young people early in June 1973. Their names and ages were given as Sandra (13), Gail (16), Ricky (17), and Jessie (19), and they had taken some rubbish to a dump off Gravel Pit Road in northwestern Jefferson County, Arkansas. During a heavy thunderstorm they waited in their car in the dumping area for the weather to clear. They first heard a noise of crunching gravel followed by a call which sounded like a woman's scream ending in a growl. Then, looking through the rear window, they saw, by the light of the car's rear lights and the lightning flashes, a dark, hairy creature 7-8 feet tall, with glowing red eyes (possibly caused by reflection from the car's rear lights, they thought) which had a foul odor like "rotting flesh."

As it peered in through the rear window, Ricky the driver started up and they left the area in a hurry. Within the next three to four hours they saw this Bigfoot (or an identical creature) three more times. It crossed the road in front of their car; later when they were at Ricky's house (some seven miles from the dumping area) they heard a noise by some rabbit cages and saw the hairy giant amble off into the woods; and finally it crossed the road behind their car when they were driving down Highway 270. The following day a search of the dump found an oversize footprint with claws instead of toes. During May and June a number of reports of hairy creatures seen or strange cries heard were made to Jefferson County authorities by the local citizenry. But as there was a lack of hard evidence the authorities dismissed the reports as imagination.

During the summer of 1973 there was a concentration of Bigfoot sightings in a number of centers in the USA, and one of these was Westmoreland County, Pennsylvania. Here the reports were investigated and recorded by the Westmoreland County UFO Study Group which had originally been set up as a UFO research body and now included Bigfoot research, as the researchers had found that the two phenomena appeared to be interlinked. At a large gathering of UFO researchers in 1974 (the Mutual UFO Network Symposium), Stan Gordon, the energetic Director of WCUFOSG, reported on the Pennsylvania UFO/Bigfoot activity, and one case he spoke of runs as follows. On the evening of 27 September 1973 at about 9:30 p.m. two girls were waiting for a lift in a country area when they saw a white, hairy creature with red eyes, standing 7-8 feet tall, in the woods. Even more surprising was the fact that it carried a luminous sphere in its hand. Shocked, the girls ran home and told what they had seen to the father of one of them. He went into the woods to search for the creature, and was away for more than an hour. The WCUFOSG investigator knew the girl's father, who confirmed that his

Figure 31: Drawing, based on eyewitness testimony and sketches, of a human-like Bigfoot, one of many seen in Pennsylvania during 1973.
Picture: Loren Coleman

daughter had seen the Bigfoot, but he denied that he had gone into the woods and forbade anyone else to go into the woods, stating that "Some things are better left alone." Several people in the area stated that during the time the man was in the woods, an object that looked like an airplane was seen stationary in the sky above the woods, and that it shone a bright beam of light down into the trees. Since the incident the man appeared to have experienced a personality change, according to people close to him. Soon afterwards he acquired a book of prophecies and would often talk about the coming end of the world. This latter part of the story is typical of UFO contactee cases, though the nature of the connection between these UFO-oriented incidents and the Bigfoot sighting remains unclear.

Early in October 1973, near Galveston, Indiana, Jeff Martin or Jim Mays (we have two reports of this case with different names, one of them presumably being a pseudonym, but we do not know which) was fishing one evening. He looked over his shoulder to see an ape-like figure watching him in the dusk from about 20 feet away. He called to it but it slipped off into the twilight. A short while later he felt a touch on his shoulder and behind him stood the creature, a sandy-colored Bigfoot. It ran swiftly away and Jeff/Jim followed behind. As it crossed a road he could hear its feet slapping on the hard surface. Then it leapt a ditch and vanished into the trees. Almost instantaneously a glowing bronze light rose from the woods and shot away in the sky. Two days later Jeff/Jim returned with his fiancée, her father, and two friends. As they drove to the area they were followed by an aerial light that disappeared before the journey's end. At the place where Jeff/Jim had last seen the creature, it was standing amid tall weeds. One of the party thought that when they turned their beams on it the beams seemed weaker. Using the surrounding herbage as a guide, they estimated its height as between 8 and 9 feet, and although two of the party had retreated to the car in fear, the others shouted questions and curses at it. As it failed to respond in any way, they tried throwing rocks, but they could not see whether the missiles bounced off, missed, or went through the creature. Whatever their aim, the creature did not move. Because of another car on the track, they had to move their own car, and when they returned the Bigfoot could no longer be seen. Of possible significance in this case is the fact that Jeff/Jim's fiancée's father had since 1965 had a dozen or so UFO sightings, and on one occasion had exchanged flashed signals with a UFO.

The final case we describe for 1973 has some of the strangest aspects of any in this book, and once more seems to link the presence of Bigfoot with mysterious hovering lights. The events started about 9:00 p.m. on 25 October at a farm near Greensburg in western Pennsylvania, the same area where so much activity had occurred during the year. On that evening about fifteen people at the farm saw a large, bright red ball slowly descending towards a pasture. The 22-year-old farmer's son, who is the chief participant in this case and has been given the pseudonym of Stephen, decided to go and investigate, and with him went two 10-year-old twin boys. As they drove towards the landing site of the object Stephen noticed his headlamps starting to dim. The three continued on foot up to the top of the hill, where they could see the luminous object on or very near the ground. It appeared to be about 100 feet in diameter, dome-shaped like a bubble, bright white, and it illuminated the surrounding area. It was making a sound like a lawn mower, and the three could also hear screaming sounds coming from its vicinity. One of the twins shouted a warning as he saw something moving along the edge of the field on their right. The air smelt of burning rubber and by the light from the object they could see two ape-like creatures with green glowing eyes. One was about 7 feet tall and the other over 8 feet tall, and they were covered with long, dark-gray hair. They seemed to be communicating with each other by making whining, baby-crying sounds. Stephen, who had brought a rifle with him, fired over the heads of the creatures, which were now walking slowly towards the witnesses. As they did not halt he fired another round over their heads, but they continued walking. One of the twins was thoroughly scared and ran away from the others back to the house. Stephen then fired three rounds directly into the larger creature. As it was hit it made a whining sound and raised its hand towards the other Bigfoot. At the same time the glowing "bubble" disappeared and its sound stopped. The Bigfeet turned slowly and walked back into the woods. Stephen returned with the youngster to the house and called the State Police. About 9:45 p.m. Stephen and a state trooper returned to the site by patrol car. Where the luminous dome had rested they could see a glowing white illuminated area that extended to a foot above the ground and was bright enough for a newspaper to be read by it. The horses and cattle in the field did not venture into the glowing area but remained just outside. As the men walked by the woods they could hear the sound of a heavy body crashing through the undergrowth, but each time they stopped moving it would stop a split second later.

It was then that the trooper returned to barracks and phoned Stan Gordon of WCUFOSG. The investigators arrived about 1:30 a.m. and checked the witness and location for radiation but found no unusual readings. The glow had now disappeared and the hard surface retained no markings. As they stood in the field interviewing Stephen, he began to shake violently, breathing heavily and growling like an animal. His father and George Lutz, one of the investigators, had to hold onto his arms to stop him falling. He suddenly flailed his arms, throwing the two to the ground. Stephen's dog then ran at him as though to attack, and when he went for the dog it ran away crying. He ran around the field swinging his arms and making animal growls before collapsing on his face into a manured area. Other investigators experienced breathing difficulties and dizzy spells, and a strong sulfur-like smell was present. Soon Stephen regained consciousness and was helped by the others down the hill. He still seemed very confused and yelled phrases like "Keep away from the corner! It's in the corner!" He was also mumbling confused predictions about the end of the world and the doom of mankind. The investigative group decided that the situation required skilled psychological counseling and investigation and called upon the services of Dr. Berthold Eric Schwarz, whose investigations into the psychological and paraphysical aspects of UFO experiences are widely known in UFO research circles.

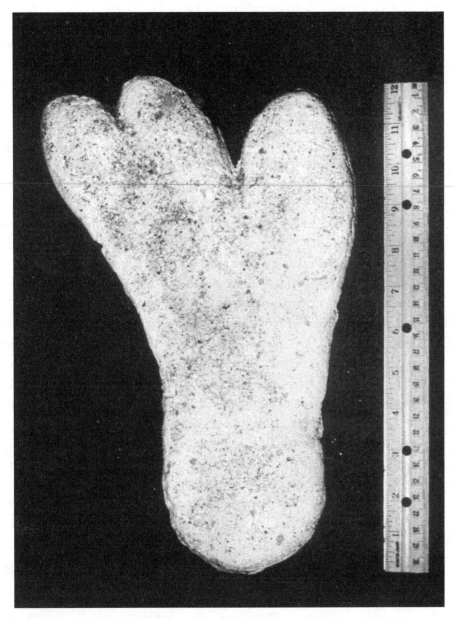

Figure 32: Cast made from a three-toed footprint found by investigator Stan Gordon at Greensburg, Pennsylvania, in August 1973.
Photo: Loren Coleman

Early in 1974 dramatic events were reported from Florida. On 9 January, in the early hours of the morning, Richard Lee Smith reported to the police that he had run over a "giant black man" on Hollywood Boulevard in the Fort Lauderdale area. Trooper Johnson was dispatched to the scene and examined Smith's car, the front of which was damaged and had bloodstains and coarse dark hair adhering to it. Richard Lee Smith explained that he had been traveling at approximately 50 m.p.h. when he overtook a huge man wearing dark clothing. As he came alongside, the man stepped into the path of his car, he swerved, and the figure lurched into the car and rolled beneath the front wheel. Smith stopped and in a state of shock watched the "man" slowly get up, stand to a full height of 7-8 feet, make a roaring sound, and lurch towards him in what he thought was a threatening manner. He jumped into his car and made off. The police began to receive other calls from motorists who had seen the "man," and soon there was a full-scale hunt in progress. At 2:12 a.m. patrolman Robert Hollemeyal saw the figure coming down the road towards him and, leaving his car, he ordered it to halt. When he turned his light onto it he was amazed to see a huge figure over 7 feet tall with long, swinging arms and covered in dark gray hair. The patrolman drew his revolver and fired two rounds at it. The creature screamed, jumped 20 feet off the road, and ran away at about 20 m.p.h. For the rest of the night the police combed the area with cars and helicopters, but no further trace of the Bigfoot was found. It had returned to the Everglades swamps from which it had probably originally emerged.

Now we return to Pennsylvania, where strange encounters continued to be reported. On the night of 6 February 1974, at Uniontown, a woman, identified as Mrs. A by the Bigfoot investigators, was sitting in her house watching television. About 10:00 p.m. she heard a noise coming from her porch. The house was set in an isolated and well-wooded area and she suspected that some wild dogs which she had seen in the neighborhood were nosing about in some tin cans. She picked up her 16-gauge shotgun intending to scare the animals away. She turned on the outside light and, stepping onto the porch, found a 7-foot hairy Bigfoot standing 6 feet from her. It raised both hands above its head and Mrs. A, assuming it was going to jump at her, reacted instantly by firing at its midriff. There was a brilliant flash like a photographer's flashbulb and the creature had disappeared, leaving no trace whatsoever. Maybe Bigfoot had been watching television, too, and hoped that putting up its hands would keep it from being shot. Imagine its surprise (and probably frustration) when it got shot anyway. We'll see this kind of interaction several more times during the next five years.

Very shaken, Mrs. A went back inside, and a moment later her telephone began to ring. It was her daughter's husband who, with his wife and children, lived 100 feet away in a trailer home. He had phoned to ask what had happened, having heard the shot. She told him and he decided to go over to her, taking with him a revolver. On his way, four or five 7-foot hairy creatures with long arms and glowing red eyes emerged from the woods and came towards him. He fired twice at them and ran into Mrs. A's house. At this time both witnesses could see a bright red flashing light that revolved like a police car beacon and looked like a Christmas tree decoration. It was hovering over the woods only 500 feet away. The cumulative effect of these incidents made them decide to phone the State Police, who quickly arrived. The police could find no tracks on the frozen ground, but noted that the domestic animals (between them the two households had several dogs and cats and a horse) were behaving in a very frightened and untypical manner.

Mrs. A's son-in-law had, interestingly, encountered some strange creatures the previous November (1973). On that occasion he was walking his dog one night when he thought he saw a trespasser on his land and called out, challenging him. The figure came towards him and he saw it was a tall, hairy Bigfoot with glowing red eyes. Because of the wild dogs in the woods, he always carried a revolver, and he promptly emptied all six rounds into the creature. The Bigfoot disappeared in front of him. He could hear it running but there was nothing to be seen where the noise came from. He went back to his trailer and then immediately returned to the woods with a rifle. Once more he saw the Bigfoot, and,

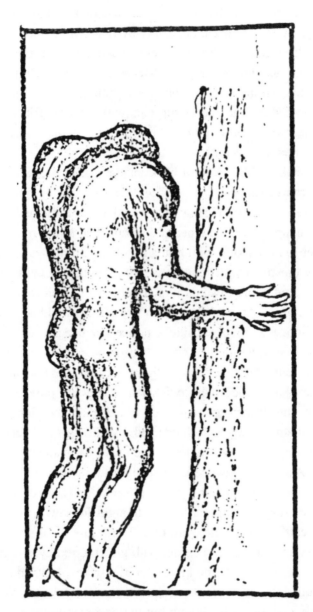

Figure 33: Logger Jack Cochran's drawing of the Bigfoot he saw in July 1974 in the Hood River National Forest, Oregon. It was standing watching loggers at work.

when he shot at it, it screamed like a crying baby. His wife, who heard the sound, said it was like "a human that was in very deep pain."

Later in 1974 Mrs. Margie Lee had repeated encounters with a 6-foot-tall Bigfoot that might even have had a sense of humor. The events began in late July in the Watova settlement near Nowata, Oklahoma. After a number of sightings over several weeks, the Lees realized that the creature was harmless and they lost their fear of it. It appeared to be a young male covered with 1-inch-long brown hair. It could run very fast, "even faster than a deer," but it ran very quietly making a noise like "moccasins over gravel." Its eyes were "normal" and not luminous as in so many other Bigfoot reports. It also seemed to be more interested in women than men, ignoring houses in which only men lived, and showing a greater interest in Mrs. Lee than in her husband John. These characteristics led them to think that it was probably seeking a mate. The Lees grew quite fond of "their" Bigfoot when it started to play a little game with them. Each day they found that it had put a feed pail in front of the barn, blocking the doorway. Every day they took it away and hid it, and every night it sniffed the pail out and replaced it in front of the door. The only time Mrs. Lee heard it make a noise was once when it seemed to laugh. Eventually it became a nuisance, thrashing around in the barn and crashing through the chicken-wired window when chased away. It also helped itself to a neighbor's chicken. It was also often seen by two sheriff's deputies, Gilbert Gilmore and Buck Field, who had been called to deal with the situation. One night they caught it in their car headlights and opened fire. The Bigfoot gave no sign of being wounded, but ran off into the woods. During the following morning a very exhausted Mrs. Lee, who had missed many nights' sleep owing to the noisy rompings of the Bigfoot, was taking a shower when there was a loud thump on the wall outside. Though she dashed to the window, she was too late to see the Bigfoot leave, having made its final farewell.

In December 1974 William Bosak, a 69-year-old dairy farmer of Frederic, Wisconsin, was driving home at 10:30 p.m. when he saw "the strangest looking thing I ever saw." Beside the road was a disc-shaped craft, the lower half hidden by a mist. But what really caught Bosak's stunned attention was the creature he saw behind the curved glass window in front. It was illuminated by a bright light, the source of which he could not see, and it looked in some respects something like a Bigfoot. It was covered all over by a dark tan fur except for face and chin. The nose and mouth were quite flat, but the strangest feature was the ears, which stuck out from the head about 3 inches on either side and reminded Bosak of a calf's ears. Its eyes did not look unusual but were large and protruding, indicating surprise or even fright; in fact Bosak thought it was "just as scared as I was." It held its arms above its head and from the waist down the body was hidden by the mist. Bosak estimated that for ten seconds he studied this apparition, then accelerated quickly past, and as he did so his car lights dimmed. He also thought he heard a soft whooshing noise. Ruminating on the sighting later, he wondered if he had perhaps seen a "spaceman" in a padded suit, but decided that, as he could see no seams or buttons, the fur had been part of the body. "I sure wish I would see it again," Bosak told investigator Jerome Clark. "Now I wouldn't hesitate to stop." If he had stopped and obtained a detailed description, perhaps we would now have conclusive proof that Bigfeet and UFOs are directly linked, at least on some occasions. As we have reported, UFOs and Bigfeet have been seen in close proximity, but we have no reliable reports of a Bigfoot emerging from or entering a UFO.

In 1975 the Bigfeet in Florida, known locally as "skunk apes" because of their strong smell and ape-like appearance, were again active. Richard Davis, living in an isolated area at Cape Coral, had for a period of three weeks been disturbed when his Alsatian dog reacted during the night to the presence of an unknown prowler. On 2 February at 2:00 a.m. the dog, an aggressive young female, was restless. It seemed there was another visitation from the prowler. Davis turned the dog loose, but she soon ran back to the house and cowered beneath the car inside the garage. The animal was not barking, but her eyes were wide open with terror. Subsequently her character changed. Davis went out to the yard carrying a revolver and saw a 9-foot-tall Bigfoot with grayish-brown hair and flat features. It was about 15 feet away and as it took a step towards him he fired into its chest and saw the bullet hit it. The Bigfoot grunted and ran off. After firing the first shot it had been Davis's intention to fire the rest of the cylinder at the animal, but to his amazement he found that he was mentally unable to pull the trigger again. A search outside the house found handprints on the air-conditioning unit; this interest by a Bigfoot in an outside air-conditioner had also been noticed by some neighbors of Richard Davis. Mr. and Mrs. Michalowski, who lived about half a mile away, had during the same three-week period been plagued with very foul smells near their home during certain evening hours and had found large fingerprints on their outside air-conditioner.

Another Bigfoot or skunk ape incident was reported on 24 March and is recorded in the files of the Dade County Public Safety Department in Florida. It seems that about midnight on that date two men, Michael Bennett and Lawrence Groom, were driving on a dirt road towards Black Point, when, nearing Goulds Canal, they saw an 8-9-foot Bigfoot standing by a stationary blue Chevrolet car and rocking it backwards and forwards with great force. A hysterical man got out and yelled for help. When the Bigfoot saw the witnesses' car arrive it ran off into the mangroves. Bennett and Groom must have left the scene very quickly too, for the report states that they did not see where the man ran to. When the police later searched the area, neither the blue car nor the Bigfoot could be found.

During September and October 1975 one or more Bigfeet were creating a furor among the populace of Noxie, Oklahoma, a few miles north of Nowata. On 1 September at 8:00 p.m. farmer Kenneth Tosh heard a scratching sound coming from a derelict house near his own residence. He and a friend saw from a distance of 10 feet a dark-brown, hairy creature 7-8 feet tall. The 1½-2-inch-long hair covered it completely except for its nose and around the eyes. They saw it again later, and fired at it, but with no effect. Other friends also tried to shoot it, from close range, but it always ran off apparently unharmed. Bigfoot investigator

Hayden Hewes found twenty-four people who had seen or heard the Noxie Bigfoot.

Another case of multiple sightings occurred on the Lummi Indian Reserve near Bellingham, Washington. The Bigfeet were seen more than a hundred times and the witnesses included the Reserve policemen. One of these, Sergeant Ken Cooper, was called out on 24 October 1975 at 2:20 a.m. to investigate a report of a prowler who had ripped a plastic storm door from its hinges. He was with several other people when the spotlight illuminated a 7½-foot-tall black, hairy creature standing in the back yard. The face was black, leathery, and wrinkled, and the head sat directly on the muscular shoulders, no neck being visible. Two of the upper and two of the lower teeth were longer than the others and the nose was flattened. Sgt. Cooper walked to within 35 feet of the Bigfoot, which had crouched down and not run away. For "many minutes" the two faced each other. The sergeant had a shotgun with him but was not sure whether the creature was some kind of human, and so was reluctant to shoot. At that time there were seven other witnesses. A noise to one side caused the man with the spotlight to shine it across the yard and announce that there was "another one over there." Before he retreated, Sgt. Cooper noted that steam appeared to be coming off the Bigfoot's body, as though it had been wet and running. Later he found large tracks. He also saw the Bigfoot again when it ran alongside his car which was traveling at 10 m.p.h., and it gave a powerful, high-pitched call.

When reading these reports we wish the police and public would carry cameras rather than guns. This did in fact happen in the following case, but unfortunately the results were no more useful. The events occurred in November 1975 in Citrus County, Florida, where seven young men were sitting around a campfire when they briefly saw three Bigfeet, the biggest 8 feet tall. The men got out their lights to search the area and 18-year-old John Sohl collected his camera with flash unit from his car. He separated from his companions, set his camera for an average range, and crouched down in the grass waiting for something to come into view. The charging circuit of the flash unit made a quiet, high-pitched note when switched on, and Sohl later thought that that may have attracted the Bigfoot towards him. He heard a noise behind him and turned slowly. Two feet away stood a Bigfoot observing him. He fired his camera and as the brilliant flash went off the Bigfoot leapt away into the darkness, spinning Sohl off his feet and throwing him a distance of 15 feet. He was not badly hurt and thought that the blow had been accidental, caused by a flailing arm of the fleeing Bigfoot. And what of the photograph? As he had not expected to be so close to a Bigfoot he had focused his camera at 40 feet. He knew that the picture was unlikely to be of any use, and in fact the only result was a large, very over-exposed blur.

Finally in 1975, on 26 December, two teenage girls were involved in a strange Bigfoot encounter at Vaughn near Great Falls, Montana. On the afternoon of that day they noticed that horses in a field near their home were behaving in a strange manner, pawing the ground, and rearing. When they went out to investigate they saw a 7½-foot Bigfoot twice as wide as a man, standing about 200 yards from the house. One girl brought a .22 rifle from the house and examined the creature with the aid of the telescopic sight on it. Its face, she said, was "dark and awful looking and not like a human's." She fired the rifle once into the air, to scare the creature away, but it took no notice, so after a short time she fired again into the air. This time the Bigfoot fell down and started to pull itself along the ground by its arms. After covering a short distance it stood up once more. This seemed to be the breaking point for the girls, who ran off. As they did so, one of them looked back and saw three or four similar creatures helping the first along towards the cover of some bushes. Their report came to the attention of Captain Keith Wolverton, a deputy sheriff for Cascade County, who was aware of the many strange happenings that had been and were still occurring in his area. The girls' genuine fright persuaded him of their truthfulness, and the results of a voluntary polygraph (lie detector) test confirmed that both girls were telling the truth.

8

Strange Encounters Continue
1976-80

During the 1970s there was an increased interest in Bigfoot reports, and an increased number of reported sightings. As public awareness of the phenomenon grew, so did the possibility that hoaxes were perpetrated, or that people unknowingly misinterpreted normal events and in good faith reported them as "Bigfoot" sightings. However, the cases we report have usually been carefully investigated, and often involve more than one witness. Also, as we have increasingly seen during the progress of this book, another equally inexplicable phenomenon, the UFO, has sometimes been reported in conjunction with a Bigfoot sighting. Our first report for 1976 is of this dual-phenomenon type.

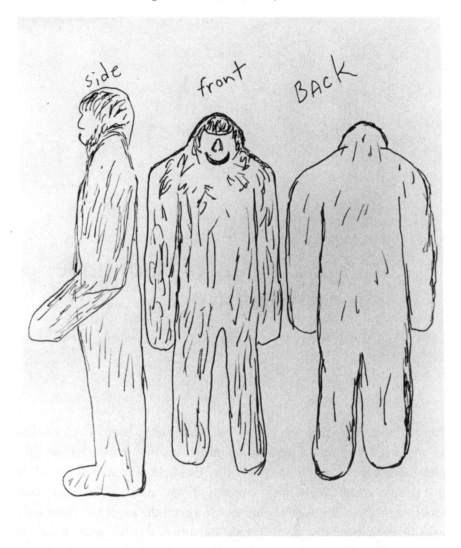

Figure 34: Drawing by 16-year-old Robert Lea of Bigfeet he saw outside his home at East Helena, Montana, on 4 April 1976.

On 22 February, a man driving near the Great Falls airport in Montana saw a 7-foot Bigfoot in a field beside the road. (One version of the report mentions three creatures.) He grabbed his gun and went after it on foot, but when it turned towards him he retreated to his car. He also reported seeing a gray, oval UFO hovering 10-15 feet above the ground about half a mile away from the road. We shall return to Montana shortly.

On 29 February, only a week after the UFO/Bigfoot sighting just described, two people walking near the Settlers Park area of Oakdale, Pennsylvania, in the mid-afternoon saw a 7-8-foot-tall, dark, hair-covered biped. It had long arms, claws, wrinkled skin on its face, and skin hanging over the eyes. Even stranger, the witnesses reported that it had bumps in place of ears, and a dent near the middle of its forehead. Is it only coincidence that the previous night a UFO was seen over the area, and there was a brief power failure in the town?

Back in Montana, the early morning of 4 April 1976 proved a frightening time for 16-year-old Robert Lea of Helena. At 4:30 a.m. he awoke and was looking out of his bedroom window, which faced fields. About 5:00 a.m. he noticed an 8-foot-tall, dark, hair-covered Bigfoot walking smoothly across the pasture, turning its head around as it did so (it appeared to have no neck). It was joined by another, slightly shorter but otherwise of similar appearance. Then the larger Bigfoot reached down and picked up a dark object "about the size of a bale of hay," with something flapping from its ends. He handed it to the other, who carried it. The larger creature walked towards the house, and looked at the window where Robert was. At this, Robert ran downstairs to wake his father, but although they were back at the window within two minutes, there was no trace of the Bigfeet. Later a 17½-inch, three-toed footprint was found. Robert was interviewed by two experienced deputy sheriffs, who believed he had seen what he reported.

During that same month of April, the residents of Flintville, Tennessee, were experiencing inexplicable events. Among the people who reported seeing a Bigfoot was a woman whose car aerial had been grabbed by one that jumped on the roof of her car. Perhaps the most frightening incident at Flintville took place on 26 April, when Mrs. Jennie Robertson nearly lost her four-year-old son Gary to a Bigfoot. Gary was playing outside in the evening when his mother heard him cry out. She rushed out and saw "this huge figure coming around the corner of the house. It was seven or eight feet tall and seemed to be all covered with hair. It reached out its long, hairy arm toward Gary and came within a few inches of him before I could grab him and pull him back inside." Mr. Robertson ran to the door when he realized something was amiss and was just in time to see a "big black shape disappearing into the woods."

Six men tracked the Bigfoot and got near enough to fire at it repeatedly, but although it screamed, it gave no sign of succumbing to the onslaught of bullets. Instead it threw rocks at its attackers for a while before running away into the brush. Next day, 16-inch footprints were found, as well as hair, blood, and mucus. The hair was scientifically analyzed but could not be identified.

In late August 1976, Bigfoot sightings were being reported from the Whitehall area of New York State. Marty Paddock and Paul Gosselin saw the creature two or three times in the same area on 24 August, and police who were called also saw it, although only from a distance. The usual description was of a 7-8-foot creature, very hairy, and with pink or red eyes. On one occasion the Bigfoot was seen at close range by a police patrolman, actually Paul Gosselin's older brother, and a state trooper. This was on 25 August, when the Bigfoot came to within 25 feet of Patrolman Gosselin's squad car. When the state trooper flashed a light in its eyes, it covered them and ran off screaming.

In September 1976 a Bigfoot hoax emerged from Cashton, Wisconsin, where four youths admitted dressing up one of their number to resemble Bigfoot and making "Bigfoot" tracks by means of large pieces of wood fixed to his shoes. However, a real Bigfoot sighting may have been hidden behind all the ballyhoo about the hoaxing. Around 1 September a farmer saw a 7-foot-tall, dark, hairy creature which smelt very strong and made a "beller which sounded something like a young bull would make." The farmer's dog rushed out and bit the Bigfoot on the leg, whereupon the creature brushed the dog aside. Some saliva fell on the dog, and the farmer and his wife noticed later that the saliva smelt the same as an odor they had noticed before on cows that had been in the same part of the woods. The farmer had heard the creature bellowing often.

Early in February 1977, a golf-course superintendent just west of Delray Beach, Florida, chanced upon another bad-smelling Bigfoot. He saw the creature, which was at least 7 feet tall, about 1:00 a.m.; it was drinking water from a lake near the second tee. The witness added that the Bigfoot was covered with long, black, shaggy hair and was very wide at the shoulders. When the pickup truck lights were shone on the Bigfoot, it looked round and then lumbered slowly away into dense woods. The superintendent left a bunch of bananas at the edge of the woods, and found them gone on his return at 5:30 a.m. The city police laughed at the witness's story, and the director of County Animal Regulation believed that he had seen a wild chimpanzee or orangutan — or "just some damn fool in a gorilla suit trying to freak out lovers on the golf course at night."

Bigfeet may themselves try to "freak out" unsuspecting citizens on occasions. Did the Bigfoot that rocked Gerald St. Louis' camper truck on the night of 7 May 1977 have a sense of humor, or was it simply angry at the truck's presence in its territory? St. Louis and his two sons were sleeping inside the camper when the rocking woke them up. St. Louis opened the door and turned on the lights. He then saw, "face to face," a "hairy, brown-colored, and eight or nine feet tall [creature] with long arms." The lights startled it and "it ran toward a fence, about four-and-a-half feet high and jumped over it with ease. I could see it standing there in the distance — just looking at us." The family had been camping by a market at Hollis, New Hampshire, but they were so scared they left immediately without the goods they had planned to sell the next day. They returned later with police, but no Bigfoot was to be seen. Interestingly, that same night Stanley Evans and Jeff Warren, both aged 15, were also camping at Hollis and had a similar experience. Said Evans: "The camper shook so bad I fell out of the bunk and a lamp fell and hit Jeff in the eye. As soon as we turned on a light, whatever it was ran away."

Less than a week after this New Hampshire Bigfoot's camper-rocking activities, about 300 miles south in the state of New Jersey a strange, well-documented, and promptly investigated series of Bigfoot sightings began. At Wantage in the north of the state, something visited a remote farm on 11 May 1977 and killed seven pet rabbits that were kept in a barn. The next evening Mrs. Sites felt "somebody was around," so she and her husband and family watched the barn from a window in the house. They soon spotted a creature at least 7 feet tall, standing on two legs below a farmyard lamp. Mrs. Sites' description of the creature was: "It was big and hairy; it was brown; it looked like a human with a beard and moustache; it had no neck; it looked like its head was just sitting on its shoulders; it had big red glowing eyes."

The family dog bravely attacked it, but was casually swept aside. The dog ran away and was not seen again until the next day. The Bigfoot ran into the woods. The following evening (Friday, the 13th), the children having been taken to stay with relatives, Mr. and Mrs. Sites and two other people waited for the Bigfoot to put in another appearance. As before, and at around the same time, it showed itself under the farmyard lamp. The watchers opened fire on it (using a .222 magnum rifle and a .410 shotgun), so it ran into a shed and out again through a window. It then stood under a tree with arms outstretched and Sites "shot at it three or four times with deer slugs in my .410 gauge shotgun, and I know I hit it." The only reaction was a growl from the Bigfoot, so Sites made for the safety of the house, where the others had already retreated, out of ammunition. The Bigfoot ran away, followed by Sites in his pickup truck, but it escaped into the fields.

Two investigators from the Society for the Investigation of the Unexplained, R. Martin Wolf and Steven Mayne, interviewed the Sites family on 17 May and were impressed by their sincerity. They also saw the dead rabbits, and claw marks on the barn where the Bigfoot had first tried to break in. On returning to the farm on 18 May, the investigators learnt that not long after they had left the night before, the creature had reappeared under the farmyard lamp. Although chased by Sites in his truck, it had again escaped into the woods. That same evening, the investigators sat

Figure 35: Mr. Sites points to the damage on his barn at the family farm in Wantage, New Jersey, said to have been caused by a Bigfoot which visited the farm during May 1977. *Photo: Peter Jordan/FPL*

and watched the farmyard, armed with movie cameras, but naturally Bigfoot stayed away. In the following weeks, strange cries from a swamp, and occasional sightings by members of the family, indicated that the Bigfoot was still around, although it did not again openly visit the house.

While a red-eyed Bigfoot was prowling around the Wantage, New Jersey, farm, a white-eyed Bigfoot was frightening two 13-year-old boys near Eaton in Ohio, about 400 miles to the west. One of the boys described what happened.

We were walking our dog, and she got excited about something. The dog tried to run away from us. I ran after her and picked her up. Suddenly, I smelled this awful stink, like rotten eggs. When my friend and I turned around, we saw a creature that was about nine foot tall, weighed about 500 pounds, and had dirty brown fur and white eyes. Its arms were real long and hung almost to the ground. The creature resembled the Bigfoot on the TV show, "The Six Million Dollar Man." It chased us down near Old Camden Pike and through a field. It seemed like it was right behind us, as it took large steps. When we almost reached my house, the thing vanished.

Again we have a clear indication that the Bigfoot had no intention of catching up with the witnesses. A 9-foot creature could easily have caught two frightened boys, had it wanted to. The puzzle is, why did it chase them? Simply to scare them from its territory? Or does such behavior have some other significance? One suggested explanation is that perhaps some of these creatures are non-physical, being formed from whatever energy source is available, and need a continued supply of energy in order to remain visible. Energy given off by humans could be utilized as one source; a frightened human would undoubtedly yield more emotional energy than one who was not afraid. What better way to obtain life-giving energy, therefore, than to frighten and chase two boys? If this theory has any validity, it could also help to explain why Bigfeet are so often attracted to houses and people.

It is not surprising that some Bigfoot witnesses refuse to talk about their experiences. A frightening encounter is best forgotten, they think, and talking about it is not the best way to consign it to oblivion. If his wife had the details correct in the story she told, it is understandable that Ronald Jones did not want to relive his adventures of the night of 30 August 1977. He was driving a truck on Route 258 in Anne Arundel County, Maryland, and saw what he thought was a human body lying near the road, so he stopped. He discovered that the "body" was in fact an 8-foot-tall Bigfoot weighing about 500 pounds and exuding a pungent smell. Jones threw a tire iron at the Bigfoot, which was now on its feet. He ran back to his truck, but the Bigfoot chased him and hit him on the back of his head. It held onto his truck when he tried to drive away, so he had to back into it before he could escape. It screamed "like a woman" and left claw marks on the door of the new Chevrolet.

The Bigfoot sightings we have recorded in this book show clearly that the witnesses come from all age groups and all walks of life. Police patrolmen and deputy sheriffs are often witnesses, since they are regularly called out to investigate sightings. In the next case the witness was a 67-year-old Baptist minister, the Reverend S.L. Whatley of Fort McCoy, Florida. He was cutting wood in the Ocala National Forest on 11 October 1977 about 2:00 p.m. and having trouble with his chain saw. He finally decided to return home, and it was at that point that he became aware that something was watching him from about 300-400 yards away. "It was this hairy-like ape animal standing there in the palmetto bushes. It looked to me to be 7 or maybe 8 feet tall. It had a dark chocolate-colored face, a face that was clear of hair, and a flat nose. The arms — I couldn't tell what kind of hands it had — the arms were down into the palmetto bushes ..." Breasts were visible too. Thinking to tackle the unknown creature, Whatley took an axe from his truck, but when he looked up again, the Bigfoot had gone.

The fall of 1977 was a season that the people of Little Eagle, South Dakota, are unlikely ever to forget. From September to December, 28 Bigfoot sightings were reported there. Although many of the sightings were made in the brush around Little Eagle, occasionally a Bigfoot came closer to houses. A witness to one of these visits was a 70-year-old Indian woman, Hanna Shooting Bear, who, one night about 10:00 p.m., looked out of her kitchen window and saw a large, hairy shape silhouetted against the lighted windows of a nearby mobile home. She could see enough to describe the creature as having "a funny big head, almost as though it had horns, and wide shoulders. Its arms were up and the hands curled down, and it swayed back and forth." She got her dogs outside, but they were scared and crawled under a car. Hanna Shooting Bear ran to the mobile home and alerted the occupants, who searched outside, but the animal had gone, leaving a smell like a dead person.

Figure 36: One of the many witnesses of Bigfeet around Little Eagle, South Dakota, during the autumn of 1977: police officer Verdell Veo.
Photo: The Mobridge Tribune, South Dakota

Figure 37: Another of the many witnesses of Bigfeet around Little Eagle, South Dakota, during the autumn of 1977: Hanna Shooting Bear. *Photo: The Mobridge Tribune, South Dakota*

Lieutenant Verdell Veo, a police officer for the Bureau of Indian Affairs, was much involved in the events around Little Eagle, and had some sightings himself. On 29 October, together with his sons and two other officers, Veo was out on Elkhorn Buttes near Little Eagle. They spotted a Bigfoot in the moonlight and two of the men began to walk towards it. Veo had a strange feeling that no weapon would have been of any use: "Something told me — I could sense it if you can understand — that I'd better just get out of there and leave the thing alone." As they began to walk back, Jeff, Veo's 15-year-old son, came rushing towards them shouting that another Bigfoot was on the scene. Jeff had watched it through an infrared scope as it walked behind the men. A few days later, on 5 November, Veo and several other people chased a Bigfoot for some hours. It was surrounded by vehicles with their lights blazing, but still it managed to escape into the brush. A rancher who had joined the hunt was puzzled by its escape. He had heard a noise like someone out of breath, and a pounding like the sound of running feet: "I put my flashlight right where I could plainly hear it, only where it should have been, there was nothing in sight! Now what I'm wondering is, can this thing make itself invisible when things get too close for comfort?" More tantalizing hints that some Bigfeet may not be completely physical creatures.

If we accept that police officers are usually reliable people, experienced in accurately observing the unexpected and keeping a cool head, then we must accept that their Bigfoot sightings cannot easily be dismissed. Lieutenant Verdell Veo saw a Bigfoot more than once around Little Eagle; and a police lieutenant was on the scene at East Brewton, Alabama, when a Bigfoot was spotted. The events of 6 March 1978 began at night when Mrs. Ruth Mary Gibson, alone at her rural home, heard a shrill screaming. Scared, she rang her brother Luke McDaniel, who came over. He too heard the screaming, but could see nothing, except that "The horses were running. The hogs were hollering. But the dogs had left." He told his sister to call the police, and soon Lieutenant Doug McCurdy arrived, as did 19-year-old Johnny Gibson. The screaming continued. Then they noticed "something" moving into the road. Lieutenant McCurdy later reported that it was large, and not human, nor any kind of animal he knew of. It crossed the road and went into the woods. Other police officers came and heard the screaming, but the Bigfoot kept out of sight. They soon left to attend to other business, and later McDaniel saw the creature again in his car lights.

It stood around about six and one-half feet to seven feet tall, weighed about 400 some few pounds and its eyes were solid red. I'd say the eyes were about 12 inches apart on its head. It had no neck at all ... hairy all over. It kind of walked like a person. It was kind of in a hurry. Its arms seemed a little longer than a human being has. I'm not saying at all it was any "Bigfoot." I've seen that on television ... but I do know what I saw. I considered it might be an ape. But I got to thinking about it and it wasn't no ape. There's no ape that high ... It wasn't a prank. There were too many guns out there ... and a human couldn't move through thick brush like it did.

The creature which prowled around 3925 North Tram Road in Vidor, Texas, scared newly married Beckie and Bobby Bussinger from their home. It regularly clawed at the window screens, howled, and yelped, yet to a certain extent the couple could tolerate its presence. Then on Sunday, 18 June 1978, they found two of their dogs dead; a third was missing. On Monday night Bobby decided to confront the intruder, a shaggy-haired, muscular creature over 6 feet tall. He took his 12-gauge shotgun outside and fired at the Bigfoot as it came towards him. Then he ran back inside and called the Sheriff's Office. Deputy Jack Reeves came and saw the broken screens for himself; he also caught a glimpse of the Bigfoot as it backed into the woods. While the deputy was there, Mr. and Mrs. Bussinger packed and left to stay with Beckie's parents.

The Bigfeet were very active during the summer of 1978. Only a week after the events at Vidor, 10-year-old Mike Lofton of South Crossett, Arkansas, had a hair-raising encounter with a 7½-foot monster outside his home. He was alone there on 26 June, and the house is several miles away from the nearest neighbor. In the circumstances, Mike acted very bravely. He was feeding his puppy when it began to whine and tremble. He looked up and saw the Bigfoot only 50 feet away. It had its arms raised above its head, and seemed to have claws for fingernails. Mike ran indoors and grabbed his father's loaded .22 rifle. He fired seven times at the "thing," which turned and toddled like a baby back into the woods. Mike then called the police, who came and found blood and hair.

A few days later, an unusual creature nicknamed "Bighead" turned up at Butler, Ohio. Sightings were made on 8, 10, and 12 July 1978, the first by Eugene Kline (17) and Ken O'Neil (15) as they walked along the railway. They heard a strange noise in the brush and, turning in that direction, saw a creature 7 feet tall and with a head larger than its body. Its red eyes were as big as golf balls, and its face was horrible. It growled, and Eugene felt compelled to communicate with it. He could not move for a while; then he threw his light at the creature and ran. He was still in a nervous state when interviewed by Ron Schaffner and Earl D. Jones two months later. Two days after his sighting Lavena Kline and others saw Bighead squatting down at a railway crossing. She too noticed its red eyes. On 12 July Theresa Kline, Eugene's 15-year-old sister, heard a freight train horn as she was pitching hay. Turning towards the railway, she saw Bighead and ran home screaming. She saw its orange-red eyes and heard its cry, like a cat only deeper. She also smelled a strong odor like cow manure.

There were a number of Bigfoot sightings around Ottosen, Iowa, between July and September 1978, some of them involving children. On 31 July three boys aged between 10 and 12 saw a 5-foot-tall, dark-brown creature which was "hunched over." It had a wide forehead, a flat nose, and deep-set eyes. Sometimes it ran on all fours, sometimes on two feet. The boys first saw the Bigfoot in an old shed. Hearing noises, they threw a rock inside, and then saw a dark furry head. They ran away, looking back to see the creature running among some bins. Later they saw it again and this time ran after it, saying that they thought "it was more scared of us than we were of it." When they spotted it in a cornfield, it just stood and looked at them. Having watched its behavior, they said that it "doesn't do anything until you do," but "when it moves, it moves real fast."

In Oceana, West Virginia, "experts" who had not seen the creature that policeman Bill Pruitt saw at 4:00 a.m. on 14 August were explaining it away as a bird, probably a crane or a heron. Pruitt was understandably annoyed. "It looked like a man," he reported. "I've never seen any bird that tall." His encounter had begun when he heard a noise like babies crying in an alley, "It made the hair stand up on the back of your neck. It wasn't no panther. I've heard a panther." Then he saw the creature under a street lamp, looking just like a huge man. "It stood 6½-7 feet tall," and as he got out of his car it ran down to the river and jumped its 30-foot width. Pruitt emptied his gun at it, and the Oceana police chief, just arrived, fired seven rounds at it with his rifle, but "it just kept going." They found no blood, only broken tree limbs and huge round footprints.

In our earlier book *Alien Animals* we wrote about several kinds of mystery creatures — lake monsters, out-of-place big cats, ghostly black dogs, giant birds and birdmen, and Bigfoot/Yeti/Yowie. We remarked that, although these creatures have a number of similar characteristics, which might suggest that they are all part of a single phenomenon, there are very few instances on record where one kind of "alien animal" has been seen side by side with another kind. The 21 August 1978 sighting in Paris Township, Ohio, is one of those rare cases. It took place at the home of the Cayton family near Minerva, and there were nine witnesses. They were out on the porch at 10:30 p.m. when they heard noises near a demolished chicken coop. They saw two pairs of large yellow eyes reflecting the light of their torches, so Scott Patterson (18) drove towards the coop in his car to try and see the animals more clearly. He saw that the eyes seemed to belong to two puma-like animals. As he watched, a Bigfoot strode on two legs in front of the cats as if to protect them. It then lurched towards Patterson's car. At this the witnesses back at the house rang the Sheriff's Office, and sat in the kitchen to wait.

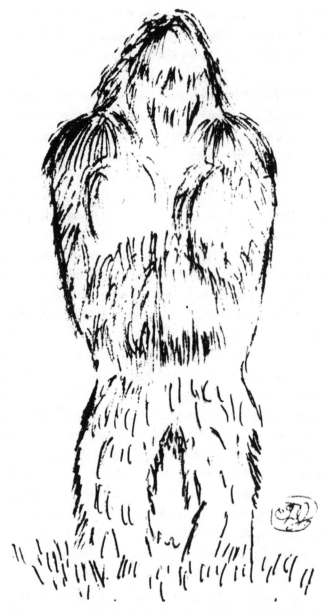

Figure 38: Drawing of the Minerva, Ohio, Bigfoot seen by the Cayton family and friends on 21 August 1978. *Picture: Ron Schaffner & Para-Hominoid Research Group*

The Bigfoot appeared at the kitchen window and was clearly seen by the yard light as it stood there for 10 minutes. The group inside had guns, but decided not to fire unless the creature attacked. Mary Ackerman (30) said: "It doesn't seem to want to bother anyone. It was just curious. We feel it wants to be friends." The Bigfoot suddenly left, and was no longer to be seen when Deputy Sheriff James Shannon arrived. He could still smell it though, an "ammonia-sulfur" smell.

Mrs. Ackerman saw the creature again the next day, 22 August, near the Caytons' house; and Howe Cayton (18) saw something strange at the house on 23 August. There were further possible sightings on 8 and 9 September, one by Mrs. Ackerman who this time saw two Bigfeet. The authorities' official explanation of the 21 August sighting of a Bigfoot and two pumas was "a bear and two cubs," but Mrs. Cayton was not convinced. She told investigators Ron Schaffner and Earl D. Jones that they were not bears, "unless they were mutated." Before the major sighting of 21 August, the Cayton family had seen a 6-7-foot, dark-haired creature around the abandoned strip mines at the beginning of the month.

We return to Michigan for the last major sighting of 1978. Morse Easterling (53) of Lansing was cleaning his garage about 9:30 p.m. on 2 December. As he was about to back his car, he noticed a figure through the rear-view mirror. It was large (about 7 feet and 400-500 pounds) and walking on two legs; he took it to be a woman in a fur coat, possibly a neighbor. He could not make out the face, though the head appeared small. He called out: "Can I help you? What do you want?" The creature, 12-15 feet away, seemed to be walking with something of a limp down the drive towards the orchard. Easterling drove forward and round a curve, but by the time he had got out of the car the creature had gone. This did not seem possible. As Easterling commented: "I just can't believe how quickly that thing disappeared!"

Figure 39: In 1978 Farrel Shook saw a Bigfoot cross his field at Casar, North Carolina, and later also saw one close-up. *Photo: Tony Healy/FPL*

The earliest interesting case in 1979 is a sighting of "Knobby," the North Carolina Bigfoot, on 15 January. This creature had been seen from time to time around Carpenter's Knob in Cleveland County during the last three months of 1978, but Gaye Smith's close encounter gave her a particularly good view of the beast. She was traveling by car with her two sisters when, on Highway 10 between Casar and Polkville, Wanda Smith screamed and it was some minutes before the other two could get her to tell what she had seen. When she did so, they turned the car round and went back. Near some woods by a farm pond they all saw "Knobby." Eighteen-year-old Gaye ran from the car towards the creature, which was on a dam. It squatted there, then stood up, faced her, and stretched out its arms. At a distance of about 150 feet, on a bright, sunny day, she could see it clearly, and later gave a good description.

"It was awful! Just terrible! He was great big, maybe bigger than Dale [a friend who is 6-foot-2 and weighs about 200 pounds] and terribly strange-looking. He was kind of pink-faced." She also added that its facial hair was shorter than that on the rest of the body, and that it was very broad-chested with wide shoulders. "He just went down to nothing at the waist. His legs were large at the thighs but very thin below the knees, almost as thin as a cow's legs." She also saw wide nostrils and a shiny black chest. "It looked almost like tar. He was sort of black and brown mixed. He looked more like a gorilla than anything else I can think of. And there was something white beside him on the dam. I don't know if it was a bird he had killed or just an empty sack or paper bag. Whatever it was didn't move, and I couldn't tell if it was some kind of animal or not."

Most people who see Bigfoot are, not unnaturally, afraid, and in a state of fear their reaction is to shoot at it, regardless of whether it shows any sign of attacking. Bigfeet are remarkably brave, or foolhardy, in the face of such belligerence. However, as the cases in this book will have shown, there is no one-hundred-percent-reliable report of a Bigfoot having been killed, and although Bigfeet have sometimes apparently been injured by gunfire, they have always been able to escape at speed.

The evidence suggests that there is little point in shooting at a Bigfoot: it is difficult to kill (perhaps impossible!), and anyway the creature shows little desire to harm humans, even when the opportunity presents itself. The next two cases both involve shooting at and injury of Bigfeet, and both demonstrate the futility of such action. Though probably the witnesses would argue that shooting at them at least scared the Bigfeet away. We do not believe that injuring an apparently harmless, albeit somewhat fearsome-looking, creature is justified, even in the circumstances described.

The first case took place at Flower Lake, near Tunica, Mississippi, in March 1979. On Friday night, 9 March, Mr. and Mrs. Tom Goff noticed a foul smell and heard a ruckus. On the Saturday night, they saw a 7-8-foot creature near the house. On Sunday night, Goff and his son Rodney armed themselves and waited for the Bigfoot. When he saw it, Rodney fired with his .22 rifle. It seemed to be hit and ran away, but later that night it returned and pushed on the front door, breaking the frame. Next day the family found blood spots around the door. They also found tracks 16-18 inches long. Nearly two months later, at the end of April, 16-year-old Tim Meissner claimed two sightings in three days in British Columbia. He was fishing with a friend on Dunn Lake near Barrière on 28 April when they heard a high screech and, across the lake, saw a Bigfoot with its arms raised. It ran off into the brush and the youths went over to investigate, finding a deer with a broken neck, hidden under branches and moss. Meissner and four others returned to the site two days later and, having separated to search, Meissner again saw a Bigfoot. "He was about 9 feet tall, black, and hairy. He had a human-like face with great big, glaring bright eyes and shoulders 4 feet wide," he reported. "He stood there glaring at me for at least three seconds. He was 50 feet away — so close I could smell him. I don't even know why I shot. I was just scared, really scared." He continued: "I was aiming for right between his eyes and he went down on one knee and one hand. At first I thought he was dead, but I guess I only grazed him, because he got up and ran away at about 30 miles an hour."

Figure 40: Tim Meissner uses his gun to show the height of the Bigfoot he shot at on 30 April 1979. *Photo: RD/FPL*

Figure 41: The Meissner ranch near Barrière, British Columbia, where 16-year-old Tim Meissner saw a Bigfoot on 28 and 30 April 1979. *Photo: RD/FPL*

Figure 42: Cast of a Bigfoot footprint 16 inches long and 10 inches wide found by agriculture teacher Jack Wood at Dunn Lake a few days after Tim Meissner saw a Bigfoot there. *Photo: RD/FPL*

Nearly 200 years have passed since the first reliable Bigfoot sighting reports were recorded — but Bigfoot is still being seen, and is still a mystery, in most of the US states. In early 1980 a previously little-visited state, Utah, became the center of attention. It was about 12:20 a.m. on 4 February when Ronald Smith of South Weber, arriving home from work, had a typical close encounter with a Bigfoot.

I was going back to feed the horse and he wouldn't come to the fence. I started out there to feed him and I heard, crunch, crunch, it was something walking on two legs through the snow. Since only the horse is out there, I thought it might have been some kids getting into something. I looked out there, it was moonlit, and I saw this dark figure walking across the pasture. I thought it was a high-school kid trying to get away before I saw him. I didn't think of how big it was. I saw it walk into some trees. The horse wasn't scared, but it was acting a little funny and looking over that way. Then I heard the screams. They were unlike anything I've ever heard. They sounded like a cougar, but only with a lot of volume. They were just different. I got out of there and into the house. My wife was telling me to get a gun or a camera, but it only lasted seconds. It screamed four times when I was outside and three more times after I got inside. I told my wife, "I think it's Bigfoot out there" and I was sort of kidding, but these screams were unbelievable.

Next morning Smith found traces of footprints in the snowy field, but the horse had trampled over them. Two journalists on the local newspaper also looked for tracks and found some in snow near a canal. They were over 15 inches long, about 4 feet apart, and had been made by something heavy. Alongside ran a smaller set of identical tracks.

When news of this and an earlier sighting got out, other people began to tell of hearing strange noises, of smelling strange smells, and of other unusual experiences possibly involving Bigfoot. Black hair found on a barbed-wire fence was analyzed and said to have come from a cow. It was the end of the month before Bigfoot was actually seen again, at Riverdale a few miles from South Weber. Lee Padilla was driving along a main highway at 3:30 a.m. on 25 February when, he says, a creature 10-11 feet tall loped across the road about 25 feet ahead of him. He saw it for only a few seconds, but that was long enough to register its graceful movement, its long arms and legs, gorilla-like head, and long, dark-brown, furry hair "in layers." Padilla estimated it weighed about 600 pounds and was running at 35 m.p.h. Apparently he was not frightened by what he saw, for he turned off the main road into a side road and directed his headlights in the direction the creature had gone, but he did not see it again. Next day Padilla and two newspapermen looked for footprints, but found none.

In June 1980, the center of attention moved to Ohio, where there were several good sightings in Logan and Union Counties. The strangest was the encounter reported by Union County legal secretary Mrs. Donna Riegler. She was driving home from work on 24 June. It was a stormy evening after a hot, muggy day. Lightning flickered, the sky darkened, and large drops of rain began to fall, but Mrs. Riegler had no inkling of what was about to happen. She told a reporter:

> I was in a good mood. I just wanted to get home. I went over the railroad tracks slow. I always do because I don't want to knock my wheels out of line. Then I saw this thing laying on the road, hunched over. I thought it was a big dog at first. Then it stood up and I thought it was a man. I thought he was crazy, laying on the road. I couldn't figure why he was out there. He had no golf clubs. No luggage. Then he turned around and looked at me.

When asked for more details of the creature's appearance, she demonstrated its posture: upright, with knees bent, and hands held out, palms up. She could not see any facial features. Mrs. Riegler escaped as fast as she could, stopping at a stranger's house where, unnerved by her experience, she broke down and sobbed.

There are several similarities in her story to that told by Patrick Pol-ing, a Union County farmer who saw Bigfoot while working in his cornfield, a week before Mrs. Riegler's encounter. The creature came out of woods bordering the field, and walked along the fence-line. Mr. Poling said it was about 7 feet tall, and walked with its knees bent. Feeling safe on his tractor, Mr. Poling drove towards it to get a closer view and to see its face. Even though he got within 30 yards of it, he still could not make out any facial features. "There was nothing there," he said. The Bigfoot stopped and turned towards him, holding its hands out, palms up.

As a newspaper reporter commented, both Mrs. Riegler and Mr. Poling are believable witnesses, and both are heartily sick of the attention paid to them since they reported their sightings. Plagued by phone calls, pestered by the media… Mr. Poling said he refused to go on radio or television. "One television station told me everybody wants to be on television. I told them I didn't." Does that sound like the attitude of a hoaxer? Usually they enjoy the publicity accompanying their escapade.

Charles Fulton and his mother-in-law Anna Mae Saunders are also unlikely hoaxers. Their brush with Bigfoot came on the night of 4 October 1980, at their rural home in a heavily wooded area of Maysville, north Kentucky. They were watching television with Mrs. Fulton and the four Fulton children, when they heard a loud noise outside. Mr. Fulton opened the front door and saw a 7-foot-tall, white-haired Bigfoot standing on the porch holding a rooster. It jumped from the porch, chased by Fulton who fired at it, apparently without effect. Mrs. Saunders also saw it, but Mr. Fulton had the closest view of the creature, and said it had glowing animal-like eyes. A week later on 10 October, J.L. Tumey of Fleming County, also in north Kentucky, had a similar visitation. He too was watching television in the evening, when he heard a noise on the back porch of his trailer home. He grabbed a pistol and ran out of the front door round to the back. He was just in time to see "what looked like a big man running towards the woods. I emptied my pistol at it as it ran." He went indoors to get more bullets, and when he came out he saw the figure again. He fired at it, but did not appear to hit it. "It was very dark," Mr. Tumey told a reporter, "so I really couldn't tell exactly what it was. It stood up like a man and it was big, but it was so dark, about all I could see was a big shadow. It made a thumping noise as it ran." Although he saw no detail, he was obviously convinced that his nocturnal visitor was not human, else he would surely not have fired at it so vigorously. It was found that the Bigfoot had broken into the back porch and raided the freezer. Frozen meat was lying around the porch and in the back yard, and two loaves of bread, a frozen chicken, and a packet of hotdogs were missing. As Mr. Tumey commented: "If it was a man, he must have been awfully hungry to break in while I was in the house. A regular animal, like a bear or a dog, couldn't have opened up the freezer and carried those packages." Sheriff's deputies and sightseers arrived soon after the incident was reported by Mr. Tumey, many of them armed, but although they scoured the woods that night, no intruder was found. Next day some footprints were found in wet sand, apparently made by a bare foot and about 14 inches long and 6 inches wide, and some long white hairs were found on the porch.

9
Elusive as Ever
1981-99

It will come as no surprise to learn that during the last twenty years of the 20th century, Bigfoot felt no inclination to come out into the open and reveal himself fully. The highpoint of the century for Bigfoot researchers remains the 1967 cine film obtained by Roger Patterson at Bluff Creek (see Chapter 6) — and as the century drew to a close, the arguments intensified over whether the film shows a genuine hairy hominid or a man in an ape suit. That 953 frames of controversial film nearly 40 years old should be the best evidence for Bigfoot's existence yet available must raise a question-mark over the persisting search for this elusive creature, and sow doubt in the minds of not a few as to the reality of its existence. Yet the sighting reports continue, keeping hope alive. In this survey of the closing years of the 20th century, we will present a representative selection of the sightings that have been reported (although as ever we cannot vouch for their authenticity).

In 1981 the Bigfoot activity in Ohio, reported towards the end of the last chapter, was continuing, especially around Rome. The events at one farmhouse were closely monitored by Dennis Pilichis' research group, and he reported some weird events that show these creatures to have definitely been in the paranormal category. The footprints found were three-toed, 14 inches long, and sinking 1½ inches into hard ground. The creatures themselves were around 9 feet tall and had glowing red eyes. Hairy and gorilla-like, they had no facial hair, but they did have fangs about 1.5 inches long. Mutilated livestock were found: ducks and chickens with heads bitten off and large bite marks in their bodies, and a horse with marks down its flank, looking as if cut open by claws. A strong, unpleasant odor was noted just before the creatures appeared, and blue lights were seen lighting up the woods. On one occasion a white "UFO-like thing" flew over the farmhouse. The witnesses tried shooting at the UFO, and at the creatures, as they stood on the edge of the woods with their red eyes glowing, but the gunfire seemed to have no effect. They appeared to have been hit, but no corpses were found, not even any blood.

Around mid-May Bigfoot encounters were being reported in three states. In Louisiana, two men out snake hunting in a cypress swamp near Ruddock noticed a terrible smell and heard something crashing through the undergrowth. They saw from a distance of 30-40 feet a tall, shaggy creature with long reddish-orange hair, so they ran the other way. In Michigan, a 7-8 foot hominid was seen in a back garden at Stockbridge, and a smell "like something was dead" was noticed. The cows, horses, and dogs "went bananas," but none of them was injured. A three-toed footprint was found, but that was all. In the Newark Watershed of New Jersey, two fishermen saw a creature covered with reddish-brown hair when it strode across the road in front of their car, so they followed it down a path and got to within 5 feet of it, when their car got stuck in the mud. They got a good look at it, and said it was about 6½ feet tall, and had a flat face and human ears. It walked with a slight hunch, swinging its arms like a cross-country skier. One of the men said, "I'll go to my grave knowing it wasn't a bear or anyone in a suit. I don't expect to ever see anything like that again." Police said that bears were being seen in the watershed area, but the description given by the men who saw it from five feet away does not in any way resemble a bear.

The big event of 1982 was Paul Freeman's Bigfoot sighting in classic Bigfoot country, Washington State. Freeman was a patrol rider in the watershed country near Walla Walla. He had a lifetime of experience with hunting and trapping and was very familiar with bears: but he was quite sure this was no bear. The date was 10 June, and Freeman had stopped his truck to look at some elk. He walked across an area where he couldn't drive because of fallen trees. Suddenly he saw an upright, hairy creature more than 8 feet tall step off a 10-foot bank onto the road. "He looked like all the pictures I've seen of prehistoric man. He was real hairy — reddish-brown hair. It was so thick you couldn't see through it on his shoulders, arms, and legs. But on his face it was thin enough to see his skin, the colour of brown leather." Freeman stood staring from around 65 yards away. The Bigfoot stared back. Freeman could hear him breathing heavily as though he'd been running, and his stomach muscles were moving. Apprehensive as to what the creature might do, Freeman backed away. When the Bigfoot saw he wasn't approaching, he turned and walked up the road.

Before the area was trampled by sightseers once the news got out, plaster casts were taken of the footprints left by the Bigfoot. These were examined by Dr. Grover Krantz, associate professor of anthropology at Washington State University, and he found dermal ridges (lines on the skin) which he believed proved that the 15-inch footprints had been made by real feet. However, recent research by Matt Crowley has shown that some dermal ridges may in fact be artifacts caused by the casting process and not necessarily representations of genuine dermal ridges.

Paul Freeman left his job after his sighting, because of all the publicity, but he then became a keen Bigfoot hunter, spending many hours in the Umatilla National Forest. He was rewarded with many footprint finds

Figure 43: Paul Freeman, who saw a Bigfoot on 10 June 1982 in
Umatilla National Forest near Walla Walla, Washington State.
Photo: RD/FPL

Figure 44: A cast of one of the Bigfoot footprints showing possible dermal ridges that was discovered by Paul Freeman in Umatilla National Forest in June 1982. *Photo: RD/FPL*

Figure 45: Dr. Grover Krantz holds a cast of one of the footprints with dermal ridges found by Paul Freeman. *Photo: RD/FPL*

and made plaster casts of hundreds of them. He even claimed to have made casts of handprints, and to have shot Bigfoot on cine film, but the sheer scale of his successes, when others were finding nothing, caused some researchers to doubt whether Freeman's claims were genuine.

There have always been hoaxes in the Bigfoot field, but the waters are even more muddied by the possibility that some of the hoax claims may themselves be hoaxes. Ray Wallace was a long-time investigator who claimed many sightings (more than 2,000!) over the years, but in 1982 his 50-year feud with another old-timer, 86-year-old Rant Mullens, came to a head when Mullens claimed that he was responsible for many Bigfoot reports. In 1924 some miners claimed to have encountered Bigfoot in Ape Canyon (see Chapter 3): Mullens said that he and his uncle scared the miners by rolling rocks down onto them. He also carved seven sets of wooden feet to make fake tracks. It is likely that some of the so-called Bigfoot tracks found down the years have been faked, but it is most unlikely that Rant Mullens has single-handedly been responsible for all the Bigfoot activity reported throughout North America since 1818.

In late August 1982, two men had a close sighting of a Bigfoot on a Connecticut farm. They had gone to check the cows just before midnight on 23 August at the Ellington farm and saw the 6-7 foot creature sitting on a feed bunk watching the cows. It was hairy and muscular with a flat nose and big "dangerous looking" teeth, and its arms hung down to its knees. It came towards them, but they screamed and ran away, looking back to see that it had thankfully turned and was itself running away. Next day they found a heavy footprint near the barn.

Through 1984, the occasional sighting was reported: people driving through a wooded area, or camping, or hunting, would catch a brief glimpse of a tall hairy hominid crossing the road or lurking in the bushes. These tantalizing reports do little other than keep the subject alive — they add nothing to our knowledge of the creature. Yet witnesses can hardly be blamed for not wanting to chase after the monster in order to get as near to it as possible so that they can take a close-up photograph.

Its behavior is unpredictable, and even a hunter armed with a powerful gun might be somewhat wary of approaching too close to it. The hunters who know about Bigfoot dream of shooting one, endlessly discussing what their tactics should be, what type and caliber of gun they should use. But this has been the case for almost a century, and no verified report of a hunter killing a Bigfoot is on record. There are enough reported sightings by hunters to suggest that someone, somewhere, could have shot one by now.

But the reports tell us that this is not as straightforward as you might expect. Some hunters, with the creature in their sights, cannot bring themselves to pull the trigger because the creature looks too human; others who do pull the trigger find that the Bigfoot seems unaffected by the gunfire, or else it might appear to be simply wounded and runs away. Is this because the gun is not powerful enough, or do some Bigfeet seem unaffected because they are non-physical beings? There are persistent reports containing elements that suggest this, but how reliable are the witnesses and the investigators? Some are clearly keen to prove that Bigfoot is a paranormal creature. Does this desire color their reports? It's indisputable that a carcass is needed in order to answer so many questions, and there have been a few reports of carcasses obtained by hunters, but these never seem to have reached officials or scientists, the very people who can independently verify that the creature really exists.

There are, of course, moral reasons why we should not go out with the intention of killing a Bigfoot: if they are closely related to humans (and even if they aren't), how can we justify killing one simply to satisfy our curiosity about it? This fact has been recognized in Skamania County, Washington State, where it is illegal to kill a Bigfoot. An ordinance was approved in 1969 which made it a felony to kill a Bigfoot in the county, but the commissioners later decided that the ordinance was probably illegal, and in 1984 passed a revised ordinance which stated that willfully killing a Bigfoot "with malice aforethought" was a gross misdemeanor punishable by a year in jail or a $1,000 fine, or both, while simply killing one without the malice aforethought would merit a $500 fine or six months in jail, or both. It would also be possible that the killer could be charged with homicide, if the coroner determined that the Bigfoot was a hominid. But such deterrents seem unnecessary, given the lack of success of hunters throughout the 20th century. Each new generation thinks they will be the ones to do it, but they are largely unaware of the large number of failed attempts that have gone before.

The early 1980s was a time of few sighting reports, compared with earlier years. Was this because the papers weren't publishing them, or were people just not seeing Bigfoot as often? Some researchers claimed there was a genuine dearth of reports, others claimed to have plenty in their files. Perhaps the unbelievable reports being published in the tabloid press had the effect of turning people against Bigfoot. Reading such headlines as "The Inspiring Story of Saint Bigfoot," "Baby Bigfoot Turns Up in U.S. Town," "I am the Father of Bigfoot Baby," "Teenage Beauty Marries Bigfoot," "Claim Bigfoot is a Space Alien," "Wolfman Snatches Kids from Moving Cars," and "Crash Survivors Rescued by Bigfoot" could make people think that the whole subject was a joke.

In August 1984 a potentially interesting report surfaced, with photographs to support it. Two men driving beside a gravel pit a few kilometers north of Agassiz in British Columbia about 8:30 p.m. saw a bear-like creature trying to climb out of the pit 35-45 meters away from them. They got a bit closer and took three photographs with a Polaroid camera. They said that the creature was well over 6 feet tall, weighing between 300 and 400 pounds, hairy, and running on its hind legs. Bill Bedry said, "I know bears and I know cougars and I know every other damned animal. I'm a hunter. What else would it be unless some circus was around and an ape got loose? What else is it? It's got to be [Bigfoot] … this thing just walked like a human being." Gorden Flanders added, "It moved very quickly. It's some type of a creature, and it more than likely is a sasquatch. I can't say for sure it was a sasquatch, but it definitely was not a bear because a bear cannot run on its hind legs. I kind of believe in sasquatches now because what I saw is some kind of creature." With this degree of certainty expressed by the witnesses, and photographs to back their claim, the case would seem to be a good one, but it was not to be. Reports of the photographs (which the men were selling for $50) described them as showing an indistinct dark object against a dark background, and even when researchers enlarged them, there was no detail to be seen. The waters were muddied further when another man claimed that the whole sighting was a hoax and that he, John Sullivan, had dressed in an ape suit and assumed a running position in the pit. But Gorden Flanders denied Sullivan's claim, saying that he was a "funny guy" he had fallen out with. In the end no one knows who is telling the truth, but an element of doubt has crept in, and the case is spoiled.

1985 produced several intriguing reports of good daylight sightings of Bigfoot. On 15 August, three golfers playing a round at the Medinah Country Club in Illinois saw a black, hair-covered creature around 6 feet tall peering at them from behind a tree. One of the witnesses started hitting golf balls in its direction, at which time it walked along the fence line, then back to the tree, before climbing the tree and vaulting over the fence. One of the witnesses said later, "At first I thought that this creature was of the ape family, or a man dressed in an ape suit. The ape theory was dispelled when I saw its walk, which was much more upright than that of an ape and, also, its physical proportions were that of a human, not of an ape. The human theory was dispelled by the agility with which it climbed the tree and jumped the fence. I think it most improbable that any human could scale a tree with the speed and agility that this creature showed." They thought that the Bigfoot might have been watching workers who were extending the golf course, cutting out a 20-acre patch of virgin forest, which was perhaps the Bigfoot's territory.

In the following month of September there were numerous sightings in Pennsylvania. On the 6th, Edward Kreamer's girlfriend thought she saw a prowler in the back garden of his parents' home in North Annville Township. He ran onto the porch and yelled at the prowler, but it didn't run away and he could see that it had long arms, an ape-like head, and was around 6 feet 4 inches tall. It had sloping shoulders and a very long stride, and Kreamer watched it for about 15 seconds as it walked upright.

At the end of the month, two men saw a tall, foul-smelling hairy creature with 2-inch fangs in East Pennsboro Township. Tom Leach described how it stood behind a guardrail waving its arms, and he passed within eight feet of it. Police Chief James Corbett was not amused: he said it was a Halloween prank (a month early!), and that someone had dressed up in an ape costume. But the policeman who investigated the case, and a neighbor who also saw the creature, were certain that it was not a bear or a person in a suit. The neighbor went outside soon after midnight, after smelling a bad smell, and he saw the creature standing about 45-50 feet away. It had shoulders about 3 feet wide and was 6-7 feet tall. The head was pointed and sat on the shoulders, with no neck being visible, a feature that has been reported before. Its hips were wide, and it was covered with shaggy brown hair. Its arms hung low, and they swung as it ran, rather than having a man's pumping action.

Despite this sounding like a genuine report of something strange, again the waters were muddied by the intervention of human jokers. Early in October, a 24-year-old man was arrested in East Pennsboro and fined $10 with $50.17 costs for impersonating Bigfoot, after he admitted going out dressed in a fur suit and a mask with fangs and standing in an area where he would be illuminated by vehicle headlights. His friends said they had dropped him off early in the morning of 29 September. He said he had done it after reading about people smelling bad smells and hearing weird noises. Was this the explanation for the East Pennsboro sightings of 29 September? It seems more than likely; and it demonstrates how easy it is for someone faced with an unfamiliar and scary sight not to see it for what it is, i.e. a man in a fur suit and mask, but instead to see all those typical Bigfoot features which he expects to see, like the long arms and the untypical running gait. Such a case as this makes one wonder, how many other witnesses have been deceived by pranksters, or have simply misidentified normal animals? After all, many sightings are only fleeting, and often take place at night.

One such occurred in southeast Indiana early in October 1985. The time was 2:00 a.m., and the witness went to the door to attend to his dog, which was chained up in the garden and was barking. He saw a large upright creature, 7-8 feet tall, standing under the outside light, watching the dog. He ran back indoors to get his gun, but in his haste he was dropping the shells as he loaded them, and then his girlfriend saw the creature, now walking away, began to scream, and hit the man on the back so that he dropped the gun. There are so many ways in which opportunities to kill a Bigfoot are lost! Some big footprints were found, and researcher Art Kapa, who came to investigate, managed to make casts of some of them, 16 inches long by 7 inches wide. He also found other people who had seen a Bigfoot, one witness reporting a white or gray creature.

Most sighting reports are of a tall figure briefly seen — but at the other end of the spectrum there are some extremely weird reports, offered in all seriousness. A family living on a ranch in coastal northwest Oregon claimed some unusual encounters. For example in June 1986 a teenage daughter and her younger sister were in the barn throwing hay down from a loft to the calves in the dark, when her hands were grabbed by large hands and she became paralyzed. Telepathically she heard the questions "Who are you?" and "Who is the other girl?", which she answered. Apparently two Bigfeet were sleeping in the barn. Later she felt their presence and communicated telepathically with them. In July her mother saw a female Bigfoot holding a baby to its breast. This was in daylight from 100-150 feet away. The Bigfoot had large breasts which looked full of milk, and it cradled the baby like a human mother. Their faces were hairy except for around the mouth and eyes, and the woman added, "It looked like a cross between a human and an ape...but more human in its mannerisms." She felt she was being told not to come closer, so she watched as the Bigfoot walked away along a road leading into the hills.

A few years earlier, she had had other sightings: of an 8-foot Bigfoot, and of a mother with a 3½-foot youngster that she touched hands with. She had also found an enormous palm print on a glass door that had been lifted out of its frame. In March 1987 she was to see them again: four of the creatures visited her while she was baby-sitting during a picnic by a remote lake, and asked her telepathically about the babies. She asked them: "The UFOs we see at our place, does that mean you are from another planet? What planet are you from?" She received no answer but felt love coming from them, and one drew a "hieroglyph" on the ground. The researcher who reported these events, Jack Lapseritis, claimed to have received other reports of telepathic communication with "the Bigfoot-people." Although bizarre, and some people might say extremely unlikely, such reports need to be mentioned as they are nevertheless a part of the whole Bigfoot scene.

That same summer, in California's Inyo National Forest, more "normal" Bigfoot encounters were being experienced. A five-man construction crew was building a bridge over a river in the mountains, and the men were camping east of Monache Mountain. They heard loud screams which unnerved them so much that one of them fired a warning shot from a rifle. The scream was "blood-curdling." "It sounded like a woman was having the flesh cut off her, but it was so loud that any creature would have had to have enormous lung capacity. Our mouths just dropped." In the twilight, about a city block away, they saw the shadowy outline of a human figure at least 8 feet tall. "We could see a silhouette of a giant, humanoid, shadowy, hulking, lumbering creature. It had a build of a human, but it seemed like it was prehistoric in a way because it had these long arms dangling by its sides and was hunched over." The men in the party who were familiar with bears and mountain lions said that the creature they saw was not a bear, and the screams they heard were different from a mountain lion's cry. They were so unnerved they left the area for a few days.

Later that same month, August 1986, a man looking for ginseng below the crest of Taylor's Ridge on the Georgia/Alabama border saw a large creature with a pointed head and arms hanging to its knees. Its left arm seemed to be useless, and its hand had long curved fingernails. Its right hand and arm appeared normal, but its left leg also appeared to be injured. It was covered with thick, long black hair falling in locks, and its face was monkey-like with thick lips to its mouth and a flat nose. It was only 20-25 feet away, but made no move to harm the terrified man. It simply grunted and walked away. Rather more aggressive were the two creatures encountered by two men, father and son, who were hunting wild turkeys on Dillon's Mountain in West Virginia on 25 October 1986. They heard branches breaking, and then they saw "a big, black gorilla about 8 feet tall." The son said, "The thing and I stared at each other for a couple of moments and then all of a sudden it growled like a gorilla and lunged at me. I turned and ran back…" His father thought it was a bear, until it came closer, and then, "It looked like a giant man dressed up in a gorilla suit. I was too surprised to pull the trigger. Besides that, I didn't know if the thing was human." Both men were waving their arms and yelling to scare it away, when suddenly the father was grabbed by a second creature, this time a female. She was covered with black hair, except on her breasts. He pulled away, and the two men were circled by the creatures which were "snarling and making terrible sounds." After about ten minutes of this, the father picked up his shotgun and fired it into the air, scaring the creatures, which ran away. Despite the terrifying situation, the men were loath to shoot the creatures because "they looked too human." They had big, yellow, human-like teeth, not fangs, and their hands and feet were like human's, but with hair on top. Their noses were a cross between a man's and a gorilla's. The men came away from their encounter with eight strands of coarse, black hair, like hair from a horse's mane or tail.

A large number of sighting reports come from the wilderness areas, and are usually made by people working or hiking in such areas, which is what would be expected of a real-life yet unidentified creature. There have been many such reports throughout this book, and they have continued to the present day. The weirder reports, however, seem to come in waves, first from one area, then from another, and the localities are often not ones where you would expect to find an unidentified hominid 8 feet tall. Perhaps such incidents are more in the nature of copycat events: someone sees something they can't identify, it gets reported, and the collective memory of Bigfoot lore takes over, helped along by hoaxing and hysteria, and also by a local investigator who goes around looking for reports. After a while, the balloon bursts and the excitement fades away. If this is what does happen, it does nothing to help the valid cause of trying to ascertain whether there is indeed an unknown species of hominid living in the North American wilderness areas.

On 14 March 1987, oilmen working on Tumbler Ridge, Calgary, Alberta, in the middle of the night, saw something "larger than an ordinary man" watching them. It ran across the road and through the bush with "an extremely long stride," moving upright, like a man. Miles Jack saw it four times in half an hour, and each time it realized it had been seen, it ran off, moving "as quick as a deer." Next day, the men found oversized tracks in the snow. Veteran investigator John Green went to the site, but by then the tracks had been damaged by the weather and by sightseers. He said that the photographs of the prints showed that "each leg was about a foot wide. The knees measured three feet apart. A human can't get his knees three feet apart no matter how big he is." Further south, in California, three out-of-work loggers parked in a deserted picnic area off Highway 89 near Truckee had a sunset sighting on 24 April 1987. They heard an eerie scream, and looked up from their coffee to see a hairy creature 9 or 10 feet tall, burnt-black in color, standing upright. Game wardens found no footprints, and surmised that the men had seen a bear, but with their logging experience they would be expected to know what a bear looked like.

Throughout 1987 reports continued to be made in Ohio, collected and researched by Mark Francis of the Ohio Bigfoot Research Group. Coshocton was a popular location, producing several clear sightings. Charles Faulkner was watching television in his trailer one June evening when he noticed a strange smell. Going into the kitchen, he saw a hair-covered animal watching him through the window. It had deep-set eyes that glowed red, a flat nose, and a face like a gorilla's. In the outside light he could see that the creature had calloused and dry breasts. It gurgled and moved out of sight. Faulkner grabbed his shotgun and ran outside, but he could hear the visitor running through the creek and up the hillside. Next day he found footprints 14 inches long on both sides of the creek. Two weeks later, while driving to work early one morning, he saw another Bigfoot running across the road. It was black, and much bigger than the first one he had seen, being 9-10 feet tall. In November, a relative of Faulkner's who was driving to see him saw a large creature run across the road, its eyes glowing red. Sightings continued into 1988.

Also in 1988, Professor Grover Krantz was hoping to see a Bigfoot in Washington State during a summer expedition in a homemade ultra-light helicopter, having first located the creature using an infrared scanner. He had no plans to try to shoot any creature he might find, but did think that killing one was the only way to be able to study it properly. Thus far, everyone's efforts to obtain substantial Bigfoot remains, or even *any* Bigfoot remains, have been unsuccessful. But sighting reports continue to come in, and during May 1988 there was a spate of reports from Arkansas. Numerous people saw the creature on roads around Jonesboro. School bus passengers riding on Arkansas 349 saw a black, furry creature 6-7 feet tall with glowing eyes and a stride like a man. It was too tall for a deer or a bear, and the bus driver, who was a hunter, was sure it was not a bear. Other witnesses agreed, but wildlife officials were saying that there had been several sightings of bears in the area and black bears from Minnesota had been introduced into Arkansas. However, they agreed it was unusual for a bear to cross the road in front of vehicles. It is also unusual for a bear to run on its hind legs for any distance. Joe Cagle was another hunter who saw it, with friends and relatives, as it crossed Arkansas 226 just after 10:00 p.m. on 5 May. At first it was running alongside the car, and they thought it was a cow — until it ran in front of the car. It crossed the highway in three strides, leaped the ditch, fell on all fours, scrambled up, and ran into the woods. It looked back at them as it fell, and one of its eyes shone. They said it was not a human or a bear. It was 7 feet tall, black and shiny, with feathery hair along its legs.

In October of the same year, Paul Freeman got another brief glimpse of a Bigfoot in Washington, at Mill Creek Watershed. On 5 October he was with his son Duane, who first noticed the Bigfoot as it came out of some trees, and he took some photographs of it. Paul put a film into his old-fashioned movie camera, and shot some footage, but it didn't come out. They were about 150 yards away, and described the creature as about 7½ feet tall, weighing 500-700 pounds, and with very long arms. Its body hair was dark, its facial hair grayish. The best photograph shows only a large, dark, humanlike shape among the trees, and no detail can be made out. In a press interview in March 1989, Paul Freeman claimed he had seen Bigfoot four times. At that time he was in the woods three days a week, and had spent $50,000 on the search.

Figure 46: The Bigfoot photographed by Duane Freeman on 5 October 1988 at Mill Creek Watershed near Walla Walla, Washington State. *Photo: Paul Freeman/FPL*

Sighting reports again seemed to be few in number in the last years of the 1980s. However, in an area with a history of Bigfoot sightings, where a keen researcher is at work, reports can still be found. For example, Don Keating filed 30 Bigfoot sightings in eastern Ohio in 1989, and Mark Opsasnick uncovered several Maryland sightings. Two boys saw a creature 3-4 feet tall, walking on two legs, on 27 May 1989 from a back garden in Odenton, Maryland. Its legs were bent or crooked, and one appeared to have a long white stripe running down the back. The creature's body was covered with a mixture of black and brown hair. It ran stiffly, making no noise, but it did leave a trail through the brush. No tracks were found because of the nature of the forest floor covering.

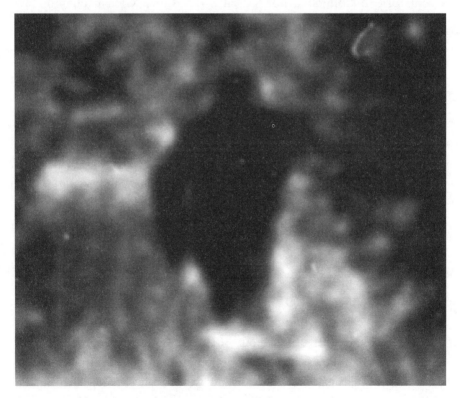

Figure 47: A closer look at the Bigfoot photographed by Duane Freeman on 5 October 1988. *Photo: Paul Freeman/FPL*

The following month, an 8-foot Bigfoot was seen on an Indian reservation at Fort Bidwell, California. Kenneth Sam saw it outside a house he was guarding at night. He shone his flashlight on it from 40 yards away and it ran towards him before turning away. Sam said later, "It was big, dark, and hairy looking. It's got silver eyes and it moves pretty fast. It's a lot bigger than a football player. It's got quite a reach. It seems like it just glides. I thought an antelope is fast, but this guy is pretty fast. It seems like it's curious." On following nights Sam lit fires outside the house. "It seems to be scared of fire. It doesn't come down when the fire is burning," he said.

Late in 1989, three people sitting around a kitchen table in Bella Coola, British Columbia, noticed an awful smell. Glen Clellamin saw something outside, and thinking it was a bear come to get some deer meat that was hanging on the back porch, they all ran over to the window. In the light from the porch they saw a 7-8 foot hairy creature with long arms and wide shoulders, running upright. The next night, the boys were alerted when the dogs started barking, and saw that the Bigfoot was in the next-door garden. They followed it towards the creek, and when they were about 30 feet away, it stopped and looked at them. They shouted at it, but ran when it started coming towards them. They also heard a high-pitched scream, and next day found three sets of tracks of differing sizes. Other people had seen the creatures, large, medium, and small, suggesting a family was in the area, searching for food.

The early 1990s seem to have been another lean time for sighting reports, and any sightings were brief ones. Peggy Nichols had heard screams during the night for several weeks from her home in Dickerson, Maryland, and then at 1:00 a.m. on 14 May 1990, she and her sister saw what may have been making them. From their back porch door, they saw a "great big hairy" creature about 30 feet away in the corner of their garden. Although they saw it only briefly before it moved into the woods, they said it was nearly 7 feet tall and walked on two legs. Until that sighting, everyone had assumed that the screams came from the wildcats that had given nearby Wildcat Creek its name.

Figure 48: 5,800 Bigfoot tracks covering several miles east of Walla Walla, Washington State, were discovered in January 1991. *Photo: Paul Freeman/FPL*

In 1992 Paul Freeman claimed further encounters in the Blue Mountains of Washington State, following his earlier sightings of 1982 and 1988. On 20 April he obtained poor-quality footage of Bigfoot on his camcorder (which he was carrying instead of a rifle). On 20 August he was near Deduct Spring where a large pond is a meeting place for forest animals. He had been visiting the pond regularly and sitting watching for several hours at a time. He found fresh Bigfoot tracks and followed them. He soon heard noises in the brush as if something was moving through, and managed to briefly film a Bigfoot. Then he saw a second, which came close enough for him to see that its face was deformed. It was snarling at him and he tried to remain calm as he filmed it. When it disappeared into the brush, Freeman followed, but he felt that something had upset them and he became scared, hiding for a while in a hole under a fallen tree before making his escape. After capturing Bigfoot on film to his own satisfaction, Paul Freeman decided that he would no longer hunt the creature. However, he did not leave the field, as later reports will show.

Also in August 1992, eight people saw a large hairy creature walking down a hillside near the Nez Perce Indian Reservation in Idaho. Becky Johnson was the first to see it, and she tried unsuccessfully to photograph the 7-8 foot tall creature. She alerted others, including a park ranger who agreed that it was tall, upright, dark in color, and not a bear. Professor Grover Krantz visited the site a few days later and found lines of tracks with a fairly long stride in a ploughed field.

On 12 September 1992, two boys had a good look at a Bigfoot near their home in Klamath, California. They had gone into the brush in the morning, looking for snakes, and while there they heard branches moving and noticed a strong smell, like rotting chicken. One of them said: "When we looked up, we saw the big hairy man standing there [about 100 feet away]. He was covered with thick dark brown hair and he was shaking a branch in his hand. We could see his face real good. My friend and I looked at him for about five seconds before we turned and ran all the way back home." Daryl Owen, the father of one of the boys, said that they were scared to death, and he went back to the place where they had seen "the big hairy man." He expected to find either bear tracks or nothing, but instead he found huge footprints, 16½ inches long and 8½ inches wide at the toes. He counted 34 prints with an average stride of 56 inches, and could hear something moving in the thick brush, so he quickly left the area. The next night screams started, "bellowing, monkey-sounding screeches" which echoed across the canyon every night. Owen explored the area with investigator Scott Herriott, and they twice saw something with glowing red eyes. Owen also saw something looking at him from behind bushes. It had deep-set eyes, large nostrils, a dark burnt-orange face, and long hair that "flowed" as it turned its head. On 12 October, they claimed to have obtained video footage showing Bigfoot, but there is apparently little detail to be made out, leading one researcher to claim that they had photographed a bear. During October-December 1992, several sightings were recorded in the same area of Northern California, including one at the Old Klamath Bridge where a family of four who were sightseeing saw an 8-9 foot creature, light brown in color, which crossed a 24-foot road in three steps. It weighed around 400-500 pounds, had no neck, and looked like a gorilla, not a man. Next day, sixteen prints were found. Only a few days later, a light-brown creature 5-6 feet tall was seen throwing rocks at the truck being used by a National Park maintenance man.

Bigfoot sightings are often reported from campsites, and there are two aspects to such reports. It seems likely that Bigfoot would be curious about people camping out in his territory, and also might look upon such places as good sources of food. At the opposite end of the spectrum, people camping out may be town-dwellers, not used to the sights and sounds of the wilderness areas, and so could mistake normal animals, especially when seen fleetingly at night, for something rather bigger and more frightening. Several interesting campsite encounters were reported in 1993/4. On 30 May 1993 at a campground 20 miles south of Molalla, Oregon, a woman saw a Bigfoot she described as about 9 feet tall, weighing 500 pounds, with brown fur with cinnamon tips, 6-inch head hair, 3-inch body hair, a bullet-shaped head, a large brow ridge, and a squashed nose. This was a daylight sighting from about 60 feet. Tracks found in the mud measured 17 inches by 8 inches. Friends also saw Bigfoot, and a 3-year-old girl said that "a really big monkey" had looked at her in the car. When the group camped at the same place three weeks later, they were again visited by Bigfoot. The little girl saw the "big monkey" eating an apple by the campfire. Pairs of reflecting eyes were seen, and there was a smell like "wet ferret." Further sightings were reported on 4 July and, when observed through binoculars during daylight, the Bigfoot was seen to have thin lips, a sloping forehead, and human-like ears.

In October 1993 there were sightings at the Crook Campground near Woods Canyon Lake in Arizona. Charlene Eairheart, campground host, was answering a call of nature while out target shooting, and felt she was being watched. She looked up and saw the creature from the waist down. It was human in appearance, with very long hair, burnt orange in color, which fell below its waist. The men found the footprints of three creatures, and also bark that had been chewed. By measuring the bark damage on the trees, they judged that the creatures were 7-9 feet tall. The footprints seemed to show that the toes were webbed, and one of the feet seemed disfigured, as if by an injury.

In January 1994 a Molalla River camping ground in Oregon was apparently visited by Bigfoot while a family was camping there. They had camped there during 1993, and now Sharon Jones's daughter found in the brush two red bowls that had disappeared from their card table during an earlier visit, as well as some missing silverware, a pair of boots, a glass bowl, and a car steering wheel. Does this show a tendency to collect interesting objects on the part of Bigfoot? Over the following days, there were signs that Bigfoot was around. The camper was rocked, they found marks on the dirt road where it looked as if something had sat down, and Sharon Jones saw a dark-brown creature looking at her from behind a tree. She saw it again later, kneeling in the brush, and took two photographs. Her husband LeRoy saw the creature that night, and the following weekend when Ed Riddle was in the brush in the dark, collecting wood for the campfire, he felt something put its hands at either side of his waist. Not surprisingly, he ran back to camp screaming.

Although sightings yet again seemed sparse during the early 1990s, Ray Crowe reported that he had had a number of reports sent to his Western Bigfoot Society of sightings mainly in Oregon and California. Yet another campsite report dates from 19 September 1994 when Tex Occanaa was at Hillson-Sanyo Camp near Baldwin Mountain, California. He saw the 7-foot creature in the campground lights, before it loped off on seeing Tex. It turned and grinned or grimaced at him, showing fangs. It had long arms, brown shaggy hair, and a bad smell.

In 1995 some detailed photographs of a massive Bigfoot were obtained. The location was Wild Creek in the Snoqualmie National

Figure 49: Professor Grover Krantz (left) and Bigfoot investigator Cliff Crook examining the Wild Creek Bigfoot photographs; December 1995. *Photo: Cliff Crook/FPL*

Figure 50: The Bigfoot photographed by a forest patrol officer at Wild Creek in the foothills of Mount Rainier, Washington State, on 11 July 1995. *Photo: Cliff Crook/FPL*

Forest foothills in Washington State, where on 11 July a forest patrol officer (who is said to have preferred anonymity) was hiking along a ridge. He heard splashing noises, and from a high bank he looked down into a swampy lagoon where he could see the Bigfoot. He shot 14 photographs, some of which were unclear because of the lighting conditions, and the best one is shown here. With any event where the subject is known to be elusive, clear photographs are naturally suspect. In this case we note that the Bigfoot seems not to have moved from shot to shot, which seems unlikely, and the photographer must have been a very brave man indeed, to have stayed around long enough to shoot 14 photographs of an unpredictable monster. Also problematic about the Wild Creek photographs is the lack of good scale, the sense that computer manipulation software is involved, and that the supposed "forest patrol officer" has never been identified.

On 5 August, Paul Freeman was with two other veteran researchers, Bill Laughery and Wes Sumerlin, on Biscuit Ridge in the Blue Mountains of Washington State, checking out some tracks which seemed to have been made by three Bigfeet. Laughery was first to see the outline of a standing figure near a tree about 35 feet away and he informed the others. But when they got to the place, there was nothing there. "It had blended right into the brush and disappeared." They followed its tracks and saw it again briefly, and felt the presence of the creatures, which they believed had been foraging for grubs, ants, etc. As well as hundreds of tracks, the men found twisted young fir trees and some long hairs of various colors.

Also in August 1995, in Jedediah Smith State Park in Northern California, some men in a camper van obtained videotape footage of a creature they saw on the road, which was believed to be a Bigfoot. It appeared to be around 7 feet 10 inches tall with a sloping forehead, and it walked with its knees slightly bent. But the footage was shot at night, the creature illuminated by vehicle headlights, and not much detail can be made out. Over the years, there have been numerous examples of footage claiming to show Bigfoot, but most are either indistinct or in some way dubious, and the clearest film still remains that obtained by Roger Patterson in 1967.

In September 1996 another sighting was reported from Washington's Blue Mountains. A couple stopped at a viewpoint 6,000 feet high, and through binoculars looked across the Mill Creek Watershed. They happened to see four creatures walking upright, two big and two smaller ones, which they were certain were Bigfoot.

Although many of the reports from the mid and late 1990s did come from the northwest United States, activity was still being reported elsewhere, especially during the summer of 1997. On 24 July, Amy Zumwalt and her family were driving out of Wyoming's Yellowstone National Park when they saw a hairy creature walking across a patch of snow near the mountaintop. It looked to be 8-9 feet tall. Around the same time, there was a spate of sightings of Florida's "skunk ape" near Ochopee in the Big Cypress preserve. A large brown creature around 7 feet tall was being seen, especially by tour guides and their parties. Some people were suspicious and felt the whole thing might be a hoax, or a publicity stunt. Anyone participating in such a stunt anywhere in North America is risking his life. There are so many trigger-happy people roaming around keen to be the first to bring in a Bigfoot that pretending to be one is a foolhardy act.

Only a month later, in August 1997, a group of children playing in the Mojave Riverbed in Hesperia in Southern California were chased by a "monkey monster" which loped casually after the boys, stopping only when it realized it was being watched by teenager Stacy Glass, who had gone out to fetch the younger children home as the sun was beginning to go down. She was walking down towards the riverbed when the boys came running out, screaming. She then saw the creature that was chasing them, and described "the monkey monster" as about 6 feet 5 inches tall, with a large "oval dome" head, and with dark brown hair all over. She couldn't see a neck or any facial features, other than a "blackish" face, but it had long arms, and ran with bent knees in a non-human way. Later a bed of fresh leaves mixed with broken sticks was found, which was thought to have been its bed, and also a footprint about 14 inches long and 8 inches wide which seemed to have only four toes. Around the time of the sighting, people in the area were mysteriously losing ducks, geese, chickens, and pigeons.

In the autumn of 1997 there was further activity in the Blue Mountains of Washington State, involving big-game hunters. A killed bear was moved while the hunters were fetching their skinning gear from their truck, and one of them spotted a Bigfoot carrying it away. An elk hunter in the mountains above Dixie shot a bull elk at sunrise and watched through binoculars as it fell down the hillside. He was then amazed to see "a big gorilla" walking out of the woods towards the elk.

As it stood there, with the hunter watching it through his binoculars, it suddenly turned and slowly sauntered back into the trees. The hunter felt it was bigger than a normal gorilla, and definitely stood upright.

Figure 51: In June 1997 Bigfoot/Sasquatch enthusiasts got together in Vancouver, British Columbia, for an International Sasquatch Symposium. *Photo: RD/FPL*

Again, it is unlikely that a human wearing a fur suit would have risked wandering about in an area where there were hunters using guns to fell game. A year later, on 26 September 1998, a group of campers had a nighttime glimpse of what appeared to be a hairy creature 9 feet tall, in a remote area near Mud Springs, south of Hayfork in California. They were roasting marshmallows at their campsite when they heard loud rustling noises in the bushes. Tim Ford shone his flashlight and saw the creature, "his arms hanging way past his knees," standing about 50 yards away on the other side of a creek. Ford and his friend James Harmon said that none of the seven men had been drinking or taking drugs. The creature stayed close to the campsite throughout the night, and they could hear its eerie screams. They also found tracks 6 inches wide and 20 inches long.

As the 20th century drew to a close, Bigfoot sightings were in short supply, but Bigfoot hunters and researchers never wavered in their enthusiasm for their quarry. Almost 200 years before (see Chapter 1), hunters and mountain dwellers were reporting seeing hairy man-beasts, yet no one was able to produce conclusive evidence of the creatures' reality: had anything been achieved in the intervening years? What would the new millennium bring?

10
Into the New Millennium

After a quiet end to the 20th century, the 21st got underway with a busy year for Bigfoot sightings, and a brief encounter late in January 2000 confirmed that Bigfoot had successfully entered the new century: he showed up in Starbuck, Washington State, at 3:00 a.m. on the morning of 27 January. The witness was an unnamed man living on the outskirts of town who went outside to fetch some wood. When he saw a 7-foot-tall, muscular figure with "grayish-brown hair" standing between the woodpile and a fir tree, he dashed back indoors and locked the door — a natural reaction in the circumstances. Brief sightings are all-too-often the norm, as witnesses, taken by surprise, do whatever is necessary to remove themselves from the location as speedily as possible. Another startled witness whose first impulse was to flee was James Hughes, driving his newspaper delivery route at 5:15 a.m. on 28 March along County Highway H 1½ miles from Granton in Wisconsin. What he saw, standing in the ditch beside the road, appeared to be an 8-foot "man" with shaggy dark-gray hair which was "in clumps and knotted," and had some lighter honey-colored patches among it. He couldn't see any facial features other than two spots where its eyes should be; the creature turned slowly as he passed, as if looking at him, and it appeared to be holding something in its left hand — a goat, Hughes thought, though later he was not sure. He reported his sighting to the local sheriff's office next day and a search was made, but no footprints were found, even in the soil of a ploughed field between the highway and the nearest wood. Another fleeting sighting was claimed by a woman driving on Route 30 between Jeannette and Greensburg in Pennsylvania early in the morning of 9 June. The 6-7-foot creature, covered with long black hair, was standing "hunched" on a back road close to the highway. She saw it turn its head towards the highway, then stride away into the woods.

The summer of 2000 brought a rash of sightings, as well as many footprint finds, especially in the Pacific Northwest. A motorcyclist claimed a Bigfoot sighting off Highway 101 at Grants Pass, Oregon, on 18 May; on 29 June a forestry manager saw one in a forest on the Kitsap Peninsula in Washington State; and two days later a psychologist, hiking with his family in the Oregon Caves National Monument, also claimed a sighting. The creature seen by David Mills, forestry manager with the Suquamish tribe, was 9 feet tall, with shiny black fur, and it ducked behind a tree when it realized it was being watched. Mills walked closer, whereupon the creature made screeching noises and also appeared to be pounding a tree with a rock. Mills then realized that there was a bear cub only 20 feet away from him, but surprisingly its mother ignored him and appeared to be more concerned with the Bigfoot — at which point Mills sensibly retreated. The Johnson family's sighting in the forests of Oregon Caves National Monument on 1 July was preceded by a strong pungent smell and a guttural noise, before Dr. Johnson saw a "half-human and half-ape" step out from behind a tree about 60 feet away. He was sure it was not a bear, having seen both grizzlies and black bears in Alaska.

Julie Davis was also sure that what she had seen, on 5 August in a remote part of the San Juan National Forest of Colorado, was not a bear.

She had been a volunteer with the Great Bear Foundation in Montana for several years, and felt justified in saying, "I've had a lot of time to get to know what bears look like up close. This animal was bigger than any bear." Ms. Davis was camping in the forest, being on a 10-day trip down the Colorado Trail with four goats and two border collies. One goat had become ill and so she had left the trail to set up camp in a remote meadow while it recovered. As the day passed, she noticed that the animals seemed nervous — until eventually she realized there was something outside the tent that was really worrying them. She expected it might be a grizzly bear and rushed from the tent with a pepper spray in her hand. The creature she saw from only 12 feet away was about 8 feet tall, with very broad shoulders, and as they stared at each other, she noted that "Its face was almost completely covered in fur but human-like, on the human side of halfway between a human and gorilla." It had "medium-chestnut fur... like an Irish setter's" covering its body. The creature made a low rumbling noise, whereupon a second animal, smaller in size and lighter in color, peered at her from behind the big one. Then they both turned, and ran into the forest. She concluded, "I know from looking at the expression on its face and from the graceful way it ran off that there was no way it could have been hoaxed. It was absolutely a beautiful lope. You could see muscles moving under the fur... I don't care if anybody believes me or not. I know what it was, and it was real. There's nothing more persuasive than staring something straight in the face."

Far away in Louisiana, a fisherman wading in a lake in the Cotton Island area in mid-August claimed that a black-haired Bigfoot, 7 feet tall, hunched over, and strong smelling, walked up to him. It was carrying a pig under its arm and darted off into the woods after stopping to stare at the startled man. Later in the month, more sightings were reported from the same area, the witnesses including logger Earl Whitstine who with a companion saw the creature in cypress swamps called Boggy Bayou. Twenty-five years earlier his father had been involved in faking giant Bigfoot tracks in the woods with plywood feet, so there was a natural suspicion about the 2000 sightings, which increased when some hair discovered at Cotton Island turned out to be from a horse. But Earl Whitstine stood by his report, as did Larry Satcher, a fisherman who saw it and said, "I know what I saw, and it was no man in a suit."

While Bigfoot was the talk of the bayous, a cousin of his was frightening hikers in the Snowmass Wilderness of Colorado. David Riley and a friend were hiking from Crested Butte to Snowmass. They returned from their trip claiming that they had been shadowed by several Bigfeet for two nights. Riley said that when he stepped out of the tent on the evening of 22 August after a heavy shower of rain, he saw a creature more than 8 feet tall, with huge glowing eyes, staring at him from the edge of camp. It had two youngsters peeking around its body.

Many other sighting and footprint reports surfaced during this active year, but as usual very few witnesses seem to have tried to photograph what they were seeing. However a creature spotted in the autumn of 2000 near the Myakka River in Sarasota County, Florida, was photographed by an elderly woman as it hid among palmetto plants in her back yard. It was heard making "woomp" noises, and a strong smell had remained long after the creature was around. It had been stealing apples from the back porch during several nighttime visits, according to the letter sent to the local sheriff, along with the photographs, by the witness, who wanted to remain anonymous. Suspicion is always aroused by a request for anonymity, because it means that no investigation can be undertaken, thus enabling a hoaxer to avoid discovery; but on the other hand the witness may have realized that to identify herself would bring a media circus to her home, and I can readily understand why such publicity may not have been desired. Although the name "skunk ape" has been given to the creature, this being a Florida name for the "swamp monsters" seen there, the photographer herself never mentioned skunk ape or Bigfoot in her letter, but said that she wondered if the creature was an escaped orangutan. Cryptozoologist Loren Coleman has been closely involved in the research into these photographs, and as he comments in his book *Bigfoot!*, "I find the comparisons of the photographed Myakka

Figure 52: Two photographs of the creature that became known as the Myakka Skunk Ape; it was photographed in Sarasota County, Florida, during the autumn of 2000. *Photo: Loren Coleman/FPL*

apes with orangutans compelling." He also reminds us that "the classic Skunk Ape…is a much different animal from the Sasquatch of the United States and Canadian Northwest" — it is well worth remembering that the terms "Bigfoot" and "Sasquatch" tend to encompass several different kinds of creature with varying appearances.

Although sightings seem to have been scarce early in 2001, October brought some sightings in a familiar Bigfoot territory, the Blue Mountains of Washington State. On the first of the month, a woman and her son heading up to their cabin on Blacksnake Ridge saw what she at first thought was a cow by the side of the road. It was sitting on an embankment apparently eating berries (not usual behavior for a cow!). As they passed by only 10-15 feet from it, she was able to look the creature in the eye, but it just ignored her and carried on eating. She said its head was broad and shaped like a baboon's. Investigator Brian Smith went to the location later and found a "big pile of rose hips discards." A fortnight after that sighting, Smith himself saw a Bigfoot, brown in color and at least 8 feet tall, as it dashed across the Mill Creek Road in the Kooskooskie summer cabin area around 10:30 p.m. It was 50-60 feet ahead of the vehicle, and crossed the road fast, in three steps. Also in late fall 2001, a hunter near Marshall, Texas, put some apples down to attract deer, but got more than he expected when he found that an ape-like creature holding the hindquarter of a deer had been attracted to his bait. It picked up some apples before leaving.

Sadly, 2001 was also the year that Bigfoot/Sasquatch research lost probably its most enthusiastic, certainly its most colorful, character, René Dahinden, who died on 18 April aged 70. He had been involved in the search for Bigfoot for almost 50 years, and an illustrated tribute to his involvement can be found in Christopher L. Murphy's *Meet the Sasquatch*, along with tributes to other long-term, dedicated researchers such as Bob Titmus, John Green, and Dr. Grover S. Krantz.

2002 was a quiet year with no major sightings. Early in the year (16 January) Linda Boydson reported that she and her son nearly ran over a slender Bigfoot that they encountered on the road near Multnomah Falls in Oregon. It was hairy, 9 feet tall, and appeared to be in need of food, for it looked bony, though she also said it was well muscled like an athlete.

In June a man living northeast of Forks, near Sappho, Washington, reported seeing a hairy, humanlike creature near his home — but attention switched to Canada late in the year when there was a flurry of sightings on Vancouver Island. Early in November three people claimed sightings between Port Alberni and Tofino, with Arnold Frank and his nephew seeing the creature twice. They heard crashing sounds and saw it in the trees — "real big orange eyes, real high off the ground" — and a few nights later it ran into the woods as they drove along the highway. They calculated it to be around 2.4 meters tall and too big for a bear, as

Figure 53: René Dahinden in 1974, hunting Bigfoot in the Stave River area 40 miles northeast of Vancouver in British Columbia. *Photo: RD/FPL*

well as walking on two legs. An elderly woman also saw a Bigfoot crossing the road ahead of her car: it stopped and looked straight at her before disappearing into the bush. Around the same time, sightings were also reported from the Squamish area on the Lower Mainland, one by a woman who was camping and heard noises early in the morning. Looking out of her tent, she saw three Bigfeet.

The death of Ray Wallace late in November 2002 stirred up a hornets' nest in the Bigfoot/Sasquatch world when it was claimed by his family that he had started the whole Bigfoot saga in 1958. Wallace was responsible for faking many Bigfoot tracks, as well as claiming hundreds

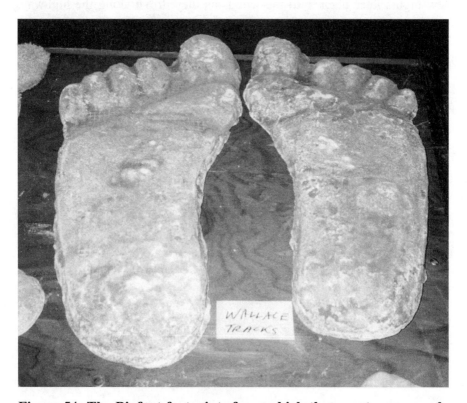

Figure 54: The Bigfoot footprints from which these casts were made were created using Ray Wallace's wooden "Bigfoot" feet. *Photo: Christopher L. Murphy/FPL*

of sightings, in addition to films and photographs of the creature, but as Loren Coleman succinctly put it, "Folks who assume Bigfoot sightings will disappear now that Wallace is dead may end up putting their big foot in their mouth." There were many sightings of Bigfoot/Sasquatch before Wallace began hoaxing, as the early chapters of this book amply demonstrate.

Bigfoot sightings during 2003 seem to have been a rarity, which perhaps explains why two vanloads of people took to the roads with cameras after emergency dispatchers in Skamania County, Washington State, received reports of a sighting in late June. Later in the year, a married couple from Mansfield, Arkansas, saw what may have been a Bigfoot beside the road a mile north of Mansfield, while they were

Figure 55: Loren Coleman photographed in 1995. *Photo: Lisa Richards/FPL*

driving home one September night from the Arkansas-Oklahoma Fair. It was crouched down beside the road, and as they passed it got up and started to walk away. The wife described it as over 6 feet tall, with long black hair, and weighing 400-500 pounds. It had legs that were too long for a bear, nor were they ape-like, though its backside looked more like an ape's.

They returned to the spot the next day and found a barbed-wire fence close to where the creature was seen which had been pulled apart as if by something climbing through, and there were several strands of long black hair caught on the wire. They took some samples of the hair, which later were lost. On the night of their sighting, they reported it to the police

Figure 56: In September 2003 numerous long-time Bigfoot researchers gathered together at Willow Creek for the International Bigfoot Symposium, and on 14 September they visited Bluff Creek, the famous Patterson-Gimlin film-site. Lined up, from left, are Dr. Jeff Meldrum, Bob Gimlin (revisiting the film-site for the first time since 1967), Dr. John Bindernagel, Daniel Perez, John Green, and Dmitri Bayanov. *Photo: Daniel Perez/FPL*

station, where they also met a local person who said that there had been another report of an ape-like creature seen in a field about a mile south of Mansfield only three days earlier. Although there are a lot of sightings of Bigfoot close to highways, this probably doesn't mean that the creatures are attracted to roads. The answer is far more likely to be that most people only travel on roads through the countryside, rather than hiking the trails, and so the sightings take place when a Bigfoot happens to be close to a road at the same time as a vehicle passes by.

Bigfoot always causes a stir when he encroaches on "human territory," such as the mobile-home park at New Town on the Fort Berthold Reservation in North Dakota where a "huge" creature was seen on 22 February 2004. The children who were playing outside began screaming when they saw it, and it was probably their noise that scared it away. More sightings in the area were made in subsequent days, including one on 24 February by two men driving near Lost Bridge south of Mandaree. They saw it walking on the road before moving into the ditch and continuing to walk along. The men returned to the area with others, but they found only footprints in the snow which showed the creature had a stride of almost 5 feet.

Another sighting of a Bigfoot on a highway came in June 2004 when two men, Marion Sheldon and Gus Jules, were driving out of Teslin in Yukon, Canada. They were on the Alaska Highway on 6 June when shortly after 1:00 a.m. they passed a figure standing beside the road. Thinking it might be someone needing a ride, they drove back — and soon realized that the figure was not a person. It was around 7 feet tall, and standing hunched over. In the lights from their truck they could see "flesh tones" under the dark hair which covered the figure. They drove away, and saw the figure cross the highway in two or three steps. No evidence was found at the site when it was examined later, probably because so many local people, on hearing of the encounter, went out to see for themselves.

In mid-August 2004, just after Hurricane Charley had passed through the area, 30-year-old Jennifer Ward, driving through the Green Swamp area of northern Polk County in Florida, ended her journey convinced of the reality of Bigfoot. She saw a creature that she estimated to be 8 feet tall standing in a drainage ditch alongside the road: it had human form, was covered in dark hair or fur, and had whitish rings around its eyes. It seemed to be doing something, possibly foraging, and it just stood and watched as she drove past. Not surprisingly, she didn't stop to investigate further, since her two young daughters were asleep in the back of her vehicle, but she did return later. However she found nothing to back up her story, no hair or footprints.

It is important to remember that throughout this book, only a fraction of the total number of Bigfoot/Sasquatch sightings has been mentioned. We have collected well over 1,000 sighting reports — and this total omits those reports where footprints only were found, of which there are very many more. It is also certain that there are plenty of sighting reports that have not come to our notice — and beyond that even more sightings that have never been reported to anyone. What we have tried to do in this book is to present a representative selection, to give readers some idea of what has been going on for well over 180 years — and is still going on. However what we cannot do is provide any answers. Those are as unattainable as they ever were, and the three opposing camps remain firmly entrenched. In the first camp are those who believe firmly that there is overwhelming evidence for the physical reality of Bigfoot: many thousands of reports of sightings and footprints, with some photographs and footage, and other signs of the creatures' presence such as damaged trees, trampled brush, feces, and hairs. In the second camp are those who can interpret all the "evidence" in a different way: misidentification, the will to believe, and downright hoaxing. For the unbelievers Bigfoot is nothing more than an example of folklore in the making. The most significant argument in favor of this viewpoint is the fact that after more than a century of sighting reports, there is still no carcass, nor even a part of one. The third camp believes that Bigfoot is part of the spirit world — real but not physically real. They point to the hundreds of sightings as evidence of Bigfoot's reality and the lack of a physical carcass as evidence that it is not physically real. As many times as Bigfoot has been shot, with no body found, including a few outright disappearances, they say that continuing to expect to capture a Bigfoot is a forlorn hope. If a carcass is found and scientific analysis shows that it is from an unknown creature, the physical camp's position will be vindicated. Otherwise, the reality of Bigfoot must remain a mystery.

Other developments have bolstered those who believe that an unknown hominid is living on the North American continent. Late in 2004 the skull and some bones of the previously unknown *Homo floresiensis* were discovered on the island of Flores in central Indonesia, north of Australia, and these small humans, weighing about 25 kg (4 stones), were still living as recently as 13,000 years ago. Indeed, some may still survive in the remotest rainforests — and there have been continuing reports of sightings of small hominids, such as that known as Orang Pendek, elsewhere in southeast Asia. This shows that it is by no means impossible for another as yet unknown hominid (albeit rather larger in size) to be living on the huge North American continent, where there are still plenty of wilderness areas.

Thanks to the diligent work of a determined band of Bigfoot researchers in the USA and Canada, the sighting reports included in this book have not remained buried in newspaper files or witnesses' memories and so lost to posterity. It seems certain that sightings will continue to be reported, however many efforts are made by skeptics to denigrate the witnesses. A single Bigfoot sighting might be explained away, but the 1,000 cases detailed in our "Chronological List of Sightings — 1818-1980" form a massive body of evidence in favor of the creature's existence.

In the future new tactics and research methods in the search for Bigfoot may help in finding out more about these creatures. Most of the sightings in this book describe brief encounters, fleeting glimpses, and interactions where both the observer and the observed have been more concerned with getting away than with trying to establish communication. Although they are seldom documented, there have been other interactions with Bigfoot of a very different nature. One example is Sali Wolford who lived in a cabin in Orting, Washington State, which was visited many times by a group of Bigfeet from 1977 to 1979. Her story of the ongoing interactions is the subject of a book, *Valley of the Skookum*, coming out in 2006.

Some researchers, for example Loren Coleman, are asking questions that show Bigfoot may no longer be considered merely something to trick or catch. He is pondering questions such as how many children are in a Bigfoot family and Bigfoot's sexual behaviour.

Autumn Williams, one of the younger generation of Bigfoot researchers, is taking a two-pronged approach in her latest research. On the one hand she is looking for people like Sali Wolford who have spent years living with Bigfoot. She has met many others who have not told their story because they don't want the notoriety or the invasion of their lives and property that would surely result. On the other hand she is planning to spend weeks in the field, as Jane Goodall did with the gorillas, trying to be accepted by a group of Bigfeet. If these creatures are real, then researchers feel it is time to do more than peek at them through the trees.

In light of all the things Bigfoot has done in the encounters described in this book, we might even start to ask the questions: Who really is the observer, Bigfoot or us? Are we really sure we are more intelligent?

Of one thing we can be sure: despite all the recorded sightings, it is Bigfoot's reclusive nature that has been his dominant trait for so long. He sensibly shuns contact with humans, preferring to lurk in the shadows — so tantalizingly close, yet always just out of reach...

Part 2

Chronological List
of Bigfoot Sightings
1818-1980

Introduction

This list gives in abbreviated form details of all the Bigfoot sighting reports we have been able to find through 1980. The date of the sighting is given first, followed by the location, the witnesses, a description of the events, and finally the source of the report. The primary sources are given where known, together with those books and magazines where further information is most easily accessible to the reader.

The most interesting cases mentioned here are described in more detail in chapters 1-8 of this book, and the chapter number following the brief description in this list shows where a fuller treatment can be found. We have sometimes quoted extensively from original sources, and in such cases the quoted passage comes from the first source listed.

The word "Bigfoot" used in the following descriptions means simply that a bipedal creature looking like a big, hair-covered man-beast was seen; it does not imply any positive identification of the creature by the witness or investigator.

U.S. State Abbreviations

AL = Alabama; AK = Alaska; AZ = Arizona; AR = Arkansas; CA = California; CO = Colorado; CT = Connecticut; DE = Delaware; FL = Florida; GA = Georgia; ID = Idaho; IL = Illinois; IN = Indiana; IA = Iowa; KS = Kansas; KY = Kentucky; LA = Louisiana; ME = Maine; MD = Maryland; MA = Massachusetts; MI = Michigan; MN = Minnesota; MS = Mississippi; MO = Missouri; MT = Montana; NE = Nebraska; NV = Nevada; NH = New Hampshire; NJ = New Jersey; NM = New Mexico; NY = New York; NC = North Carolina; ND = North Dakota; OH = Ohio; OK = Oklahoma; OR = Oregon; PA = Pennsylvania; RI = Rhode Island; SC = South Carolina; SD = South Dakota; TN = Tennessee; TX = Texas; UT = Utah; VT = Vermont; VA = Virginia; WA = Washington; WV = West Virginia; WI = Wisconsin; WY = Wyoming

Names of Canadian provinces are given in full, except for British Columbia, abbreviated as BC, and Ontario, abbreviated as Ont.

Source Abbreviations

For fuller details of books listed, see Bibliography.

AS = Sanderson, *Abominable Snowmen: Legend Come to Life*

BAOTC = Place, *Bigfoot All Over the Country*

BB = *Bigfoot Bulletin* (produced by the late George F. Haas of The Bay Area Group, 1969-71)

BFN = *Bigfoot News* (produced by Peter Byrne of the Bigfoot Information Center)

Bigfoot (N) = Napier, *Bigfoot*

Bigfoot (PRL) = *Bigfoot: Tales of Unexplained Creatures* (A Page Research Library Newsletter Special Report, 1978)

Bigfoot (S&B) = Slate & Berry, *Bigfoot*

BSIS = Bigfoot/Sasquatch Information Service (photocopied news clips – produced by D.E. Gates, and later by Edd Kaye)

COTOE = Clark & Coleman, *Creatures of the Outer Edge*

DASOARE = Patterson *Do Abominable Snowmen of America Really Exist?*

FN = *Forteana News* (produced by Lucius Farish; see Bibliography for contact details)

FSR = *Flying Saucer Review*

Hall (1) = Mark A. Hall, "Contemporary Stories of 'Taku He' or 'Bigfoot' in South Dakota as Drawn from Newspaper Accounts," *The Minnesota Archaeologist*, vol. 37, no. 2 (May 1978) pp. 63-78

Hall (2) = Mark A. Hall, "Stories of 'Bigfoot' in Iowa during 1978 as Drawn from Newspaper Sources," *The Minnesota Archaeologist*, vol. 38, no. 1 (Feb. 1979) pp. 2-17

JG = John Green

OTTOTS = Green, On *the Track of the Sasquatch*

RD = René Dahinden

RP = Roger Patterson

Sasquatch = Hunter & Dahinden, *Sasquatch*

SCFTAS = Keel, *Strange Creatures from Time and Space*

STAAU = Green, *Sasquatch: The Apes Among Us*

TSF = Green, *The Sasquatch File*

TSFBF = Byrne, *The Search for Big Foot*

UIRTCSIP = Stan Gordon, "UFOS, in Relation to Creature Sightings in Pennsylvania." (MUFON UFO Symposium Proceedings, 1974)

Other Abbreviations

ft = foot/feet

in = inches

int. = interviewed by

Mt = Mount

quot. = quoted in

repr. = reprinted in full in

1818-1900

Early 1800s / Mt Katahdin area, ME / Trapper named Cluey / Saw Bigfoot near camp at night, and again next day; possibly fictional / *Camping Out,* noted STAAU p. 228.

6 Sept. 1818 / Ellisburgh, NY / "Gentleman" / Saw hairy "animal" which ran away (see ch. 1) / *Exeter Watchman* 22 Sept. 1818, located by Howard Koval, NJ.

c. 1834 / St. Francis, Poinsett & Greene Counties, AR / Sportsmen & hunters / "Wild man" seen over many years / New Orleans, LA, *Times Picayune* 16 May 1851, quot. OTTOTS pp. 117-18 & STAAU pp. 28-9.

1830s / Bridgewater, PA / Man picking berries / Small Bigfoot ran off when chased (see ch. 1) / Dorchester County, MD, *Aurora* 27 Aug 1838, quot. STAAU pp. 26-7.

Summer 1838 / Silver Lake Township, PA / 16-year-old boy / Frightened by seeing small black-haired Bigfoot (see ch. 1) / Dorchester County, MD, *Aurora* 27 Aug. 1838, quot. STAAU pp. 26-7.

Late 1830s / Around Fish Lake, IN / - / "Wild child" seen near and swimming in lake (see ch. 1) / Philadelphia, PA, *Saturday Courier* 28 Dec. 1839.

13 May 1849 / SW of Eagle (later Eagletown), OK / One-Eye Bascomb / Hunter-trapper saw "strange critter" in swamps; description fits Bigfoot / Diary of Bertrand Tonihkah, noted in "McCurtain County Has a Manbeast," McCurtain, OK, *Sunday Gazette* 9 July 1978, repr. FN Sept. 1978 p. 16.

c. 1850 / Mt St. Helens, WA / Rocque Ducheney / Bigfoot beckoned to witness, who turned and ran / Told by witness's daughter, Agnes Louise Eliot, in *Told by the Pioneers* (U.S. Work Projects Administration, Olympia, 1937-8) & noted TSF p. 5.

Mar. 1851 / Greene County, AR / Mr. Hamilton / Gigantic "wild man" pursued cattle (see ch. 1) / New Orleans, LA, *Times Picayune* 16 May 1851, quot. OTTOTS pp. 117-18 & STAAU pp. 28-9.

2 Jan. 1855 / Waldoboro, ME / J.W. McHenri / 18-in hairy manlike creature captured / Washington State *Pioneer and Democrat* 12 May 1855, repr. BFN 19 p. 3.

1856 / AR-LA border / - / "Wild man" dragged man from horse and bit and scratched him before riding off on horse / Caddo, LA, *Gazette* date unknown; *Arkansas Gazette* 27 June 1971, quot. *Pursuit* vol. 4 no. 4 p. 89.

1850s / Mt Shasta area, CA / Gold prospector / Saw Bigfoot smash sluiceway against tree (see ch. 1) / Letter in *True* magazine 1959 or 1960 from John R. Weeks, Providence, RI, quot. OTTOTS pp. 113-14 & STAAU pp. 37-8.

Mid-19th century / Nr Wisdom River in the Bitterroot Mtns, ID-MT border / Hunter named Bauman / Something, thought from footprints to be Bigfoot, haunted hunters' camp and eventually killed one (see ch. 1) / Theodore Roosevelt, *Wilderness Hunter* (1892), quot. AS pp. 134-7, TSFBF pp. 18-22, STAAU pp. 29-34.

1864 / Fraser River canyon, BC / Alexander Caulfield Anderson / Fur trader and party attacked by "hairy humanoids" which threw rocks at them / Anderson's journal, noted BAOTC p. 45.

After 1865 / Saline County, AR / - / 7-ft "wild man" captured (see ch. 1) / Otto Ernest Rayburn, *Ozark Country* (Duell, Sloan, & Pearce, 1941) pp. 313-14, quot. *INFO Journal* 1 pp. 48-9.

Sept. 1869 / Area of East Davenport & Gilbert, IA / Huntsman / Saw ugly, sandy-haired "wild boy" eating fish in river / Hartford, CT, *Courant* 27 Sept. 1869, located by Gary Mangiacopra.

Autumn 1869 / Orestimba Creek area, CA / Hunter / Watched Bigfoot swinging lighted sticks from his fire (see ch. 1) / Antioch, CA, *Ledger* 18 Oct. 1870, repr. Oroville, CA, *Butte Record* 5 Nov. 1870; quot. OTTOTS pp. 118-20, STAAU pp. 41-3, *Sasquatch* pp. 143-6, BB 5 pp. 4-5.

1860s / Northern NV / A large party / Pursuers saw "the object" carrying a club and a rabbit; bloodhounds refused to chase it (see ch. 1) / New York *Tribune* report repr. Lansing, MI, *Republican* 4 Aug. 1870, located by Tim Church & quot. STAAU pp. 39-40.

1860s / Arcadia Valley, Crawford County, KS / Many / "Wild man or animal" seen around houses; unsuccessfully hunted (see ch. 1) / Letter from M. S. Trimble dated 15 Aug. 1869 printed in the St. Louis, MO, *Democrat* in that year & quot. STAAU pp. 38-9.

Sept. 1870 / Orias Timbers (Orestimba) Creek, CA / F.J. Hildreth & Samuel de Groot / Two hunters saw "gorillas" / Oakland, CA, *Daily Transcript* 27 Sept. 1870, quot. STAAU pp. 40-1.

1870 / Crow Canyon nr Mt Diablo, CA / "Wild man" seen but evaded capture; 13-in tracks / San Joaquin, CA, *Republican* 19 Sept. 1870, quot. STAAU p. 40.

1871 / Harrison River area of BC / Amerindian woman / Kidnapped by Bigfoot (see ch. 1) / Told by abductee to J.W. Burns & noted AS p. 68.

Feb. 1876 / 10 miles E of Warner's Ranch, CA / Turner Helm / Prospector saw and spoke to Bigfoot, which did not reply (see ch. 1) / San Diego, CA, *Union* 9 Mar. 1876, quot. STAAU pp. 43-4.

1878 / TN / - / "Wild Man of the Woods" reportedly captured; 6 ft 5 in tall, large eyes, "fish scales" on body. Exhibited in Louisville, KY / Louisville, KY, *Courier-Journal* 24 Oct. 1878, noted SCFTAS p. 117.

Oct. 1879 / Nr Williamstown, VT / Two young huntsmen / Red-haired Bigfoot chased witnesses after being shot at (see ch. 1) / New York *Times* 18 Oct. 1879, quot. STAAU pp. 230-1.

Early 1880s / Nr Happy Camp, Siskiyou County, CA / Jack Dover / Hunter saw 7-ft "wild man" picking berries or shoots / L.W. Musick, "The Hermit of Siskiyou" (booklet published 1896) pp. 79-80, quot. OTTOTS p. 123.

1882 / Owens Valley, CA / Several, including John Clarke, Paul Myrtengreen, & Jack Ferral / Many reports of large, shaggy beast roaming the foothills of Round Valley. Clarke came upon it asleep and tried to lasso it, but it ran off yelling. Myrtengreen fainted when he saw it coming towards him. Ferral hunted it and on 25 March came upon it feeding. He fired five bullets into it, but it came for him. His horse broke two legs in its mad escape and Ferral was bruised / CA, *Inyo Register* 19 Mar. 1981 referring to articles in the Bishop Creek *Times* of 1882, noted *Bigfoot Co-op* Apr. 1981 p. 2.

June or July 1884 / 20 miles from Yale, BC / - / Hairy "half man, half beast," nicknamed Jacko, 4 ft 7 in tall and weighing 127 lb, captured (see ch. 1) / Original report in Victoria, BC, *Daily Colonist* 4 July 1884. See AS pp. 63-7, *Bigfoot* (N) p. 75, COTOE p. 29, OTTOTS pp. 35-8 & 109, *Sasquatch* pp. 18-21, STAAU pp. 83-8.

1885 / Cascade Mtns nr Lebanon, OR / Mr. Fitzgerald & others / Hunters saw hairy "man" eating deer flesh (see ch. 1) / Carson City, NV, *Morning Appeal* 31 Dec. 1885, repr. STAAU pp. 44-5.

c. 1880s / Horseshoe Bend area of Bear Creek, AL / Jade Davis / Fisherman watched by Bigfoot which jumped into creek when noticed / Red Bay, AL, *News* 6 May 1976, quot. STAAU pp. 438-9.

Oct. 1891 / Nr the Tittabawassee River, MI / George W. Frost & W.W. Vivian / 7-ft Bigfoot killed bulldog with one blow (see ch. 1) / Colfax, WA, *Commoner* 6 Nov. 1891, quot. STAAU pp. 199-200.

1892 / Anaconda, MT / "a wild-eyed individual" / Saw hairy "varmint" in the mountains / Anaconda, MT, *Standard* report repr. New Haven, CT, *Evening Register* 11 Nov. 1892, located by Gary Mangiacopra.

Autumn 1893 / Rockaway Beach, Long Island, NY / Several, including "Red" McDowell & George Farrell / Large "wild man" frightened local people / New York *Herald* 29 Nov. 1893 p. 7, located by Gary Mangiacopra.

Jan. 1894 / Nr Dover, NJ / Bertha Heatig, Lizzie Guscott, Katie Griffin, Mike Dean, Bill Dean, William Mullen, & others / Bearded 6-ft "wild man" with club seen in woods (see ch. 1) / New York *Herald* 9 Jan. 1894 p. 12, located by Gary Mangiacopra.

May 1894 / Deep Creek, KY / Jack Agee, Joseph Ewalt, Eph Boston, Tom Boston, James Boston / Man-beast which raided farms was tracked to cave (see ch. 1) / Letter to Louisville, KY, *Courier Journal* repr. Hartford, CT, *Daily Courant* 16 May 1894, located by Gary Mangiacopra.

Aug. 1895 / Colebrook, CT / Riley W. Smith / Bigfoot ran out of bushes, yelling as witness picked berries / Hartford, CT, *Courant* 21 Aug. 1895, quot. STAAU p. 232.

Aug. 1895 / Delamere County, NY / Peter Thomas / "Wild man" seized traveler's horse, killed it, and dragged it away / ? *Daily Press* 29 Aug. 1895, located by Gary Mangiacopra.

Late April 1897 / Nr Sailor, IN / Adam Gardner & Ed Swinehart / Two farmers saw Bigfoot run into woods (see ch. 1) / Cleveland, OH, *Plain Dealer* 1 May 1897, quot. George M. Eberhart, "The Ohio Airship Story," *Pursuit* vol. 10 no. 1 p. 7.

Late April 1897 / Nr Stout, OH / Several / "Wild man" seen in woods on several occasions (see ch. 1) / Akron, OH, *Beacon and Republican* 28 Apr. 1897; Cincinnati, OH, *Enquirer* 27 April 1897; Portsmouth, OH, *Blade* 28 April 1897; noted George M. Eberhart, "The Ohio Airship Story," *Pursuit* vol. 10 no. 1 p. 7.

26 May 1897 / Nr Rome, OH / Charles Lukins & Bob Forner / Struggled with curly-haired Bigfoot which escaped (see ch. 1) / Cleveland, OH, *Plain Dealer* 27 May 1897, noted George M. Eberhart, "The Ohio Airship Story," *Pursuit* vol. 10 no. 1 p. 7.

Summer 1897 / Nr Tulelake, CA / An Indian / Bigfoot took fish offered by witness (see ch. 1) Tawani Wakawa, "Encounters with the Matah Kagmi," *Many Smokes* (National American Indian magazine) Autumn 1968, repr. *INFO Journal,* vol. II no. 2 pp. 39-40.

1899 / Headwaters of South Sixes River, OR / Prospectors named Robbins & Benson / Saw 6½-ft, yellow-furred "devil" push camp gear off cliff; ran away when shot at / Article by Dale Vincent, 1947, noted TSF p. 5.

Late 1800s / Nr Moncton, New Brunswick / - / "Squatty, hair-covered creature with long arms" seen on edge of woods several times / Information from Revd A. Fulton Johnson of Moncton, noted TSF p. 6.

1900 / E of Thomas Bay, AK / 3 prospectors / Hairy creatures, "neither men nor monkeys," smaller than men, seen (see ch. 2) / Harry D. Colp, *The Strangest Story Ever Told* (privately published in New York, 1953), noted in Ivan T. Sanderson, *"Things"* (Pyramid Books, 1967) pp. 100-2 & STAAU p. 303.

1900 / Sixes River area, OR / William Page & Johnnie McCulloch / Miners saw 9-ft hairy "animal-man" drinking at stream (see ch. 2) / Myrtle Point, OR, *Enterprise* report repr. Roseburg, OR, *Daily Review* 24 Dec. 1900 & quot. STAAU pp. 45-6.

c. 1900 / Kildeer Mtns, ND / People in sleigh / Saw large gorilla-like animal which first ran towards them, then ran off through snow leaving huge manlike tracks / Letter from Mrs. Myrtle Paschen to RP, see STAAU p. 172.

1901-1920

July 1901 / Pensbury Township, PA / Milton Brint, Taylor Brint, Tom Lukens / 3 coon hunters one rainy night saw creature with man's head and neck, wild beast's body and legs, jump from tree. Dogs terrified. Same beast seen by Lewis Brooks and Jack Murphy in same woods not long after, walking on all fours. Seen to pass *through* fence; bullets did it no harm. (Not clear if this was a Bigfoot-type creature.) / COTOE pp. 63-4.

1901 / Campbell River area of Vancouver Is., BC / Mike King / Saw "man-beast" washing roots in water and placing them in neat piles (see ch. 2) / Victoria, BC, *Colonist,* report noted *Sasquatch* p. 21, AS p. 72, TSF p. 9, STAAU p. 57.

14 Jan. 1902 / Chesterfield, ID / Several young people / Skaters chased by 8-ft hairy creature with club (see ch. 2) / Wilkesboro, NC, *The Chronicle* 5 Feb. 1902, quot. *INFO Journal* vol. V no. 4 p. 13.

Feb.-March 1904 / Sixes mining district nr Myrtle Point, OR / William Ward, Mr. Burlison, Mr. Harrison / Miners' cabins shaken by "wild man" (see ch. 2) / Myrtle Point, OR, *Enterprise* 11 March 1904 repr. Cottage Grove, OR, *Lane County Leader* 7 April 1904 & quot. STAAU pp. 46-7, OTTOTS p. 108, TSFBF pp. 24-5.

Dec. 1904 / Nr Horne Lake, Vancouver Island, BC / A.R. Crump, J. Kincaid, T. Hutchins, W. Buss / Hunters in uninhabited area saw young, hairy "wild man" with "long matted hair and a beard" who ran off at speed through impenetrable undergrowth; had also been seen by others in past few years / Victoria, BC, *Colonist* & Vancouver, BC, *Province* 14 Dec. 1904, former quot. TSF p. 9 & STAAU p. 47.

Between 1900 & 1905 / Nr Mt Shasta, CA / An Indian / Bigfeet treated him for snakebite and carried him part-way back to camp (see ch. 2) / Tawani Wakawa, "Encounters with the Matah Kagmi," *Many Smokes* (National American Indian magazine) Autumn 1968, repr. *INFO Journal* vol. II no. 2 pp. 39-40.

Sept. 1906 / Violet Mine nr Cobalt, Ont. / Group of men / Creature nicknamed "Yellow Top" because of light-colored mane seen / North Bay, Ont, *Nugget* 27 July 1923, quot. STAAU p. 249.

March 1907 / Bishop's Cove, Vancouver Is., BC / Indians / Villagers scared by hairy "monkey" which dug clams and howled on beach at night (see ch. 2) / Vancouver, BC, *Province* 8 March 1907, quot. STAAU p. 48, TSF p. 9.

May c. 1909 / Nr Chehalis Indian reserve, BC / Peter Williams / Bigfoot chased witness home and then pushed against walls of wooden house / J.W. Burns, "Introducing BC's Hairy Giants," *MacLean's Magazine* 1 April 1929, repr. TSF pp. 10-11.

c. 1910 / Mirrow Lake, WI / 10-year-old girl / Followed by man-like furry creature in woods (see ch. 2) / Letter to *Argosy* magazine, see STAAU pp. 197-8.

c. 1911 / Northern MN / 2 hunters / Followed strange footprints and found "human giant" with long arms and short, light hair on body; searchers later found nothing / Letter to Ivan Sanderson, see his *"Things"* (Pyramid Books, 1967) p. 103.

Autumn 1912 / Nr Oakville, WA / Mrs. Callie Lund's mother / Saw tall, ape-like creature looking in at window of lonely farm (see ch. 2) / Letter from Mrs. Callie Lund of Rochester, WA, in 1969 to JG, quot. OTTOTS pp. 130-1 & STAAU pp. 389-90.

c. 1912 / 10 miles from Gallipolis, OH / Mother & son / Witnesses berry-picking, followed by "strange dark cloud" and saw dark, wide-shouldered monster (see ch. 2) / Ron Schaffner, "A Report on Ohio Anthropoids and Other Strange Creatures," *Bigfoot* (PRL) pp. 40-2.

c. 1912 / Nr Effingham, IL / 2 boys / Witnesses' sister recalled the hairy creatures seen near their home from time to time / Letter from Mrs. Beulah Schroat in Decatur, IL, *Review* 2 Aug. 1972, quot. COTOE pp. 65-6, STAAU p. 202, FSR vol. 19 no. 1 p. 24.

c. 1913 / Traverspine nr Goose Bay, Labrador / Michelin family / Isolated house often visited by tall, hairy creatures (see ch. 2) / Elliott Merrick's account in his *True North* (Charles Scribner's Sons, 1933) quot. Ivan T. Sanderson, *"Things"* (Pyramid Books, 1967) pp. 104-5 & STAAU pp. 252-3; Bruce Wright's account in his *Wildlife Sketches Near and Far* (University of New Brunswick Press, 1962) quot. STAAU pp. 253-4.

1914 / Churchville, MD / Boy (8) / Saw Bigfoot sitting on log behind his home (see ch. 2) / Bel Air, MD, *Aegis* 19 June 1975, quot. S. Stover, "Does Maryland Have a Sasquatch?," *INFO Journal* vol. VII no. 6, p. 2; STAAU p. 227.

1915 / Cougar Lake nr Holy Cross Mtns, BC / Charles Flood, Donald McRae, Green Hicks / Prospectors watched Bigfoot eating berries / Sworn Statutory Declaration by Charles Flood dated Sept. 1957, quot. AS pp. 76-7, TSF p. 12, STAAU pp. 58-9.

c. 1915 / SE of Wann, OK / Crum King / Saw Bigfoot near house gate (see ch. 2) / COTOE p. 65.

1917 / Cowlitz River, WA / Albert M. Fletcher / Was followed at night; hid behind tree and saw 7-ft Bigfoot (see ch. 2) / Report from witness quot. BB 4 p. 2.

c. 1920 / Nulato, AK / Albert Petka / Witness, who lived on his boat, attacked there by a "bushman"; dogs drove it away but Petka died of injuries / STAAU p. 335.

1921-1940

Nov. 1922 / Babylon, Long Island, NY / Several / 4-ft "baboon" seen in woods; known to have lived in vacant house for two weeks, and attacked 13-year-old Willie Erlinger / Washington, DC, *Post* 6 Nov. 1922, located by Gary Mangiacopra.

July 1923 / Nr Cobalt, Ont. / J.A. MacAuley & Lorne Wilson / Prospectors saw Bigfoot in blueberry patch (see ch. 3) / North Bay, Ont, *Nugget* July 1923, quot. STAAU pp. 248-9.

July 1924 / The Muddy, a branch of the Lewis River, 8 miles from Spirit Lake, WA / Marion Smith, Roy Smith, Fred Beck, Gabe Lefever, John Peterson / Prospectors saw and shot at several Bigfeet; their cabin was attacked (see ch. 3) / Portland, OR, *Oregonian* 13 July 1924, quot. STAAU p. 89; Fred Beck int. RP in 1966, quot. STAAU pp. 91-6; see also *Bigfoot* (N) pp. 81-2, OTTOTS pp. 75-6, *Sasquatch* pp. 23-5, TSFBF pp. 22-8.

Summer 1924 / Nr head of Toba Inlet, BC / Albert Ostman / Camper kidnapped and kept prisoner by Bigfoot (see ch. 3) / Account written by Ostman and often quoted, e.g. AS pp. 85-94, *Bigfoot* (N) pp. 76-9, OTTOTS pp. 20-34, *Sasquatch* pp. 45-59, TSFBF pp. 54-9, STAAU pp. 97-112.

1924 / Nr Flagstaff, AZ / Woman & her mother / Watched Bigfoot in garden take corn and turnips (see ch. 3) / STAAU p. 176.

June 1925 / Nr Alton, MO / Man / Saw from 50 yds a man-like animal covered with brown hair and having a monkey-like face; 2 other sightings. Said to be a hair-covered *man*, but man interviewed had *black* hair and wore clothes / Mountain View, MD, *Standard* 26 June & 13 Aug. 1925, noted STAAU p. 195.

Spring 1926 / Nr Goodwater, OK / Doctor / Saw "the thing" running across lane in the lights of his Model T Ford / "McCurtain County Has a 'Manbeast'," McCurtain, OK, *Sunday Gazette* 9 July 1978, repr. FN Sept. 1978 p. 16.

1926 / Mountain Fork River, OK / 2 hunters / Saw "manbeast" which later killed their dog (see ch. 3) / "McCurtain County Has a 'Manbeast'," McCurtain, OK, *Sunday Gazette* 9 July 1978, repr. FN Sept. 1978 p. 16.

1926 / Yankton, OR / 28 people / Many sightings, including one of a Bigfoot running alongside a moving truck and looking in cab / *The Oregon Journal* 12 Aug. 1963, quot. TSF p. 15 & noted SCFTAS p. 114.

Sept. 1927 / Agassiz, BC / Indian named Point & Adaline August / While walking on railroad track, saw Bigfoot coming towards them / Letter from Point quot. J.W. Burns, "Introducing BC's Hairy Giants," *MacLean's Magazine* 1 April 1929, repr. TSF pp. 10-11.

c. 1927 / Nr Salem, NJ / Taxi driver / Bigfoot shook car while witness changed tire (see ch. 3) / James F. McCloy & Ray Miller, Jr., *The Jersey Devil* (The Middle Atlantic Press, 1976) pp. 85-7.

1928 / Conuma River, Vancouver Is., BC / Muchalat Harry / Indian kidnapped and kept prisoner by Bigfeet (see ch. 3) / TSFBF pp. 1-5.

1928 / South Bentinck Arm, nr Bella Coola, BC / George Talleo / While trapping, saw and shot at Bigfoot, which fell; witness did not stay. Earlier had found excrement covered by moss / Witness to JG, noted TSF p. 14.

25 July 1929 / Elizabeth, IL / - / "Huge gorilla" seen wandering in woods near town / Washington, DC, *Post* 26 July 1929, located by Gary Mangiacopra.

1920s / Gambrill State Park, MD / - / Huge hairy creature, the "Dwayo" or "Dwayyo," seen from time to time / Contemporary Frederick, MD, newspaper reports noted in "BHM in the NE USA," *INFO Journal* vol. III no. 3 p. 27.

c. 1930 / Kwakwa Kitasu Bay, Swindle Island, BC / Tom Brown / Bigfoot seen in shallows at night; screamed when shot at, but no body to be found next day / Witness to JG, noted TSF p. 14.

June 1931 / Mineola, Long Island, NY / 6 people / 4-ft Bigfoot seen briefly by people at nursery; armed police found nothing / New York *Times* 30 June 1931, noted SCFTAS pp. 95-6 & Charles Fort, *Wild Talents (The Complete Books of Charles Fort,* Dover Publications, 1974) pp. 902-4.

18 July 1931 / Nr Huntington, Long Island, NY / Stockman family / Nurseryman's family saw gorilla-like animal running through shrubbery / SCFTAS pp-95-6; Charles Fort, *Wild Talents (The Complete Books of Charles Fort,* Dover Publications, 1974) pp. 902-4.

July 1931 / Nr Huntington, Long Island, NY / Mr. Bruno / Farmer saw "strange animal"; police found tracks / SCFTAS pp. 95-6; Charles Fort, *Wild Talents (The Complete Books of Charles Fort,* Dover Publications, 1974), pp. 902-4.

21 Jan. 1932 / 5 miles N of Downingtown, PA / John McCandless / "Half-man, half-beast" seen in brush / COTOE p. 65.

19 Aug. 1933 / Tillamook Head, OR / 3 woodsmen / Saw "shaggy-appearing human"; other reports in same area (see ch. 3) / Tulare County, CA, *Visalia Times-Delta* 19 Aug. 1933, quot. BB 26 p. 11.

c. 1933 / Head of Pitt Lake, BC / 2 men / Saw Bigfoot through field glasses, eating berries / STAAU pp. 59-60.

March 1934 / Chehalis Indian reserve nr Harrison River, BC / Frank Dan / "Hairy giant" seen by Indian near his home (see ch. 3) / Vancouver, BC, *Province* March 1934, quot. *Sasquatch* pp. 30-1.

July 1936 / Morris Creek nr Harrison River, BC / Frank Dan / Bigfoot threw rocks at witness's canoe (see ch. 3) / Report by J.W. Burns, quot. AS pp. 102-4.

1937 / Saginaw River, MI / Fisherman / Saw "manlike monster climb up the river bank, lean upon a tree, and then return to the river." Had a nervous breakdown / Folklore Archives, Indiana University Library, quot. STAAU p. 200.

c. 1937 / Nr Bridesville, BC / Mrs. Jane Patterson / Saw Bigfoot sitting in abandoned garden (see ch. 3) / STAAU pp. 63-4.

1939 / Borrego area, CA / Los Angeles man / Camper approached by several Bigfeet (see ch. 3) / Witness int. Ken Coon, see STAAU p. 306.

Aug. 1939 or 1940 / Headwaters of Silver Creek, Harrison Lake, BC / Burns Yeomans & another prospector / Saw 4 or 5 Bigfeet wrestling (see ch. 3) / Int. JG *c.* 1965, quot. STAAU pp. 60-3.

1930s / Nr Priest Lake, ID / Several / Saw Bigfoot kneeling on bench looking in at ranch window; walked away on 2 legs / Letter to JG noted STAAU p. 284.

1930s / Nr Alert Bay, BC / Ellen Neal / Saw Bigfoot walk along beach and into trees / Witness to JG, noted TSF p. 14.

1930s / Head of Mosby Creek, nr Cottage Grove, OR / Bob Bailey / Hunter saw Bigfoot / Cottage Grove, OR, *Sentinel* 13 July 1972, noted TSF p. 15.

c. 1940 / Nr Kaluka, AK / - / Female, black-haired Bigfoot captured and fed on raw fish; its hair fell out and it died / TSF p. 16.

1941-1960

Summer 1941 / Gum Creek nr Mt Vernon, IL / Revd Lepton Harpole / Struck at Bigfoot with gun barrel; also many other sightings in the area (see ch. 4) / *Hoosier Folklore* vol. 5 (March 1946) p. 19, quot. AS pp. 124-5; see also SCFTAS p. 105.

Sept. 1941 / Ruby Creek, BC / Mrs. Jeannie Chapman & 3 children aged 9, 7, & 5 / Bigfoot visited lonely house; adult witness grabbed children and fled to village (see ch. 4) / Mrs. Chapman int. Ivan T. Sanderson, see AS pp. 99-102; Mrs. Chapman int. JG, see OTTOTS pp. 8-9, 11-15; see also STAAU pp. 51-2, *Sasquatch* pp. 60-2, DASOARE pp. 92-7.

Oct. 1941 / Port Douglas at head of Harrison Lake, BC / Many Indians / Fled in canoes after seeing Bigfoot nearly 14 ft tall at their village / Vancouver, BC, *Province* 25 Oct. 1941 p. 2, quot. OTTOTS pp. 9-10.

1941 / Above Lake Lichtenwaash, WA / - / "Naked man" seen "leaping from rock to rock on a mountainside"/ Report from Clarence Fox, noted OTTOTS p. 129.

Late summer 1942 / Todd Lake, OR / Don Hunter, head of Audio Visual Dept at University of Oregon, & Mrs. Hunter / Saw tall figure in meadow; when they got out of car, it strode into woods on 2 legs / Don Hunter int. Lee Trippett 1963, quot. OTTOTS pp. 79-80 & DASOARE pp. 32-4.

Oct. 1942 / Mt Ashland, OR / Red Edwards & Bill Cole / Hunters saw Bigfoot, and one may have been carried by it a short distance / Account written by Edwards, quot. STAAU pp. 412-15; see also OTTOTS pp. 77-9 & *Sasquatch* pp. 97-8.

1942 / Alaska coast, probably Wrangell Narrows / Bob Titmus / Witness on board ship saw "upright ape" on beach / STAAU p. 303.

c. 1942 / Central Sandwich, NH / *c.* 14-yr-old boy / 6-7-ft "gorilla-looking" creature followed him for 20 mins as he cut spruce / Int. Brent Haynes, noted STAAU p. 230.

1943 / DeWilde's Camp nr Ruby, AK / John McQuire / Killed by Bigfoot (see ch. 4) / STAAU p. 335; report from Bob Betts in BB 21 p. 2.

Early 1940s / Nr Coombes, Vancouver Is., BC / Alex Oakes / Bigfoot ran across road in front of witness's car (see ch. 4) / STAAU pp. 57-8.

April 1946 / Nr Gillies Lake, nr Cobalt, Ont. / Woman & son / Saw dark hairy animal with light head in the bush; thought to be "Yellow Top" (see July 1923) / North Bay, Ont, *Nugget* 16 April 1946, quot. STAAU p. 249.

Spring 1947 / Old Highway 99, S of Shasta, CA / Man & wife / Two Bigfeet seen crossing road; one looked in car window (see ch. 4) / Letter to JG 1974, noted STAAU pp. 405-6.

11 May 1947 / Nr Fall River Mills, CA / Mr. & Mrs. Russ Tribble / While fishing, saw 2 smelly Bigfeet walking along river bank eating fish and reeds; left tracks, the longest 17½ in / Witness's report noted TSF p. 16.

1947 / Piney Ridge, MO / Several hunters / Bigfoot was killing sheep and goats. When hunted, it killed the dogs and overthrew the hunters' jeep / Report by Glenn Payne, noted STAAU p. 194.

1947 / Grouse Mtn, North Vancouver, BC / Mr. & Mrs. Werner / Driving along logging road, witnesses came upon 2 tall beings, with "a skin wrapped round them" (see ch. 4) / Witnesses to RD, noted *Sasquatch* p. 103.

1947 / Lakeland, FL / Child (4) / Saw Bigfoot standing under tree near home / Letter to JG, noted STAAU p. 271.

1948 / Nr Mobile, AL / 5 boys / Saw 11-ft Bigfoot in swamp / STAAU p. 214.

c. 1948 / Harrison Mills, BC / Henry Charlie / Indian on bicycle chased by Bigfoot, which kept up with him for over a mile / Witness to JG, noted TSF p. 14.

c. 1948 / Mad Lake nr Leavenworth, WA / Clarence M. Foster / Saw thin, black-haired, 6-ft Bigfoot squatting on lake shore / TSF p. 15.

1949 / New Hazelton, BC / Frank Luxton / Highway foreman saw 8-ft Bigfoot while driving; it ran into the bush / Vancouver, BC, *Sun* 21 June 1957, noted OTTOTS p. 142.

1949 / Thorntown, IN / Nearly 30 Thorntown residents / "Gorilla" with protruding teeth seen frequently in the area; chased two fishermen / International News Service report, 17 July 1949, quot. STAAU p. 204.

Late 1940s / Nigger Wool Swamps, SE MO / - / Gorilla-like animal killed cows and horses; someone shot it. (This may be the same case as Piney Ridge 1947.) / SCFTAS p. 111.

1940s / Jacobsen Bay, 20 miles W of Bella Coola, BC / Clayton Mack, game guide / Saw Bigfoot from boat as it walked along beach and into timber (see ch. 4) / Report from witness quot. *Sasquatch* p. 28; int. JG 1967, quot. OTTOTS pp. 57-60.

1940s / Yukon Territory / - / Witness saw 10-ft Bigfoot and shot at it with .30-06; tracks were 18-22 in long / Letter from witness to JG, noted STAAU p. 242.

c. 1950 / Nr the Eel River above Eureka, CA / Girl (10) / Walking in a meadow, saw Bigfoot dressed in torn clothes (see ch. 4) / Letter from witness to Ivan T. Sanderson, quot. AS pp. 169-70.

Autumn 1951 / Charlotte, MI / Many / "Gorilla Swamp" the haunt of a "strange monster" on 2 legs, seen by many different people / Folklore Archives, Indiana University Library, quot. STAAU p. 200.

c. 1951 / Nr Boston, GA / Woman & husband / Dogs cornered hairy giant on house porch; husband shot at it, but it ran away / STAAU p. 215.

Summer 1952 / Northwest Territories / Murray Lloyd / Saw 9-ft Bigfoot standing watching him from blackberry bushes 75 ft away; it then walked away / Witness wrote to RP, noted TSF p. 23.

1952 / nr Orleans, CA / Man / Had hair-raising encounter with Bigfoot while driving through forest on a rainy night (see ch. 4) / Part of witness's 1966 letter to RP repr. STAAU pp. 344-6, & int. JG.

Summer 1953 / Alder Creek canyon, nr Portland, OR / Middle-aged man / While fishing apart from 2 companions, saw huge, hairy Bigfoot watching him from thicket / Unidentified newspaper report of 5 Aug. 1963, probably a Portland, OR, paper, repr. BSIS vol. 2 no. 4 p. 5.

Sept. 1953 / Nr Courtenay, Vancouver Is., BC / Jack Twist / At dusk saw 8-ft Bigfoot on road ahead; it moved into forest / Witness to JG, noted TSF p. 18.

1953 / Fouke, AR / - / Probable earliest sighting of "Fouke Monster" / *Fate* no. 264 p. 28.

1952 or 1953 / Nr Lewiston, CA / Logging mechanic / Bigfoot with glowing red eyes watched him grease tractor / Reported to Bob Titmus, noted TSF p. 21.

1954 / Nr Padanaram, OH / Dean Averick / Saw tall, hairy creature wade into 3 ft of water, then head for small island / Miami, FL, *Homestead City News* 29 Aug. 1977, noted STAAU pp. 208-9.

20 July 1955 (1), 24 July 1955 (2), 25 July 1955 (3) / Three Springs Ranch, nr Edison, GA / Tant King (1), Mrs. Alberta Donnell & son Toby (2), Martha Donnell (3) / Witnesses separately saw a "hairy little gray man" about 3½-ft tall walking in the fields; tracks also found / Best report, including letter from ranch-owner, given in Isabel Davis & Ted Bloecher, *Close Encounter at Kelly and Others of 1955* (Center for UFO Studies, 1978) pp. 161-5; see also SCFTAS p. 104 & STAAU p. 215.

1 Aug. 1955 / Nr Kinchafoonee Creek on Bronwood-Smithville Highway, GA / Joseph Whaley / Man cutting grass fought Bigfoot with scythe (see ch. 4) / Isabel Davis & Ted Bloecher, *Close Encounter at Kelly and Others of 1955* (Center for UFO Studies, 1978) pp. 170-7 has best report and analysis; see also Evansville, GA, *Press* 4 Aug. 1955, quot. STAAU pp. 215-16.

14 or 21 Aug. 1955 / Ohio River nr Dogtown, IN / Mrs. Darwin Johnson / Left leg grabbed by hand with claws and furry palm as she swam in river (see ch. 4) / Evansville, IN, *Press* 15 or 22 Aug. 1955; see COTOE pp. 52-3 & Isabel Davis & Ted Bloecher, *Close Encounter at Kelly and Others of 1955* (Center for UFO Studies, 1978) pp. 181-2 (which also includes a letter from someone who knew Mrs. Johnson).

Oct. 1955 / Mica Mountain, BC / William Roe / Watched female Bigfoot eating leaves at a distance of 20 ft (see ch. 4) / William Roe's sworn affidavit dated 26 Aug. 1957 quot. AS pp. 108-11, STAAU pp. 53-6, OTTOTS pp. 16-20, *Sasquatch* pp. 45-8; see also *Bigfoot* (N) pp. 79-80.

1955 / Fouke, AR / James Lynn Crabtree / Fired at "Fouke Monster" / *Fate* no. 264 p. 28.

c. 1955 / Between Vancouver & Banff, BC / Woman & boy / Witnesses on bus saw Bigfoot standing beside road / TSF p. 18.

17 May 1956 / Trans-Canada Highway nr Flood, BC / Stanley Hunt, auctioneer / Slowed down as gray, 7-ft Bigfoot crossed road to join another, which was "gangly, not stocky like a bear" / AS pp. 111-12 & *Sasquatch* p. 104.

May 1956 / Nr Marshall, MI / Otto Collins, Philip Williams, Herman Williams / First 2 witnesses picked up and carried by Bigfoot (see ch. 4) / SCFTAS p. 107.

Aug. 1956 / Inside Passage, AK / Bob Everett / Sighting of Bigfoot on beach made from Fisheries boat / STAAU p. 303.

Summer 1955 or 1956 / Mount St. Helens, WA / Paul McGuire & about 10 other hikers / Saw Bigfoot with longish dirty-white hair, which ran away fast over fallen logs / McGuire to JG, noted TSF p. 19.

c. 1956 / About 13 miles from Wilberton, OK / Several / Hairy, long-armed Bigfoot seen to walk by pond near house; and seen hanging over neighbor's fence. Writer's sister saw huge, hairy leg while berry picking / Letter to JG, noted STAAU p. 182.

c. 1956 / Nr Columbus, GA / 7-ft, long-haired Bigfoot seen along certain road by numerous witnesses / Letter from Jamie O'Riley to RP, noted TSF p. 24.

Spring 1957 / Big Cypress Swamp, FL / 2 hunters / As they slept in hammocks, a Bigfoot stood and watched them. They awoke and saw it was tall and dark with glowing eyes. After about 2 mins it walked away / Letter from one witness, quot. STAAU pp. 271-2.

Autumn 1957 / N of San Antonio, TX / Man / Saw Bigfoot 8-9 ft tall and with gray-white hair through telescopic sight as it moved tree limbs near a lake / Witness wrote to Dr. Grover Krantz, noted TSF p. 24.

Autumn 1957 / Wanoga Butte, nr Bend, OR / Gary Joanis & Jim Newall / Joanis shot a deer, which was then stolen by a Bigfoot (see ch. 4) / STAAU pp. 377-8 & DASOARE p. 42.

1957 / Nr Jackson, TN / James M. Meacham (15) / Witness shot repeatedly without effect at small ape / Letter from witness to Ivan T. Sanderson, quot. AS pp. 122-3.

12 Oct. 1958 / Bluff Creek, CA / Ray Kerr & Leslie Brezeale / From pickup truck, saw Bigfoot cross road in 2 strides at night / TSF p. 22, AS p. 157, SCFTAS p. 100, DASOARE p. 38.

17 Oct. 1958 / Bluff Creek, CA / George Smith / Saw 8-ft Bigfoot cross road / TSF p. 22.

8 Nov. 1958 / North Main Street nr Riverside, CA / Charles Wetzel / Creature, scaly "like leaves," leapt at witness's car and fell back gurgling as he drove on. It had a round head, long arms, a protuberant mouth, and shining eyes. Scratches were found on the windshield / Los Angeles, CA, *Examiner* 9 Nov. 1958, quot. AS pp. 149-50; see also SCFTAS p. 100, STAAU pp. 306-7, 309.

Dec. 1958 / Bella Coola Valley, BC / George Robson & Bert Solhjell / Hunters saw 7-ft Bigfoot watching them; ran off when they stared at it / Witnesses to JG, noted TSF p. 18.

c. 1958 / Nr New Hazelton, BC / 2 women / Bigfoot crossed road in front of witnesses' car / Witnesses to Bob Titmus, noted TSF p. 18.

Feb. 1959 / Cincinnati, OH / Trucker / Saw a "hulking creature" climb out of Ohio River on a cold, windy night / Report by George Wagner, noted STAAU p. 209.

Feb. 1959 / Covington, KY / Motorist / Saw large, 2-legged creature on bridge / Report by George Wagner, noted STAAU p. 209.

March 1959 / Aristazabal Island, BC / Lawrence Hopkins / Saw strong-smelling Bigfoot in brush / Witness to Bob Titmus, noted TSF p. 18.

June 1959 / Between Weed & MacDoel, CA / - / While parked, witness heard walking noise and turned on lights, to see Bigfoot / Letter to Ivan T. Sanderson, quot. DASOARE p. 57.

Sept. 1959 / Clapps Chapel Road, nr Knoxville, TN / Earl Taylor & John Rosenbaum / Fired at Bigfoot which came up to house / Knoxville, TN, *Journal* 24 Sept. 1959, noted STAAU p. 221; see also SCFTAS p. 117.

Sept. 1959 / Hidden Lake, nr Enderby, BC / Mrs. Bellvue / While collecting wood at dusk for campfire, saw 6-ft Bigfoot watching her (see ch. 4) / Witness to JG, noted TSF p. 18; witness's husband to RD, noted *Sasquatch* pp. 100-1.

Oct. 1959 / Ten Mile nr Roseburg, OR / Wayne Johnson & Walter Stork / Boys shot at and hit Bigfoot, but no corpse found (see ch. 4) / Boys int. Bob Titmus within 2 days; reported in STAAU pp. 378-9, OTTOTS p. 77, SCFTAS p. 115, DASOARE p. 49.

1959 / Carroll County, MD / Policeman / Saw Bigfoot cross road and step over fence; yelled "Halt!" Bigfoot walked towards him so he fired at it but it kept coming. Drove away fast / Baltimore, MD, *News American* a 1959 edn, noted S. Stover, "Does Maryland Have a Sasquatch?", *INFO Journal* vol. VII no. 6 p. 2.

1959 / Wind River, WA / Deputy Sheriff of The Dalles Sheriff's Dept / Saw Bigfoot coming through trees as he was fishing; it saw him and turned away / TSFBF p. 31.

1959 / Nr Seeley Lake, MT / R.W. Rye, game guide / Bear hunter saw Bigfoot but did not shoot it / *Saga* Dec. 1960; Billings, MT, *Gazette* 4 Dec. 1960; *Daily Missoulian* 2 Dec. 1960; *Montana Sports Outdoors* 1960; first & last quot. STAAU pp. 292-3.

c. 1959 / Pottawatomie Indian Reserve, KS / Man / Saw "real hairy man" standing beside house, so drove across lawn and ditch to escape / Letter from Nadine Goslin to RP, noted TSF p. 23.

c. 1959 / Pottawatomie Indian Reserve, KS / Woman / About same time as previous sighting, witness saw "wildman" run into trees beside field where she was working / Letter from Nadine Goslin to RP, noted TSF p. 23.

1950s / Pine Barrens, NJ / 2 men camping / 2 sightings of Bigfoot at night, one from only a few yards; "overpowering foul odor" noticed / Letter in SITU files, noted STAAU p. 265.

Late 1950s / Cambridge Springs, PA / Group of young people / 8-10-ft Bigfoot approached farmhouse one night while people were sitting waiting for it as it had been reported banging on house at night; ran off when shot at / Letter from friend of farmhouse occupant, on file with Grover Krantz and noted STAAU p. 255.

Late 1950s / Nr New Hazelton, BC / Man / Bigfoot crossed road in front of witness's car / Witness to Bob Titmus, noted TSF p. 18.

Feb. 1960 / Price Island, BC / Joe Hopkins / While digging clams, saw small Bigfoot walk up beach and into trees / Witness to JG & Bob Titmus, noted TSF p. 18.

Aug. 1960 / Nr Prospect, OR / Sidney Morse / 7-ft Bigfoot ran beside witness's vehicle on logging road / Witness wrote to RP, noted TSF p. 20.

Summer 1960 / Around Parson, WV / Many / Saw 8-ft shaggy Bigfoot with huge eyes "like big balls of fire" / SCFTAS p. 121.

Summer 1960 / Nr Davis, WV / Group of young men / Confronted by 8-ft shaggy Bigfoot in woods (see ch. 4) / Letter dated 7 Jan. 1961 from witness to John Keel & noted SCFTAS pp. 120-1.

Oct. 1960 / Monongahela National Forest, nr Marlinton, WV / W.C. "Doc" Priestley / Car stalled when witness saw Bigfoot with "hair standing straight up" (see ch. 4) / Charleston, WV, *Daily Mail* 5 Jan. 1961. Details given in SCFTAS p. 121, COTOE p. 45, & Jerome Clark & Loren Coleman, "Anthropoids, Monsters & UFOS," FSR vol. 19 no. 1 p. 19.

Autumn 1960 / Walnut Creek nr Clanton, AL / Several, including Revd E.C. Hand / Tall, hairy "Booger" seen and hunted, but only "giant ape" footprints found / SCFTAS pp. 98-9.

30 Dec. 1960 / Nr Hickory Flats, WV / Charles Stover / Bakery truck driver saw 6-ft Bigfoot on road late at night, standing watching him / Charleston, WV, *Daily Mail* 31 Dec. 1960, noted STAAU p. 224; see also SCFTAS p. 122.

1960 / Oroville area, CA / Leonard Mack / Saw Bigfoot near a spring / Witness to Jim McClarin, noted TSF p. 23.

1960 / Hoopa area, CA / Leroy Dolittle / Saw Bigfoot standing in meadow / Witness to Jim McClarin, noted TSF p. 23.

1960 / Northern CA / President of a Portland company on a fishing trip / Saw Bigfoot in pine trees 30 yds away; it walked off. His fishing companion felt he was being watched / TSFBF p. 32.

c. 1960 / Conser Lake nr Albany, OR / - / Many sightings of 7-8-ft Bigfoot with shaggy white hair. Once kept pace with truck traveling at 35 m.p.h. / *The Oregon Journal* 16 Aug. 1963, quot. TSF p. 20; see also AS pp. 164-5 & DASOARE pp. 58-9.

Winter, *c.* 1960 / Watson Bay, Roderick Island, BC / Timothy Robinson & Samson Duncan / Shot at small Bigfoot on beach and found blood on snow where it had been, but were afraid to follow the creature / Witnesses to JG & Bob Titmus, noted TSF p. 18.

Early 1960s / Nr Orchard, WA / Lopez / On foggy night, drove round 8-9-ft black Bigfoot with flat face and no neck / Witness to RP, noted TSF p. 27.

Early 1960s / Nr Orleans, CA / Benjamin Wilder / Saw Bigfoot at night / Witness to Jim McClarin, noted TSF p. 29.

Early 1960s / Diamond Mtns nr Eureka, NV / Dion Pollard / Saw Bigfoot / TSF p. 31.

1961-1970

June 1961 / Leakin Park, MD / Mr. & Mrs. Fergeson / Saw huge eyes staring in car window; Fergeson followed tall Bigfoot, but ran back when it began to growl / Int. S. Stover, see his "Does Maryland Have a Sasquatch?", *INFO Journal* vol. VII no. 6 p. 3.

Summer 1961 / Small town nr Wilmington, OH / Woman / 9-ft Bigfoot chased from house by man with shotgun / Ron Schaffner, "A Report on Ohio Anthropoids and Other Strange Creatures," *Bigfoot* (PRL) p. 42.

Sept. 1961 / W of Ross Lake, WA / Man / Saw Bigfoot from 400 ft; it walked away / Witness to Dick Grover, noted TSF p. 27.

Oct. 1961 / Kokanee Glacier Park, BC / John Bringsli / Bigfoot hunter saw ape-like creature on trail at night / Witness to JG, noted TSF p. 26.

Winter 1961-2 / Nr Yakima, WA / Man / Saw white Bigfoot a dozen times at his rubbish dump / Witness to RP, noted TSF p. 27.

1961 / Nr Alpine, OR / Larry Martin & friends / Saw tall Bigfoot at close range while deer hunting (see ch. 5) / Martin int. Barbara Wasson, text in her *Sasquatch Apparitions* (1979) pp. 14-17.

1961 / Nr Moricetown, BC / Couple / Sitting at breakfast, watched black, 8-ft Bigfoot walk across field and road / Witnesses to Bob Titmus, noted TSF p. 26.

c. 1961 / Swede's Pass nr Bossburg, WA / Man & wife / Saw Bigfoot / Witnesses to RD, noted TSF p. 27.

April 1962 / Bella Coola, BC / Woman & 2 children / Saw female Bigfoot holding youngster by hand, on Bella Coola River bank; others saw Bigfoot in village at night / Witness to JG, noted TSF p. 26.

June 1962 / Trimble County, KY / Owen Powell or Pike / Saw black, 6-ft creature attacking his dogs; other activity in the area (see ch. 5) / Louisville, KY, *Courier-Journal* June 1962, noted STAAU p. 223; see also SCFTAS p. 106.

June 1962 / Nr Fort Bragg, CA / Robert Hatfield & Bud Jenkins / Bigfoot made 11-in handprint on house wall and 16-in 4-toed footprints near house (see ch. 5) / Witnesses int. Chuck Edmonds, quot. STAAU pp. 14-15; see also OTTOTS p. 76, DASOARE p. 60.

July 1962 / Nr Mt Vernon, KY / 4 young people / Bigfoot growled at witnesses in parked car (see ch. 5) / Jim Brandon, *Weird America* (Dutton, 1978) p. 95.

July 1962 / Stoney Lake nr Hixon, BC / Alex Lindstrom / While on lake saw heavy, light-gray, 8-ft Bigfoot on shore; it left quickly as he approached / Witness to JG, noted TSF p. 26.

7 Aug. 1962 / Lemon Creek nr Nelson, BC / John Bringsli / Woodsman and hunter, picking huckleberries, suddenly saw 7-9-ft Bigfoot with 4-in gray-blue body hair walking slowly towards him. It seemed curious. At 40 ft, witness sprinted for his car and drove away / Nelson, BC, *Daily News* Oct. 1962; int. JG, quot. STAAU pp. 416-17.

10 Aug. 1962 / Siskiyou County, CA / Joseph Wattenbarger / While driving in daylight, saw 8-ft dirty silver Bigfoot with flat face / TSF p. 29.

Aug. 1962 / Blue Clay Springs nr Richmond, IN / Group of young people / 6-7 ft, white-haired, 4-toed Bigfoot with red eyes seen in Indian graveyard; more sightings in September / Report by witnesses sent to Ivan T. Sanderson, noted STAAU p. 204; see also SCFTAS p. 106.

Aug. 1962 / Nr Hixon, BC / Woman / Saw 7-ft black Bigfoot walking along creek towards her; it jumped into bush on seeing her / Witness to RD, noted TSF p. 26.

Late Aug. 1962 / Between Quesnel & Prince George, BC / Mrs. Calhoun / Bigfoot seen in woods, 10 yds away (see ch. 5) / Witness int. RD, see *Sasquatch* p. 102.

Oct. 1962 / Spokane area, WA / Dutch Holler & uncle / Hunters saw 7-ft Bigfoot walking with swinging arms / Holler to RP, noted TSF p. 27.

Oct. 1962 / Between Vedder Crossing & Yarrow, BC / Joe Gregg, bus driver off duty / Bigfoot crossed road in front of car at night / Int. RD, see *Sasquatch* pp. 63-5; int. JG, see STAAU pp. 398-9.

Nov. 1962 / Off East William Street Road, E of Decatur, IL / Steven Collins, Robert Earle, & 2 other men / Gray Bigfoot seen standing in creek / Int. Loren Coleman, noted SCFTAS p. 105.

Nov. 1962 / Lost Trail Pass, MT / Reed Christenson, wife, & daughter / Saw 6-7-ft Bigfoot run up embankment beside road at 2 am / Report in *Bitterroot Journal*, noted STAAU p. 296.

1962 / Madison, IN / Several farmers / Saw Bigfoot which left tracks; searchers unsuccessful / Ron Schaffner, "Creature Chronicles, Vanishing Bigfeet," *Unusual News* Oct. 1977, p. 3.

1962 / Lost Gap, E of Meridian, MS / Many / Green-eyed Bigfoot seen in woods; search with bloodhounds and helicopter found nothing / SCFTAS p. 110.

27 Jan. 1963 / Cold Springs, off the Sonora Highway, CA / Man / Phoned Sheriff's Dept to report Bigfoot; Sheriff and deputy went and heard horrible screams in woods (see ch. 5) / Sonora, CA, *Union Democrat* 29 Jan. 1963, noted *Bigfoot* (S&B) pp. 4-6.

28 Feb. 1963 / Nr Confidence, nr Sonora, CA / Lennart Strand & Alden Hoover / Pilots saw 10-ft, cinnamon-brown creature on the ground, "half bear, half gorilla"; took photographs which were blurred / Strand int. Basil Hritsco, see TSF pp. 29-30.

March 1963 / Strawberry, nr Angel's Camp, CA / Mr. & Mrs. Campbell / Honeymoon couple on hike saw 8-9-ft Bigfoot / Mrs. Campbell phoned JG on phone-in, see TSF p. 30.

Spring 1963 / Toppenish Ridge, base of Hambre Mtn, WA / "A respected businesswoman" / Hairy, ape-like face peered in through window as she was reading; watchdogs panicked / *Bigfoot* (S&B) p. 147.

June 1963 / Lewis River Canal nr Yale, WA / Stan Mattson / Watched female Bigfoot with hanging breasts and young Bigfoot under left arm as it drank water or caught small fish / TSF pp. 27-8.

July 1963 / Hoopa Valley, CA / A resident identified as "Peters" / Bigfoot jumped out in front of witness, leapt 5-ft fence and was lost in darkness / Humboldt, CA, *Times* 20 July 1963, quot. DASOARE p. 54, noted SCFTAS p. 101.

July 1963 / Lewis River, nr junction with the Columbia, OR / Mr. & Mrs. Martin Hennrich / Saw Bigfoot standing by river; later 16-in tracks found which came from and returned to river / OTTOTS p. 76 (tracks seen & cast by JG).

Late July 1963 / Satus Pass between Toppenish & Goldendale, WA / Paul Manley & 2 passengers / Driving at night, saw tall, shaggy "tree stump" which then stepped out of ditch as car passed / Story printed in *Oregon Journal* (of which Manley was business manager) & noted TSF p. 28.

c. July 1963 / Nr Satus Pass, WA / Gladys Herrarra / Saw 9-ft figure look in window at night; dogs were scared / Witness to RP, noted TSF p. 28.

Aug. & Sept. 1963 / Quartz Creek nr Grants Pass, OR / Family camping / Saw Bigfoot on 3 weekend trips / Letter to RP, noted TSF p. 28.

Early Oct. *c.* 1963 / Nr Lebanon, OR / Former deputy sheriff / Saw Bigfoot cross road in front of car / TSF pp. 28-9.

1963 / Nr Mt Shasta, CA / Deer hunter / Badly hurt after fall, witness carried back to camp by white-haired Bigfoot 8-9 ft tall and with musty smell / Witness to JG on phone-in, noted TSF p. 31.

1963 / Nr Cincinnati, OH / Wallace Wright, girlfriend, & several men / First 2 witnesses, parked in car, saw very tall creature "like a huge tree walking." Fetched several men to see it / Mrs. Wright wrote to RP, noted TSF p. 32.

1963 / Mansfield, OH / Many, including C.W. Cox / 7-8-ft, gray-haired monster like a gorilla, with large luminous eyes, seen; search revealed nothing / SCFTAS p. 114, TSF p. 32.

1963 / Holopaw, FL / Several / Bigfoot seen running across field / SCFTAS p. 102.

1963 / Goose Point, nr Anahim Lake, BC / Harry Squiness / Hairy monkey face looked into tent; four Bigfeet at edge of camp walked into forest (see ch. 5) / Witness int. RD, noted *Sasquatch* p. 29.

1963 / Nr Bella Bella, BC / Jack Wilson / Saw Bigfoot on island shore / Witness to Bob Titmus, noted TSF, p. 27.

17 May 1964 / Brown's Gulch, 15 miles from Butte, MT / Boy Scout / Woken at 4 am, looked out of tent to see Bigfoot which ran off leaving tracks 20 in long by 7 in wide (see ch. 5) / Report by Dr. Joseph Feathers, quot. STAAU pp. 293-4.

May & June 1964 / Sister Lakes, Cass County, MI / Mr. & Mrs. John Utrup, Gordon Brown, Joyce Smith, Patsy & Gail Clayton, & many others / 9-ft Bigfoot with shining eyes frequently seen over several weeks (see ch. 5) / SCFTAS p. 108; TSF p. 32; STAAU p. 200; Jim Brandon, *Weird America* (Dutton, 1978) p. 115; U.K. *Sunday Express* 14 June & 6 July 1964 cited in Odette Tchernine, *The Yeti* (Neville Spearman, 1970) pp. 75-6; *National Observer* 22 June 1964, repr. BSIS vol. 2 no. 8 p. 3.

June 1964 / Nr Estacada, OR / 4 men / Saw Bigfoot by lakeshore / TSF p. 29.

June or July 1964 / Between Neah Bay & Sekiu, Clallam County, WA / Air Force man / Driving on Highway 112, witness saw Bigfoot cross road in 3 bounds / Port Angeles, WA, *Evening News* 3 July 1964, noted SCFTAS p. 118; see also TSF p. 27.

4 July 1964 / Nr Cultus Lake, nr Chilliwack, BC / 2 youths / Saw 2 7-ft, shaggy white Bigfeet beside road at 2:30 am / Witnesses to JG, noted TSF p. 27.

20 July 1964 / Delia, KS / Bread truck driver / Saw 5-ft Bigfoot / Topeka, KS, *Daily Capital* 21 July 1964 pp. 1-2; Jim Brandon, *Weird America* (Dutton, 1978) pp. 87-8.

July 1964 / NW of Lake Stevens, WA / Man / In moonlight, saw 10-ft brown-haired Bigfoot outside his house at midnight / Witness to Dick Grover, noted TSF p. 28.

July 1964 / State Highway 89 nr the IL-WI border / Man / Shortly after midnight, saw a Bigfoot run across road, jumping fences on either side / Letter from witness to JG, noted STAAU p. 198.

Aug. 1964 / Grid Creek, MT / Lou Bigley / Truck driver saw brown 5-ft Bigfoot standing in middle of road / *Bitterroot Journal* report noted STAAU p. 296.

Summer 1964 / Between Mt Adams & Spirit Lake, WA / Prospector / Saw Bigfoot in his camp at night / Witness wrote to George Haas, quot. TSF p. 28.

13 Sept. 1964 / Blue Lake, NW CA / Benjamin Wilder / When asleep in his car, woken by Bigfoot shaking it (see ch. 5) / Blue Lake, CA, *Advocate* 24 Sept. 1964, quot. STAAU p. 338 & DASOARE p. 55.

Sept. 1964 or 1965 / Garrison, PA / Glen Varner / Saw Bigfoot peering in window of his mother's home at dusk / STAAU p. 255.

Nov. 1964 / Nr Fillmore, Ventura County, CA / Several youngsters / While playing in an abandoned dairy they saw a hairy "animal-man" / Los Angeles papers of Nov. 1964, noted STAAU p. 307.

1964 / Point Isabel, Clermont County, OH / Mr. & Mrs. Lew Lister / Sitting in parked car, saw Bigfoot which changed shape and vanished (see ch. 5) / Mrs. Lister int. L.H. Stringfield, his notes published in *Ufolog* 25 Feb. 1975 & repr. Leonard H. Stringfield, *Situation Red, The UFO Siege!* (Doubleday & Company, 1977) pp. 64-5.

1964 / Nr S.R. 28, Milford, OH / Several / Residents reported that an ape-like animal was destroying property and killing cattle / Ron Schaffner, "A Report on Ohio Anthropoids and Other Strange Creatures," *Bigfoot* (PRL) p. 43.

1964 / Ape Canyon area, WA / "High rigger" / Workman saw Bigfoot / TSF p. 28.

1964 / Nr Elsie, OR / Man / Saw Bigfoot standing looking inside station wagon at sleeping man / Witness to Keith Soesbe, noted TSF p. 29.

1964 / Pretty Boy Dam, MD / Workmen / While building house saw "Blueberry Hill Monster" come out of woods near reservoir / S. Stover, "Does Maryland Have a Sasquatch?", *INFO Journal* vol. VII no. 6 p. 2.

c. 1964 / Cradle Lake, head of Icicle River, WA / Father & son / When camping by lake, saw Bigfoot by moonlight / Report by Clarence Fox, noted OTTOTS p. 129.

March 1965 / French Lick, IN / Youngsters / Saw 10-ft green monster with glowing red eyes, named it "Fluorescent Freddie" / Indianapolis, IN, *News* 15 March 1965, noted STAAU p. 205.

31 May 1965 / Nicomen Island nr Mission, BC / Mrs. Seraphine Jasper / Saw tall, black Bigfoot in field in daytime; cows stared at it / Witness to JG, noted TSF p. 33.

28 June 1965 / Pitt Lake, 25 miles NE of Vancouver, BC / two prospectors / Found Bigfoot tracks; later realized they were being watched. Sketched Bigfoot before it walked off (see ch. 5) / *Sasquatch* pp. 40-1; OTTOTS pp. 140-2; STAAU pp. 435-8.

July 1965 / Nr Butedale, BC / Jack Taylor / Man fishing saw 2 Bigfeet on shore and another in the water swimming strongly (see ch. 5) / Witness int. Bob Titmus, see STAAU p. 432.

9 Aug. 1965 / Nr Smithville, Ont. / Truck driver / Saw 6-7-ft, long-armed Bigfoot weighing about 500 lb / Hamilton, Ont, *Spectator* 16 Aug. 1965, noted STAAU p. 250; Loren E. Coleman & Mark A. Hall, "Some Bigfoot Traditions of the North American Tribes," *INFO Journal* vol. II no. 3.

13 Aug. 1965 / Nr Monroe, MI / Christine van Acker & mother Mrs. Ruth Owens / Black 7-ft Bigfoot reached into car and gave Christine a black eye (see ch. 5) / *True* magazine June 1966; STAAU p. 201; Curt Sutherly, "Case History of a UFO Flap," *Official UFO* Dec. 1976, p. 59; *Strange Life Sourcebook* (compiled by William Corliss, 1976) vol. B1 p. 21; BAOTC pp. 105-6; TSF p. 40.

Aug. 1965 / Campden, Ont. / Several people including Wayne Beach, Manfred Berg, Hector McDonald / Saw something 7 ft tall, black, and furry "like a big gorilla"; 16-in prints found / Beamsville, Ont., *Express* 25 or 28 Aug. 1965, noted STAAU p. 250, TSF p. 39.

Aug. 1965 / Rutherford County, TN / Roy Hudson, Terry Ring, Dorris Barrett, Terry Lester / Saw 7-ft, reddish-brown Bigfoot with 3-in teeth and pug nose / Nashville, TN, *Tennesseean* 24 Aug. 1965, noted STAAU p. 221.

Summer 1965 / Clio Bay nr Kitimat, BC / Group of men / Saw Bigfoot on rock beside sea; walked away upright / Several witnesses to Bob Titmus, noted TSF p. 33.

Summer 1965 / Bowen's Ranch, San Gorgonio Mtns, CA / Jim & Jan Gorrell / Couple having night-time barbeque were watched by 9-10-ft Bigfoot; they left hurriedly / BB 19 p. 2, quot. STAAU pp. 307-8; witnesses to Ken Coon, noted TSF p. 38.

Sept. 1965 / Montezuma Hills nr Decatur, IL / 4 young people / Black Bigfoot approached their car and they fled; later police search found nothing / Decatur, IL, *Review* 22 Sept. 1965, noted SCFTAS p. 105.

Sept. 1965 / Tillsonburg, Ont. / Several people / Bigfoot seen in tobacco fields; 18-in tracks found / Kitchener-Waterloo, Ont., *Record* 4 Sept. 1965, noted STAAU p. 250, TSF p. 39.

Oct. 1965 / Nisqually Hill, nr Olympia, WA / Russell Geis & Dennis Lensgrave / Saw white, 7-ft Bigfoot in car headlights and shot at it. Later large tracks and broken trees found / *The Sunday Olympian* 24 Oct. 1965, noted TSF p. 35.

Autumn 1964 or 1965 / Nr LaPorte, CA / Herb Brown / Saw 4 deer followed by a Bigfoot / Witness wrote to RP, noted TSF p. 34.

Autumn 1965 / Nr Harrison Mills, BC / Man / Saw female Bigfoot in brush near road / Witness told JG & RD, noted TSF p. 33.

Autumn 1965 / Little Jedito Wash, N of Winslow, AZ / Roger Heath (school teacher) / Creature 3 ft high with shining black fur and long arms seen hopping and scrambling at roadside / Letter from Heath to Loren Coleman quot. COTOE pp. 109-10; letter from Heath to JG quot. STAAU p. 176.

Nov. 1965 / Green Bay, nr Bella Coola, BC / Jimmy Nelson / Watched Bigfoot cross loggers' slash in 10 mins; witness took 2 hours to cross the same area (see ch. 5) / Int. JG, quot. OTTOTS pp. 60-2.

1965 / Fouke, AR / James Lynn Crabtree (14) / While squirrel-hunting, 7-8-ft Bigfoot approached; boy fired at its face 3 times and ran off (see ch. 5) / STAAU pp. 189-90.

1965 / Tarrytown, GA / Man / Saw Bigfoot over 8 ft tall which "appeared mangled" / Report from Gordon Strasenburgh, noted STAAU p. 217.

1965 / Morristown, NJ / Young woman & 3 other people / Sitting in parked car at night, drove off in panic when Bigfoot thumped on the back / SCFTAS p. 113.

1965 / Nr The Dalles, OR / Dalene Brown & other girls / Saw Bigfoot near gravel pit on several occasions / Witness to RP, noted TSF p. 37.

Mid-1960s / Yakima River, Yakima, WA / Jim Mission & 3 others / Saw tall animal with head set on shoulders / Mission to RP, noted TSF p. 35.

Jan. 1966 / Wildwood, CA / Bob Kelley & Archie Bradshaw / Kelley shot a Bigfoot which looked in cabin window at 2 am; big tracks found / Report in Redding, CA, *Record Searchlight,* noted TSF p. 38.

Spring 1966 / Brooksville, FL / Mrs. Eula Lewis / Bigfoot with roundish head and shoulders chased her into her house; she saw it swinging its arms as dogs yapped at it / Brad Steiger & Joan Whritenour, *New UFO Breakthrough* (Award Books/Tandem Books, 1968) p. 80; Brad Steiger, *Alien Meetings* (Ace Books, 1978) p. 99; SCFTAS p. 103.

April 1966 / Trinity Alps N of Weaverville, CA / Nick Campbell, Larry Browning, Bill Crockett, Bill Combe, Frank Magnussen / Campers saw Bigfoot several times: it watched campers, threw rubbish bins around, and took food left for it / Campbell to Ken Coon, noted TSF p. 38.

21 May 1966 / Morristown, NJ / Raymond Todd & 3 friends / Saw a 7-ft black Bigfoot walking through park / SCFTAS p. 112.

21 July 1966 / Richmond, Lulu Island, BC / John Osborne / "Big hairy man 6 ft 8 in to 7 ft tall" seen in woods / Vancouver, BC, *Sun* 22 July 1966, noted in SCFTAS p. 123; see also TSF p. 33.

21 July 1966 / Richmond, Lulu Island, BC / Darlene Leaf / Saw head and shoulders of Bigfoot above 6-ft raspberry bushes at night / Witness to JG & RD, noted TSF p. 33.

22 July 1966 / Nr Fraser River, Richmond, Lulu Island, BC / John McKernan / In car, saw Bigfoot cross dirt road / Witness to JG & RD, noted TSF p. 33.

July 1966 / Nr White Rock, BC / Mr. Letoul / Saw light Bigfoot come up to his house in the moonlight; it "fooled around" / TSF p. 34.

July 1966 / Richmond, Lulu Island, BC / Don Gilmore / "A big woolly animal" stampeded about 100 cattle / Witness to JG & RD, noted TSF p. 33; see also SCFTAS p. 123.

July 1966 / San Diego, CA / 5 people / Tall, reddish Bigfoot ransacked car while they were picnicking / SCFTAS p. 101.

July 1966 / Fontana, CA / Teenage boys / One, grabbed by Bigfoot, received scratches and torn clothing (see ch. 6) / Report by Ken Coon, quot. STAAU p. 308.

27 Aug. 1966 / N of Fontana, CA / Jerri Mendenhall (16) & friend / Smelly Bigfoot with muddy, slimy hair scratched girl's arm through car window (see ch. 6) / Jerri int. Ken Coon & Bill Early, & Coon's report quot. STAAU p. 308; see also SCFTAS p. 101.

Summer 1966 / Nr Anclote River, Elfers, FL / Ralph "Bud" Chambers / Bigfoot seen standing in trees had a "rancid, putrid odor" / SCFTAS p. 102; Bryan Stevenson, "On the Trail of the Sasquatch, America's Abominable Snowman," *True Frontier* Dec. 1975 p. 64.

Summer 1966 / Nr Richland, WA / Greg Pointer, Roger True, Tom Thompson, Carl & Jim Franklin, John McKnight, Alvin Anderson, Selby Green, Roger Howard, Bob McDonald, Ron Blackburn / 8-ft, whitish-gray Bigfoot was repeatedly shot at with no effect (see ch. 6) / Boys int. RP, RD, & JG, see *Sasquatch* pp. 108-9 & TSF p. 35.

Summer 1966 / Sawyer, WA / 3 boys / Saw the "white demon" / Told to RP, noted TSF p. 35.

Summer 1966 / Nr Yakima, WA / A youth / Chased by white Bigfoot which climbed out of tree at night; was found lying on ground shocked and clutching white hairs / Witness to RP, noted TSF p. 35.

19 Sept. 1966 / Nr Yakima, WA / Ken Pettijohn / 7-ft, grayish-white Bigfoot examined car and driver / Int. JG & RD, quot. STAAU pp. 399-401 & OTTOTS pp. 81-2; see also *Sasquatch* pp. 107-8 & SCFTAS p. 119.

Sept. 1966 / Parke County, IN / Various / 10-ft Bigfoot left 21-in tracks and killed 2 dogs / *Fate* Aug. 1973 article noted STAAU pp. 205-6.

Early Oct. 1966 / Nr Yakima, WA / Carl Timberbrook / Saw tall, gray Bigfoot walking by canal near road at 8 am / Witness to RP, noted TSF p. 35.

Oct. 1966 / Albuquerque, NM / Clifford McGuire & family / Over a period of several weeks a 5-ft Bigfoot that cried like a baby roamed round their property, and the radio would stop when it was near / Albuquerque, NM, *Journal* 14 Oct. 1966, noted COTOE p. 110.

Oct. 1966 / Nr Yakima, WA / Mike Corey / His dog attacked Bigfoot; Corey shot at it as it ran away; dog later mysteriously killed / Corey to RP, noted TSF p. 35.

Autumn 1966 / Lower Bank, NJ / Married couple / Bigfoot looked in through window, and witnesses left food out for it which it ate (see ch. 6) / Report from Bob Jones of Vestigia, noted STAAU p. 269.

c. 7 Nov. 1966 / Nr Winona, MS / William & James Cagle / 7-ft Bigfoot with 2-in diameter red eyes "waved" its arm at witnesses' passing truck / Unsigned letter received by Winona, MS, *Times* in 1967 quot. COTOE p. 90 & STAAU p. 193; different report quot. SCFTAS p. 110.

30 Nov. 1966 / Nr Brooksville, FL / Miss M.B. / While changing a wheel on lonely road, witness watched by green-eyed Bigfoot / Brad Steiger & Joan Whritenour, *New UFO Breakthrough* (Award Books/Tandem Books, 1968) p. 79; Brad Steiger, *Alien Meetings* (Ace Books, 1978) p. 98; SCFTAS pp. 103-4; TSF p. 40.

Nov. 1966 / Mason County, WV / Cecil Lucas / Saw "three bear-like creatures sniffing around an oil pump"; ran off erect / John Keel, "West Virginia's Enigmatic 'Bird'," FSR vol. 14 no. 4 p. 11; TSF p. 40.

Dec. 1966 / Nr Lakeview, OR / Youths / While they were cutting Xmas trees their Alsatian dog rushed frightened out of brush, and they saw a Bigfoot; tracks in snow later found / TSF p. 37.

Dec. 1966 / Anclote River, FL / 2 hunters / Saw Bigfoot / TSF p. 40.

1966 / Quartz Hill nr Lancaster, CA / 2 young men / Saw Bigfoot on hilltop / STAAU p. 309.

1966 / Maquoketa, IA / Gary Koontz / Shot at 4-5-ft Bigfoot which screamed like a woman and disappeared into the brush / Unidentified newspaper report quot. STAAU p. 196.

1966 / Cass County, MI / Various / Bigfoot seen in sparsely populated area near Detroit / *True* magazine, June 1966; New York *Times* 17 Aug. 1966; noted *INFO Journal* 1.

1966 / Wayne National Forest, OH / - / A 7-ft ape-man was reported roaming the forest / Report from Tom Archer, noted STAAU p. 209.

1966 / Bluff Creek, CA / Richard Sides / Saw Bigfoot drinking from creek with cupped hands / Report from Jim McClarin, noted TSF p. 38.

Jan. 1967 / Elfers, FL / Four teenagers / Smelly Bigfoot with glowing green eyes jumped onto car hood / Int. Joan Whritenour, noted Brad Steiger & Joan Whritenour, *New UFO Breakthrough* (Award Books/Tandem Books, 1968) pp. 78-9; see also SCFTAS p. 104 & Brad Steiger, *Alien Meetings* (Ace Books, 1978) pp. 97-8.

Jan. 1967 / Wildwood Inn, Shasta-Trinity National Forest, CA / Bob Kelley / Heard moaning and saw Bigfoot, dark-brown with silver-tipped hair, a flat nose, and no hair on face or hands, looking in at window / Report from Ben E. Foster, quot. BB 7 p. 2.

Feb. 1967 / Hartley Bay, BC / 2 men / Saw Bigfoot on an island and shot at it; it screamed / Witnesses to Bob Titmus, noted TSF p. 34.

May 1967 / The Dalles, OR / Dennis Taylor (19), Dave Churchill, & others / Bigfoot followed witnesses, who returned with friends and guns on several nights (see ch. 6) / Taylor int. RD, quot. *Sasquatch* pp. 129-31; int. RP quot. OTTOTS pp. 198-202 & STAAU pp. 375-7.

Spring or summer 1967 / Nr Willow Creek, CA / Russel Summerville / Saw 8-9-ft, smelly Bigfoot walk downhill along road and into trees / Report from Jim McClarin, noted TSF p. 38.

Summer 1967 / Nr Anclote River, Elfers, FL / Ralph "Bud" Chambers / Saw Bigfoot in yard / SCFTAS p. 102; Bryan Stevenson, "On the Trail of the Sasquatch, America's Abominable Snowman," *True Frontier* Dec. 1975 p. 64.

Mid-Sept. 1967 / Nr Marietta, Nooksack River, WA / John Davis / Saw 8-ft Bigfoot at 3 am cross road and go towards river / TSF p. 36.

21 Sept. 1967 / Nr Marietta, Nooksack River, WA / Mrs. Brudevold / In fishing skiff, saw Bigfoot rise up from water beside her (see ch. 6) / STAAU p. 429, OTTOTS p. 204.

21 Sept. 1967 / Nr Marietta, Nooksack River, WA / Mrs. Martha Washington / Saw dark-brown Bigfoot sitting on oil drum in neighbor's yard; had human face but reflecting eyes, and sat with arms straight, hands on drum / TSF p. 36.

Sept. 1967 / Nr Marietta, Nooksack River, WA / Harold James / Smelled strong animal smell and saw Bigfoot sitting by river at dawn / Witness to JG, noted TSF p. 36.

Sept. 1967 / Nr Marietta, Nooksack River, WA / Mr. & Mrs. Joe Brudevold / Black 8-ft Bigfoot with flat face and no neck seen standing in river; bent down and disappeared. Tracks later seen coming into and out of water (see ch. 6) / TSF p. 36.

Sept. 1967 / Nr Marietta, Nooksack River, WA / John Green, Reynold James, Randy Kinley / Night-time fisherman's net hauled in by Bigfoot (see ch. 6) / STAAU p. 430; OTTOTS p. 204; TSF p. 36; Robert and Frances Guenette, *The Mysterious Monsters* (Sun Classic Pictures, 1975) pp. 129-30.

Sept. 1967 / Nr Bellingham, WA / Mrs. Carol Davis / Saw Bigfoot wading out of sea / TSF p. 36.

20 Oct. 1967 / Bluff Creek, CA / Roger Patterson & Bob Gimlin / Saw and photographed Bigfoot on cine film (see ch. 6) / *Sasquatch* pp. 116-28, 180-6, 199-202; OTTOTS pp. 70-4; STAAU ch. 4; *Bigfoot* (N) pp. 89-95; Ivan T. Sanderson, *More "Things"* (Pyramid Books, 1969) pp. 65-79.

Late Oct. 1967 / Nr Estacada, OR / Glenn Thomas / Watched 2 adult and a young Bigfoot eating rodents (see ch. 6) / Witness's taped story quot. OTTOTS pp. 83-8 & STAAU pp. 421-5; see also *Sasquatch* pp. 131-2.

Late Oct. 1967 / Marietta, WA / Rita Lawrence / Saw hand, covered with dark hair except for fingers and knuckles, reach into bedroom through window and feel around / Witness's brother to JG, noted TSF p. 36.

Late Oct. 1967 / Marietta, WA / Frank Lawrence, Jr. / A few days after previous case, saw 7-ft Bigfoot outside house; it ran away / Witness to JG, noted TSF pp. 36-7.

Autumn 1967 / By Chehalis River nr Chehalis, WA / Billy Brown / Hunter saw white, 8-ft Bigfoot; shot at its head and it screamed and ran into swamp. Found blood later / Witness to RP, noted TSF p. 37.

Autumn 1967 / Dead Horse Creek nr Grande Ronde River, NE OR / Joe Jackson / Saw Bigfoot standing by road; it ran into brush / Witness to Russell Gebhart, noted TSF p. 37.

Early Dec. 1967 / Nooksack River, nr Marietta, WA / Frank Lawrence, Jr., & another man / Saw 6-ft Bigfoot with red eyes walk out of river at night and into misty fields / Witness to JG, noted TSF p. 37.

Dec. 1967 / Teton Forest nr Jackson Hole, WY / Two university students from Marshalltown, IA / Saw what they thought was a bear and shot it. They examined the corpse and found it was dark brown, humanlike, about 7 ft tall, and hair-covered except for soles and palms. They left the body where it was / Witnesses wrote to RP, noted TSF p. 39.

6 Jan. 1968 / Confidence Ridge, CA / Robert James, Jr., & Leroy Larwick / Saw 10-12-ft Bigfoot from aircraft (see ch. 6) / *Fate* Oct. 1968 p. 10; UPI report noted TSF p. 45.

Feb. 1968 / Broughton Island, BC / Tom Brown & Harry Whonnock / While digging clams, were watched by 6-ft Bigfoot / BC, *Powell-River News* 29 Feb. 1968, quot. SCFTAS pp. 123-4; *Fate* Oct. 68 p. 11.

6 April 1968 / Trinity Alps N of Weaverville, CA / Larry Browning / Saw Bigfoot wading in river at night / TSF p. 45.

7 April 1968 / Trinity Alps N of Weaverville, CA / Larry Browning / Female Bigfoot chased him after watching him for 30 mins / TSF p. 45.

8 April 1968 / Trinity Alps N of Weaverville, CA / Mike Melton / Saw Bigfoot leaning over river to drink / TSF p. 45.

22 April 1968 / Cleveland, OH / William Schwark & another boy / 8-ft Bigfoot knocked Schwark down slope, chased boy, tore his jacket and scratched shoulder / Cleveland, OH, *Plain Dealer* 24 April 1968, noted SCFTAS p. 114.

Spring 1968 / Salem, OH / Mrs. Alice Allison & family / Bigfoot watched home from nearby woods; also other strange phenomena (see ch. 6) / COTOE pp. 17-18.

Spring 1968 / Clackamas River area, OR / Glenn Thomas / Watched female Bigfoot eating willow leaves (see ch. 6) / Int. JG & RD, see STAAU p. 425.

Spring 1968 / Monteagle Mtn, TN / Brenda Ann Adkins / 7-ft Bigfoot with nauseating odor came within 6 ft of witness and stared at her before walking away / Witness's account from *Saga* July 1969, quot. SCFTAS p. 117.

16 June 1968 / French Creek, ID / Frank Bond / While fishing, saw 2 silver-gray-haired Bigfeet 7 and 8 ft tall / Grangeville, ID, *Idaho County Free Press* 27 June 1968, noted TSF p. 49 & STAAU p. 284.

Mid-June 1968 / Nr Clipper, WA / Frank Lawrence, Jr. / Logger saw male and female Bigfeet and child, all black haired; he ran off on seeing them 100 yds away / Witness to JG, noted TSF p. 42.

27 June 1968 / Salmon Arm Inlet, BC / Gordon Baum / Saw 5-ft, black-haired Bigfoot leap over pile of logs; "He was gone in two seconds" / Vancouver, BC, *Sun* 24 June 1968, repr. BB 3 p. 4; see also SCFTAS p. 124 & *Fate* April 1969 p. 9.

June 1968 / Nr Estacada, OR / Man / Saw Bigfoot with no neck standing on edge of woods / Witness to Millie Kiggins, noted TSF p. 44.

June 1968 / Between Bluff Creek & Fish Lake, CA / Steve Martin & Bruce Cornwall / Saw smelly Bigfoot at night in clearing / TSF pp. 45-6.

11 July 1968 / Trinity River nr Salyer, CA / Family / Saw Bigfoot walk by their camp at night / TSF p. 46.

July 1968 / Nr Borrego Springs, CA / Harold Lancaster / Saw "giant ape-man" walking across desert towards him / *Saga* July 1969, noted SCFTAS p. 102.

July 1968 / Kinlock, St. Louis, MO / Boy (4) & his aunt / Bigfoot picked up boy but dropped him when aunt screamed / STAAU p. 339, SCFTAS p. 111.

Early Aug. 1968 / Nr Rogue River, OR / Anthony Anable / Silver and charcoal Bigfoot, 12 ft tall and with amber reflecting eyes, came to within 5 ft of witness sleeping outdoors; left 15-in tracks with 78-in stride / TSF p. 44.

11 Aug. 1968 / Nr Chittyville, IL / Tim Bullock & Barbara Smith / Witnesses in parked car were frightened by 10-ft black Bigfoot which threw earth at them through the window / SCFTAS p. 106, & Carbondale, IL, *Southern Illinoisian* 19 Aug. 1968, noted STAAU p. 203.

Mid-Aug. 1968 / Nr Stewart, BC / 2 hunters / Bigfoot over 7 ft tall with short neck, flat nose, and long arms, ran up hillside at dusk / One witness to JG, noted TSF p. 41.

23 Aug. 1968 / Between Easterville & Grande Rapids, Manitoba / Three men / Short-haired Bigfoot walked onto road, 100 yds from witnesses' car; another sighting in the area shortly afterwards / Winnipeg, Manitoba, *Free Press* Aug. 1968, noted STAAU pp. 242-3.

Late Aug. 1968 / N of Hyder, AK / 2 men / Stopped to shoot what they thought was a bear; it walked off uphill on 2 legs / Witness int. JG, noted STAAU p. 303.

Aug. 1968 / Banff National Park, Alberta / Gerald Martin & family / Watched black Bigfoot walking on ridge / Witness wrote to RP, noted TSF p. 48.

Summer 1968 / Yukon River nr Galena, AK / Hazel Strasburg / Saw Bigfoot on river bank at dusk; other Bigfoot sightings in the area during 1968 / Report from Bob Betts, noted TSF p. 48; see also STAAU p. 302.

Summer 1968 / Clearwater River nr Golden, ID / C.E. Ricketts & Fred J. Richardson / Eventually saw cinnamon-colored Bigfoot which had visited their camp unseen, left tooth marks on a bag and tin, and took a sack of flour / Ricketts wrote to JG & sent him letter by Richardson printed in Centralia, WA, *Daily Chronicle* 10-11 May 1969, noted TSF pp. 49-50.

Summer 1968 / Nr Leavenworth, KS / Dennis Williams & others / 7-8-ft light Bigfoot seen in daylight by group of "monster hunters" / Letter to RP, noted STAAU p. 179 & TSF p. 50.

Summer 1968 / N of Anthony, NM / Couple / While driving, saw Bigfoot with long black wavy fur eating an animal killed on the road / STAAU p. 177.

Summer 1968 / Nr The Dalles, OR / 2 girls / Woke up while sleeping outdoors and saw Bigfoot on haunches watching them; it ran when they screamed / TSF p. 44.

11 Sept. 1968 / Nr Billings, MT / Harold E. Nelson / Opened door of his motor trailer and was faced by Bigfoot with reddish-brown hair / *Saga* July 1969, noted SCFTAS p. 111.

14 Sept. 1968 / Nr Chetwynd, BC / Eddie Barnett & another game guide / Saw Bigfoot / TSF p. 41.

Sept. 1968 / Hamburg, AR / - / People reported seeing "a thing that looks like a man but has a gorilla head" / *Arkansas Gazette* 26 Sept. 1968, noted STAAU p. 192.

Oct. 1968 / Nr Estacada, OR / Fisherman / Chased back to truck by Bigfoot waving its arms. When he fell, Bigfoot waited till he got up and never tried to catch him / Witness to Millie Kiggins, noted TSF pp. 44-5.

Autumn 1968 / Nr McCall, ID / Roy Fleetwood / Logger saw Bigfoot while driving a skidder / Letter to RP, noted STAAU p. 286 & TSF p. 50.

Autumn 1968 / LaCrescent, NM / Man / Black Bigfoot surprised man in duck blind / Eric Norman, *The Abominable Snowman*, noted STAAU p. 197.

Autumn 1968 / Point Isabel, OH / Larry Abbott (15), his father, & Arnold Hubbard / Men fired at 10-ft Bigfoot which disappeared in a white mist (see ch. 6) / Larry Abbott int. L.H. Stringfield, see Leonard H. Stringfield, *Situation Red, The UFO Siege!* (Doubleday & Company, 1977) pp. 65-6.

9 Nov. 1968 / Lorain, OH / Mr. & Mrs. Cataldo / 6-ft Bigfoot about 600 lb looked through bedroom window at couple, then ran away on 2 legs / COTOE p. 112.

12 Nov. 1968 / N of Floodwood, MN / Uno Heikkila / Hunter saw 4½-ft Bigfoot about 125 ft away; jumped from tree and walked into woods / Witness wrote to RP, noted STAAU p. 197 & TSF p. 50.

30 Nov. 1968 / Deltox Marsh, Fremont, WI / 12 deer hunters including Bob Parry, Dick Bleier, & Bill Mallo / Gave detailed description of Bigfoot which watched them; had been seen before in same area (see ch. 6) / Investigated by Ivan T. Sanderson & Dr. Bernard Heuvelmans, see Ivan T. Sanderson, "Wisconsin's Abominable Snowman," *Argosy* April 1969, quot. STAAU pp. 198-9; see also OTTOTS p. 176, SCFTAS p. 122.

Nov. 1968 / Between Oakwood & Canton, OK / Roger Boucher / "Gorilla-like" animal ran across road at night; other sightings during the winter / COTOE p. 85, STAAU p. 180.

Nov. 1968 / Clackamas River area, OR / Glenn Thomas / Studied two female Bigfeet while they slept and ate (see ch. 6) / Witness int. JG & RD, see STAAU pp. 425-6, OTTOTS pp. 175-6.

Nov. 1968 / Tannum Valley nr Yakima, WA / 2 students / Saw 8-9-ft Bigfoot by moonlight; it came to within 12 ft. Tracks found next day / Recorded by RP, noted TSF p. 42.

Dec. 1968 / Clackamas River area, OR / Glenn Thomas / Turned to find 9-ft Bigfoot standing behind him (see ch. 6) / Int. JG & RD, see STAAU p. 426, OTTOTS pp. 175-6.

1968 / Evans, WA / Mrs. Gruber / Saw Bigfoot walking nr Columbia River / TSFBF p. 83.

1968 / Murray, KY / Dr. Richard Young & Charles Denton / Saw Bigfoot on road / Nashville *Banner* 11 July 1977, noted STAAU p. 223.

Late Feb. 1969 / Khutze Inlet, BC / Ronnie Nyce & 2 other men / Shot at Bigfoot which ran screaming into woods / Nyce to Bob Titmus, noted TSF p. 41.

Feb. 1969 / Nr Truman, AR / Nathan Russell / Saw creature a cross between dog and ape, with human head and shoulders; jumped from tree and chased him briefly / *Midnight* 19 Oct. 1970, noted TSF p. 50.

5 March 1969 / Beacon Rock State Park, WA / Don Cox / 8-10-ft Bigfoot crossed road at 4 am in front of witness's car and leapt up 40° slope / Int. JG, see OTTOTS p. 133; Portland, OR, *Oregonian* 6 March 1969, repr. BB 3 p. 1 & see BB 3 p. 4; see also *Sasquatch* pp. 135-6, SCFTAS pp. 119-20 & Stevenson, WA, *The Skamania County Pioneer* special "Bigfoot" edition, summer 1969.

March 1969 / North Saskatchewan Valley, Alberta / Mark Yellowbird / Saw Bigfoot / OTTOTS pp. 161, 195.

March 1969 / Nr Skamania, WA / Mrs. Ellen Satterthwaite / Saw legs and body of Bigfoot which crossed road in front of her car (her lights were too low to show more) / Stevenson, WA, *The Skamania County Pioneer* special "Bigfoot" edition, summer 1969, noted TSF p. 42.

16 April 1969 / Road between Paradise & Stirling City, CA / Robert & Mrs. Behme / Saw 6-ft Bigfoot with short black hair flecked with white limp across road / Letter from Mrs. Behme in BB 5 p. 3, TSFBF pp. 29-30 & TSF p. 46.

24 April 1969 / Port Huron, MI / Children / Frightened in woods by 6-ft gray Bigfoot / Port Huron, MI *Times Herald* 24 April 1969, noted TSF p. 50.

April 1969 / Between Bossburg & Northport, WA / Woman / Saw two Bigfeet looking in dustbins / OTTOTS p. 204.

April 1969 / Oroville area, CA / Ed Saville & Eldon Butler / 8-ft, greenish-eyed Bigfoot came to their rabbit call at night / Report from Jim McClarin, noted TSF p. 46.

Early Spring 1969 / Clackamas River area, OR / Logger / Saw Bigfoot standing in small lake / OTTOTS p. 161.

Spring 1969 / Nr Kettle Falls, WA / Mrs. Betty Peterson / Two black Bigfeet over 7 ft tall, and heavy, ran quickly across road / Witness to JG, noted OTTOTS p. 205 & TSF p. 42.

Spring 1969 / Nr Marietta, WA / Sailor & three others / When parked, car lights lit up 7-8-ft, white, long-armed Bigfoot which ran into woods / TSF p. 43.

Early 1969 / Rochester, MN / Larry Hawkins / Student saw Bigfoot crouching at roadside; it ran off when he stopped, leaving a dead rabbit / *Saga* June 1969, noted STAAU p. 197.

18 May 1969 / Nr Merritt, BC / David Ludlam & army cadets / Witnesses saw hairy 10-ft Bigfoot near their camp, by day and night / Witnesses to JG, noted OTTOTS p. 162 & TSF p. 41.

19 May 1969 / Nr Rising Sun, IN / George Kaiser / Watched muscular black Bigfoot with no neck 25 ft away; 3-toed tracks found / SCFTAS pp. 94-5; COTOE pp. 75-6; Jerome Clark & Loren Coleman, "Anthropoids, Monsters and UFOS," FSR vol. 19 no. 1 p. 18.

26 June 1969 / Dallas, OR / Mrs. Doris Newton / Saw two black Bigfeet walking upright across a field 150 yds away / Int. John Fuhrmann, noted BB 7 p. 1 & TSF p. 45.

June 1969 / Wildwood Inn, Shasta-Trinity National Forest, CA / Several people including Bob Kelley & family / 6-ft, dark-brown Bigfoot seen fighting dogs (see ch. 6) / Report from Ben E. Foster, quot. BB 7 p. 2.

June 1969 / Mamquam, BC / Gordon Ferrier / Saw hairy biped with bushy tail; 3-toed tracks found later / OTTOTS p. 163.

June 1969 / Nr Orofino, ID / Mr. Moore / Several Bigfeet often heard and seen around sawmill (see ch. 6) / Int. Russell Gebhart, noted BB 25 p. 4; also quot. STAAU pp. 288-9.

June or July 1969 / Trinity Alps nr Trinity Center, CA / Don Ballard & friend / Saw Bigfoot over 8 ft tall by daylight / Report from Jim McClarin, noted TSF pp. 46-7 & OTTOTS p. 163.

4 July 1969 / N of Wildwood, CA / Eldon Brackett / Saw 7½-ft Bigfoot with no neck; left 16½-in tracks / TSF p. 47.

Early July 1969 / Twain, CA / Lester Orlinger (16) & two girls / Witnesses in car saw Bigfoot crouched in road, swerved to avoid it and stopped, but it had gone / *Klam-Ity Kourier* 22 July 1969 & Oroville, CA, *Mercury-Register* 15 July 1969, noted BB 7 p. 2; see also BB 9 p. 3.

12 July 1969 / Oroville, CA / Charles Jackson & son Kevin (6) / 7-8-ft Bigfoot with 3-in gray hair and large breasts watched witnesses burning rubbish in yard (see ch. 6) / Chico, CA, *Enterprise-Record* 14 July 1969 & Oakland, CA, *Tribune* 14 July 1969; RD investigation see *Sasquatch* pp. 141-2; see also OTTOTS pp. 207-8 & BB 7 p. 2, BB 9 p. 3.

Mid July 1969 / North Saskatchewan Valley, Alberta / Edith Yellowbird (16) / Saw 4 Bigfeet / OTTOTS pp. 165, 195.

26 July 1969 / Deekay Road, Copalis Beach, WA / Deputy Sheriff Verlin Herrington / Saw Bigfoot at night while driving home (see ch. 6) / JG's interview with Herrington published in the Agassiz, BC, *Advance* 7 Aug. 1969, in BB 8 pp. 2-3, in OTTOTS pp. 135-8, & in part in STAAU pp. 401-4; RD's interview with Herrington published in *Sasquatch* pp. 42-4.

July 1969 / Nr Bradfield Canal, AK / J.W. Huff & companion / Witnesses setting up camp saw Bigfoot watching them from 500 yds away / Letter from Huff quot. BB 11 p. 3 & TSF p. 48, & noted STAAU p. 303.

July 1969 / Nr Oroville, CA / Homer Stickley / By moonlight saw dark Bigfoot walk across field / Witness to JG, noted TSF p. 47.

4 Aug. 1969 / Nr Cub Lake, E of Darrington, WA / Mark Meece & Marshall Cabe / Chased back to camp by 3 Bigfeet / Investigated by Dick Grover, noted OTTOTS p. 165 & TSF p. 43.

24 Aug. 1969 / Big Horn Dam, North Saskatchewan River, Alberta / Harley Peterson, Stan Peterson, Guy L'Heureuse, Floyd Engen, Dale Boddy / Construction workers were watched for about half an hour by 15-ft figure half a mile away (see ch. 6) / Investigated by JG, see OTTOTS pp. 193-7 & STAAU p. 239, & by RD, see *Sasquatch* pp. 146-9; see also Leicester, UK, *Mercury* 1 Sept. 1969.

Aug. 1969 / East fork of Coquille, OR / Jack Woodruff / Something shook trailer home. Next night witness saw Bigfoot running away fast through trees; later found track 12 in long x 5 in wide / TSF p. 45.

Aug. 1969 / Sixes River nr Port Orford, OR / Joe Bayless / Saw Bigfoot several times during 2-month dredging operation. 6 ft tall, heavy, black haired. Sat and watched him for 30 mins, with elbow on knee, head resting on hand / TSF p. 45.

Summer 1969 / Easterville, Manitoba / Schoolteacher & Indian couple / Saw Bigfoot leaping small bushes / Indian int. JG, noted STAAU p. 245.

Summer 1969 / Nr South Sulphur River nr Commerce, TX / Jerry Matlock, Kenneth Wilson, & others / 8-ft, brown-haired Bigfoot with wide shoulders came fast over levee towards car at night; men drove away, trying unsuccess-fully to fire a gun at it / Mark Jones & Teresa Ann Smith, "Has Bigfoot Moved to Texas?", *Fate* vol. 32 no. 7 pp. 30-2.

Summer 1969 / Nr North Bend, WA / Robert Parker & friends / Fishermen heard a scream and saw brown Bigfoot walk across hillside / Parker to JG, noted TSF p. 43.

Late summer 1969 / Nr Maple Springs, N of Orleans, CA / Woman / Prospector saw adult male and female Bigfeet several times; took apples and grapes she left out / Reported to John Dana, noted OTTOTS p. 165.

13 Sept. 1969 / Nr Deception Pass, WA / A youth / Saw black Bigfoot 5 ft 3 in tall cross road at night / OTTOTS p. 166.

20 or 30 Sept. 1969 / Fife Heights nr Tacoma, WA / Dick Hancock & Gary Johnson / Bigfoot ran across road and hit metal road sign, leaving it bent / Investigated by Dick Grover, noted OTTOTS pp. 129-30.

Sept. 1969 / Bellingham, WA / Woman / Witness opened curtains at 4 am and saw huge, sad-looking face covered with white hair / STAAU p. 14.

Sept. 1969 / Lost Trail Pass, MT / Man / Wood-cutter watched by 7-ft "ape-man"; the hair on its neck stood up when he started his power saw (see ch. 6) / *Bitterroot Journal* report quot. STAAU p. 296.

Sept. 1969 / Kananasis Lake–Ribbon Creek area, nr Banff, Alberta / Three men / Prospectors saw female Bigfoot 7-8 ft tall, squatting near camp at noon; it chattered its teeth and moved its arms up and down / One witness wrote to JG, noted TSF p. 49.

25 Oct. 1969 / Nr Anahim Lake, BC / Pan Phillips / Game guide watched brown Bigfoot through telescopic sight for 10 mins; it sat by snow hole (apparently its home) at edge of glacier at 6,000 ft / TSF pp. 41-2.

31 Oct. 1969 / Nr Oroville, CA / Wes Strang / Saw squatting Bigfoot outside his house; looked at each other; witness returned indoors to watch TV! / TSF p. 47.

Oct. 1969 / Little Cricket, SW of Yakima, WA / Ross Hendrich / Deer hunter saw two dark-brown Bigfeet 7-9 ft tall, reaching down to take something from under rocks as they walked uphill / Witness to RP, noted TSF p. 44.

Oct. 1969 / Feather River nr Oroville, CA / Charles Mauldin / Witness in boat saw Bigfoot running on abandoned road / Witness to RP & Dennis Jensen, noted TSF p. 47.

Autumn 1969 / French Creek nr Oroville, CA / Ron Sanders / Saw two Bigfeet turning over rocks and eating something / Witness to Homer Stickley, noted TSF p. 47.

Autumn 1969 / S of Twin Falls, ID / Man / Rabbit hunter saw 8-10-ft Bigfoot momentarily step into spotlight beam / Int. Robert Walls, noted STAAU p. 290.

1 Nov. 1969 / Nr St. Clair Lake, nr Fort Lewis, WA / Army Sergeant Lloyd Stringer / Driving on foggy night, hit 6-ft brown Bigfoot standing in road / Reported to sheriff's office, noted TSF p. 44.

7 Nov. 1969 / Lake Worth, TX / Charles Buchanan / Thrown to ground, while sleeping in pick-up, by Bigfoot (see ch. 6) / STAAU p. 186, COTOE p. 53.

20 or 22 Nov. 1969 / Trans-Canada Highway nr Lytton, BC / Ivan Wally / Gray-brown Bigfoot about 7 ft tall stood in road with hands above head as Wally drove by at night / Agassiz, BC, *The Advance* 27 Nov. 1969, repr. BB 12 p. 4; see also OTTOTS p. 139.

23 Nov. 1969 / Calkins Ranch on Neimi Road nr Woodland, WA / Charles Kent / Saw "bear" standing near ranch in moonlight; 18 tracks found later were 11¾ in long x 4 in wide and not a bear's / Woodland, WA, *Lewis River News* 27 Nov. 1969, noted BB 13 p. 4 & TSF p. 44.

Nov. 1969 / Calaveras Big Trees National Park, CA / Mike Scott & another / Scott fired 3 rounds at a Bigfoot 30 yds away / *Bigfoot* (S&B) p. 9.

Nov. 1969 / Neah Bay, WA / Loggers / Bigfoot seen / OTTOTS p. 167.

Nov. 1969 / Nr North Bonneville, WA / Mrs. Louise Baxter / Gray Bigfoot crossed road in front of car at 10 pm / Witness to JG, noted STAAU p. 16.

July to Nov. 1969 / Lake Worth, TX / Many people including Jack E. Harris / White Bigfoot often seen during this summer; threw car wheel 500 ft at one group of watchers (see ch. 6) / Harris story in Fort Worth, TX, *Star Telegram* 11 July 1969, quot. STAAU pp. 185-6; see also SCFTAS p. 118.

Dec. 1969 / Nr Bridgewater, MA / - / Bigfoot seen near teachers' college / *Herald-Traveler* 9 April 1970, noted STAAU p. 232.

1969 / Nr Davie, FL / Charles Robertson / Met smelly, growling Bigfoot in abandoned guava orchard / Duane Bostick, "Florida's Incredible Manhunt for a Supernatural Suspect," *Startling Detective* March 1976.

1969 / Nr Davie, FL / Henry Ring / Saw huge black Bigfoot treed by dogs in orange grove; it swung away through the trees and dived into canal / Duane Bostick, "Florida's Incredible Manhunt for a Supernatural Suspect," *Startling Detective* March 1976.

1969 / Nr Massett, Queen Charlotte Islands, BC / Indians / Saw Bigfoot on at least two occasions / Witnesses rang Bob Titmus, noted TSF p. 41.

1969 / Klickitat Valley, WA / Woman / Passed Bigfoot standing by roadside at night / TSFBF pp. 30-1.

1969 / Nr The Dalles, OR / Four young people / Got out of car to watch Bigfoot sitting on rocky bluff / TSFBF p. 32.

1960s / Mt Elbert, CO / Twelve climbers / Saw 7-ft Bigfoot with shiny black fur; followed tracks in snow for a mile / Letter to RP, noted STAAU p. 173.

1960s / Nr Columbia Falls, MT / Tom Tiede, journalist / Gray-haired Bigfoot heard wailing and seen walking through woods / Witness's story repr. STAAU p. 291.

1960s / Nr Invermere, BC / Man / Saw white or gray Bigfoot / Witness to RD, noted TSF p. 26.

1960s / Denison, IA / Barry Bergamo & another / 2 students saw Bigfoot in woods behind college / Bergamo wrote to RP, noted TSF p. 32 & STAAU p. 178.

Late 1960s / Chuska Mtns, NM / Two Navaho shepherds / Shot at 8-ft Bigfoot which ran wounded into canyon; two others helped it / Letter from Mrs. Cheeseman, noted TSF p. 50.

Late 1960s / Nazko River, S of Nazko, BC / Samial Paul / Saw Bigfoot near river / Paul to JG, noted TSF p. 41.

Winter, late 1960s / Vancouver Is., BC / Paul Griffith / After exploring a cave, saw 7-ft Bigfoot with long arms, flat face, and reflecting eyes at 3 am; later saw large tracks in snow near same cave / Griffith to JG, noted TSF p. 41.

Early Jan. 1970 / Whitewater, NM / Clifford Heronemus, Robert Davis, Carl Martinez, David Chiaramonte / Bigfoot ran beside witnesses' car at 45 m.p.h. until they shot at it (see ch. 6) / Gallup, NM, *Independent* 29 Jan. 1970, noted BB 16 p. 3; see also COTOE pp. 110-11, STAAU pp. 176-7.

7 Jan. 1970 / Cheakamus Canyon nr Squamish, BC / Bill Taylor, road works foreman / 7-ft Bigfoot crossed road in front of Taylor's car, carrying a fish in its hand / Int. JG, quot. STAAU pp. 406-8 & OTTOTS pp. 143-5; int. Peter Byrne, noted TSFBF pp. 79-81; see also *Sasquatch* pp. 1-2.

Jan. 1970 / Route 45, Centre County, PA / Teenage girl / Witness saw from her house, Bigfoot watching her for more than 2 mins / Pat Morrison, "UFOs and Bigfoot Creatures: An Adventure into the Unexplained," *Bigfoot* (PRL) pp. 28-9.

Early Feb. 1970 / Nr Klemtu, BC / Andrew Robinson / While in boat, saw 6-ft, light-brown Bigfoot on beach / Witness to Bob Titmus, noted TSF p. 51.

Feb. 1970 / Big Cypress Swamp, FL / H.C. Osbun & another man / At 3 am saw smelly Bigfoot with no neck running away from tent; 17½-in tracks found / *National Observer* 16 Aug. 1971, noted TSF p. 58.

March 1970 / Below Priest Rapids Dam, WA / Bill Harwood / Camper saw 8-9-ft Bigfoot by flashlight at night / Int. RP, noted TSF p. 52.

March 1970 / Nr Route 28, Bridgewater, MA / - / Bigfoot seen / *Herald-Traveler* 9 April 1970, noted STAAU p. 232.

c. March 1970 / Queen Charlotte Islands, BC / Tina Brown / Saw 7-ft Bigfoot in car headlights at night / Vancouver, BC, *Sun* 24 June 1970, noted TSF p. 51.

Early 1970 / Nr Juskatla, BC / Boy / Saw Bigfoot run away with arms raised / TSF p. 51.

2 April 1970 / Harrison Hot Springs, BC / Keith Shepard / 8-ft tall, dark hair-covered Bigfoot "ambled" across road in front of witness's car / Int. Jim McClarin, noted Agassiz, BC, *The Advance* 9 April 1970, repr. BB 16 p. 1; see also TSF p. 51.

8 April 1970 / Nr Bridgewater, MA / - / 7-ft "bear" nearly run down; tracks found by police / *Herald Traveler* 9 April 1970, noted STAAU p. 232.

23 April 1970 / Nr Klemtu, BC / Crew of seiner *Bruce I* / Saw beige Bigfoot on shore / TSF p. 51.

April 1970 / Nr Bridgewater, MA / Police officer / In patrol car in dark, felt rear end of car picked up and saw "bear" running away / *Herald-Traveler* 9 April 1970, noted STAAU pp. 232-3.

April 1970 / Hyampom, CA / Buzz McLaughlin & others / Several nights saw bad-smelling, 9-ft Bigfoot like "giant gorilla" from ranch school window / Witness's account repr. BB 24 p. 1.

12 May 1970 / Butte Creek Canyon nr Chico, CA / Clifford Brush / Shot Bigfoot 4 times with .22 caliber rifle after it waved its arms and growled at him as he went to get water at his well; went away making cries of pain / Sacramento, CA, *The Sacramento Bee* 14 May 1970 & Chico, CA, *Enterprise-Record* 14 May 1970, noted BB 17 p. 2.

May 1970 / Footedale, PA / Parents & three children / Driving home from church, saw reddish-brown Bigfoot walking slumped / BAOTC p. 158.

May 1970 / Nr Copalis Crossing, WA / Diane Higby, Becky Figg, Rosemary Tucker / Saw 7-ft Bigfoot with silver-tipped hair in headlights at midnight / TSF p. 52.

14 June 1970 / Nr Yakima, WA / Two young couples / Witnesses besieged in their car at night by "enraged" 9-ft Bigfoot / One young man int. RP, quot. STAAU pp. 342-4.

18 June 1970 / Trinity National Forest, CA / Archie Buckley / Bigfoot researcher attracted Bigfoot to camp by friendship and fish (see ch. 6) / Correspondence with witness, and Paul Ciotti, "Ape-man on the Loose!", *Coast* magazine, Oct. 1974, pp. 29-32.

June 1970 / Nr Taholah, WA / Allan Ebling & other youths / Investigating rock-throwing report, saw dark, 8-ft Bigfoot leaning against tree in car headlights / Ebling int. JG, noted TSF p. 52.

June 1970 / Nr Carlisle, WA / Three teenage girls / Witnesses in car chased by Bigfoot / 16-in footprints later found / BAOTC pp. 50-1.

9 July 1970 / Nr Salt Creek, nr Farmer City, IL / Don Ennis, Beecher Lamb, Larry Faircloth, Bob Hardwick (all 18) / Camping at night, saw Bigfoot with gleaming eyes circling camp fire / COTOE p. 68.

9 July 1970 / Mt Rainier National Park, WA / Wayne Thureringer & companion / Two youths watched Bigfoot nearly 8 ft tall for 10-15 mins as it walked, bent at knees and waist, across country / Thureringer int. JG, quot. STAAU pp. 392-3.

10 July 1970 / Yakima, WA / Several men / Saw dark Bigfoot standing on dike by swimming hole watching them; did not move when they fired at it, so they left / TSF p. 52.

31 July 1970 / Beacon Rock Park, E of Skamania, WA / Man / Saw Bigfoot asleep in cave; had human-shaped foot with flat nails / TSF p. 52.

Early Aug. 1970 / Kickapoo Creek, IL / Three youths / Saw creature "as big as a cow" walking on hind legs; partly eaten fish found / Champaign-Urbana, IL, *News-Gazette* 10 Aug. 1970, noted STAAU p. 203.

Early Aug. 1970 / Nr Bloomington, IL / Vicki Otto / While driving at night saw "ape running in the ditch" / COTOE p. 70.

2 Aug. 1970 / Boston Basin, nr Cascade Pass, WA / Ronald Zimmerman / 6-ft tall, whitish-haired Bigfoot with very large stomach seen walking along ridge / Report obtained by Dick Grover & repr. BB 22 p. 4.

5 Aug. 1970 / Cobalt, Ont. / Bus driver Aimee Latreille & miner Larry Cormack / Latreille nearly crashed busload of miners when Bigfoot walked across road in front of them / North Bay, Ont, *Nugget*, report repr. STAAU p. 249.

11 Aug. 1970 / Nr Waynesville, IL / Steve Rich, George Taylor, Monti Shafer / Saw Bigfoot / Bloomington, IL, *Daily Pantagraph* 12 Aug. 1970, noted TSF p. 57.

11-20 Aug. 1970 / Basin Gulch, Trinity National Forest, CA / Sharon Gorden, Richard Foster, Ben E. Foster, Jr. / During fishing trip, several Bigfoot sightings made: threw a rock, prowled round campfire, flipped car aerial, and communicated by gesture. Tracks, dead fawn, and feces found (see ch. 6) / *Klam-Ity Kourier* 23 Sept. 1970; BB 20 pp. 1-3.

15 Aug. 1970 / Blue Mtns nr Walla Walla, WA / Rich Myers / Motorcyclist saw in brush 10-12-ft Bigfoot, with pale palms (its arms were outstretched) at dusk / Walla Walla, WA, *Union-Bulletin* 30 Aug. 1970, noted TSF p. 52.

16 Aug. 1970 / Kickapoo Creek, IL / Don Lindsey & Mike Anderson / Bigfoot 6 ft 5 in tall crossed road in front of their car / COTOE p. 20.

19 Aug. 1970 / Nr North Bonneville, WA / Louise Baxter / Stopped to examine her tire and saw a Bigfoot was watching her (see ch. 6) / Witness's account quot. STAAU p. 16 & TSF p. 53.

29 Aug. 1970 / Wilsonville, OR / Young woman / Bigfoot picked up witness as she climbed through fence and threw her back over fence (see ch. 6) / Int. JG, noted STAAU pp. 340-1 & TSF p. 54.

Aug. 1970 / Winslow area, IN / Various / Over 2-week period people reported 10-ft Bigfoot with top speed of 60 m.p.h. / Evansville, IN, *Press* 15 Aug. 1970, noted COTOE p. 76 & STAAU p. 205.

Aug. 1970 / Benton, WI / About 15 / Witnesses described 7-ft white-haired ape-like creature with pink eyes and claws / Dubuque, IA, *Telegraph-Herald* report, quot. STAAU p. 198.

Summer 1970 / Cub Lake E. of Darrington, WA / Man / Looking for Bigfoot in area where they have been seen, saw one looking out of bush and photographed it / TSF p. 52.

Summer 1970 / McCall, ID / About 5 men / Studied 7-ft Bigfoot through binoculars from half a mile away / Two witnesses int. Grover Krantz, noted STAAU p. 286.

Summer 1970 / Nr Reynolds, Manitoba / Man / Saw Bigfoot near road by day / Investigated by Brian McAnulty, noted STAAU p. 246.

Sept. 1970 / Nr Coos Bay, OR / Edward Flowers / Saw two Bigfeet, one 8 ft and dark, the other 6 ft and dark but with long silver-tipped hair on head, neck, and calves; they ran on hillside / Int. Ron Olson, noted TSF p. 54.

Oct. 1970 / S of Huron, OH / Young woman / Witness in car nearly hit 7-ft dark brown Bigfoot with pointed head and unusually long arms / STAAU p. 209.

Nov. 1970 / Easterville, Manitoba / Schoolteacher / Saw Bigfoot / Investigated by Brian McAnulty, noted STAAU p. 245.

1970 / Lake nr Priest Lake, ID / Two fishermen / Saw Bigfoot swimming across lake (see ch. 6) / TSFBF pp. 31-2.

1970 / Nr Reynolds, Manitoba / Man / Saw 7-ft dark Bigfoot stand up by roadside at night / Investigated by Brian McAnulty, noted STAAU p. 246.

1970 / Talihina, OK / Several / Saw Bigfoot / Report from The International Association for the Investigation of the Unexplained, noted STAAU p. 180.

1970 / Timothy Lake, OR / Young man / Witness in fire tower saw Bigfoot walking up road to tower / TSFBF p. 31.

1971-1980

23 Jan. 1971 / Nr Flagstaff, AZ / 2 students / 5-ft Bigfoot looked in parked car window at 1 am / Flagstaff, AZ, *Daily Sun* 23 Jan. 1971, noted STAAU p. 176.

Jan. 1971 / Dutchess County, NY / Young man / Saw Bigfoot on 3 occasions: while snowmobiling, in lovers' lane, and while Bigfoot-hunting, when 8-9-ft Bigfoot approached pickup carrying 4-ft stick / Investigated by Bob Jones, noted STAAU p. 233.

Feb. 1971 / Big Cypress Swamp, FL / H.C. "Buz" Osbon (or Osborn) & other archaeologists / 8-ft, light-brown Bigfoot, strongly smelling, approached close to their tent at 3 am; 17½-in, 5-toed tracks found later / *National Enquirer* 7 Nov. 1971, noted STAAU pp. 272-3; BAOTC pp. 165-6; *INFO Journal* vol. II no. 4 p. 17.

2 March 1971 / Tenino, WA / Charles Smith & Margie Baker / 7-ft Bigfoot came up to car at night and patted roof / *Daily Olympian* 3 March 1971; witnesses int. Mrs. Elmer Dodge, noted TSF p. 53.

2 May 1971 / Jonesville area, Fouke, AR / Bobby Ford, his wife, and brother Douglas Ford / 6-ft Bigfoot seen several times during night (see ch. 7) / "Arkansas has a Problem" (based on newspaper reports), *Pursuit* vol. 4 no. 4 pp. 89-90; "Love that Monster!", *Fate* vol. 25 no. 3 pp. 24-8; Jim Brandon, *Weird America* (Dutton, 1978) pp. 16-17; *Arkansas Democrat* 3 May 1971, repr. BB 26 p. 2; TSF p. 58.

23 May 1971 / Nr Fouke, AR / Mr. & Mrs. D.C. Woods, Jr., & Mr. & Mrs. R.H. Sedgass / 6-7-ft Bigfoot ran across road in front of car; reported by other drivers on Highway 71 / "Arkansas has a Problem," *Pursuit* vol. 4 no. 4 pp. 89-90; also *Arkansas Democrat* 25 May 1971, repr. BB 26 p. 4.

Early June 1971 / Pinewood Trailer Court, nr The Dalles, OR / Dick Ball, Jim Forkan, Frank Verlander, Joe Mederios / 8-ft, silvery-gray Bigfoot seen on several occasions by groups of witnesses (see ch. 7) / Investigated by Bigfoot Information Center, see TSFBF pp. 73-6; aerial photograph of location reproduced in BFN 41 p. 2; see also TSF p. 55.

2 June 1971 / Pinewood Trailer Court, nr The Dalles, OR / Richard & Mrs. Brown / At night saw 10-ft gray Bigfoot with red eyes standing in grassy field. Although had rifle, could not shoot (see ch. 7) / *Wall Street Journal* 10 Aug. 1972; report by officer of Wasco County Sheriff's Office; Hood River, OR, *News* 26 June 1975, quot. *Bigfoot* (S&B) p. 56; see also TSF p. 55.

June 1971 / Greenville, MS / Mae Pearl Young / Saw 6-ft black Bigfoot standing beside her daughter's home at night / Greenville, MS, *Delta Democrat Times* 22 June 1971, noted STAAU p. 193.

July 1971 / Highway 79, N of Louisiana, MO / Joan Mills & Mary Ryan / Young women were picnicking when "ape man" came out of woods and trapped them in their car (see ch. 7) / Jerome Clark & Loren Coleman, "Anthropoids, Monsters & UFOS," FSR vol. 19 no. 1 pp. 19-20; see also "'MO' & Others," *INFO Journal* vol. III no. 1 p. 50.

Aug. 1971 / W of Fort Lauderdale, FL / Henry Ring / Rabies control officer saw Bigfoot with long dangling arms cross road, during a search following many other reports from the area / *National Enquirer* 7 Nov. 1971.

Summer 1971 / Stone State Park, nr Sioux City, IA / Gary Parker & two friends / Saw Bigfoot on hilltop; earlier, group of teenagers in car had hit a "man-like" creature in the same park / Jerome Clark, "Are 'Manimals' Space Beings?", *UFO Report*, summer 1975, p. 49.

1 Sept. 1971 / Nr Mammoth, CA / Sheriff's lieutenant / Saw 8-ft, brown, shaggy Bigfoot with outstretched arms / *Bigfoot* (S&B) p. 10, TSF p. 56.

Early Sept. 1971 / Allison Pass Manning Park, BC / Man / Saw dark, 8-ft Bigfoot with small head and long arms walk across lighted highways dept. yard at 4 am / TSF p. 51.

2 Oct. 1971 / Yale Reservoir, WA / Elmer Wollenburg / Heard 10-sec. bellow across lake, and watched while two Bigfeet walked from beach across logging road / Witness's account quot. STAAU p. 391.

Autumn 1971 / Nr Sechelt, BC / Prospector / Saw two Bigfeet, the color of a collie dog, run away from small lake where they may have been pulling up lily roots / Int. JG, noted STAAU p. 420.

Beginning June or July 1971, until autumn 1972 / Nr Sharpsville, IN / DK, a farmer / 9-ft Bigfoot with strong odor often seen on farm and always eluded capture (see ch. 7) / Investigated by Don Worley & Fritz Clemm, noted COTOE pp. 76-80.

Beginning July 1971 & continuing into 1972 / High Sierras, CA / Warren Johnson, Lewis Johnson, Larry Johnson, Bill McDowell, & a family friend / Bigfeet frequently prowled around camp at night; shadowy figures seen and vocalizations recorded / *Bigfoot* (S&B) pp. 11-13, 19-34.

15 Dec. 1971 / Nr Bremerton, WA / Woman & her three children / Watched from house 8-ft Bigfoot looking into the house from 5 ft away / Woman int. JG, noted STAAU p. 14.

Winter 1971 / W of Sherman Pass, WA / George Hildebrand / Saw Bigfoot jump from road into snow as he approached in car / Investigated by Bigfoot Information Center, noted TSFBF pp. 83-6.

1971 / Nr Davie, FL / Sgt. Harry Rose & Sgt. Joseph Simboli / Heard Bigfoot around deserted buildings and watched as it escaped by swinging through orange trees / Duane Bostick, "Florida's Incredible Manhunt for a Supernatural Suspect" *Startling Detective* March 1976.

1971 / Chuska Mtns, NM / - / Bigfoot taking sheep from corrals; one seen walking with sticks on its arms / Mrs. Cheeseman to JG, noted TSF p. 57.

c. 1971 / Little Rock Dam nr Palmdale, CA / Youth / Says he shot at Bigfoot 4 times with a .30-30 / Int. California Bigfoot Organization, noted STAAU p. 313.

2 Jan. 1972 / A canyon, ID / Justin Phelps / Railway engineer saw 6-ft, grayish-brown Bigfoot; had seen smaller ones in same place before / Pocatello, ID, *Journal* 25 Feb. 1972, noted TSF p. 57.

14 Jan. 1972 / Nr Drexel, NC / Deputy Sheriff & volunteer deputy / Saw 6-ft gray Bigfoot cross road in front of their car / Associated Press report dated 14 Jan. 1972, noted STAAU p. 220; Witnesses int. E.M. Murray noted TSF p. 58.

Late Jan. 1972 / Nr Balls Ferry, CA / John Yeries (16), James Yeries, Darrell Rich (16), & Robbie Cross / Saw 7-ft lumpy creature; car would not start, and fireworks effects in field changed into a human figure / COTOE pp. 44-6.

Jan. 1972 / Springdale, AR / Mrs. G.W. Humphrey / Barking dogs alerted witness who saw Bigfoot outside trailer home on 2 occasions / Jerome Clark & Loren Coleman, "Anthropoids, Monsters, and UFOS," FSR vol. 19 no. 1 p. 23.

Jan. 1972 / Nr Stone State Park nr Sioux City, IA / Jim Britton / Saw 7-ft Bigfoot with 6-in brown hair; when he shot at it, it ran away on all fours / Int. Dr. Laurence Lacey, noted STAAU p. 178.

Feb. 1972 / Nr Kapowsin, WA / Farmer / Studied Bigfoot in telescopic sight after seeing it cross field; it was 8 ft tall and had glowing amber eyes / Int. JG, noted TSF p. 54.

Feb. 1972 / Bremerton, WA / Woman / Saw by daylight a 7-8-ft Bigfoot with red-brown hair standing 25 ft from her house / Int. JG, noted STAAU p. 14.

Feb. 1972 / Nr Triangle Lake, OR / Jim Kunkle & another man / Hunters saw Bigfoot on hillside at night; it ran away flailing its arms when they fired at it / Investigated by Mike Jay, noted STAAU p. 375.

Feb. 1972 / Lake Isabella, CA / Four young people / Watched a Bigfoot prowling around campground in the moonlight / STAAU p. 313.

Feb. 1972 / Nr Aloha, WA / Don Waugh / Saw black Bigfoot jump ditch / Int. JG, noted TSF p. 54.

Early 1972 / Nr Sherman Pass, Ferry County, WA / - / Bigfoot sighting / Peter Byrne in article in *Explorers Journal* June 1972.

26 May 1972 / Nr Copalis Crossing, WA / James Figg / Saw black Bigfoot on road in daylight; it walked into brush / Int. JG, noted TSF p. 54.

27 June 1972 / McKenzie River valley, nr Eugene, OR / Three timber fellers / Workmen observed Bigfoot 100 yds away; it walked off quickly when it saw them / Investigated by Ron Olson, noted STAAU p. 418.

29 June 1972 / Mountains in VA / Three people / As they walked up mountain-side, witnesses scattered as 7-8-ft Bigfoot running on 2 legs passed them on its way down / Investigated by John Lutz, noted STAAU p. 225.

c. 30 June 1972 / Cuivre River, nr Cuivre State Park, MO / Named as V.M. & Tim / Fishermen saw Bigfoot wade river and walk along bank towards them / Investigated by John F. Schuessler, noted Brad Steiger, *Mysteries of Time and Space* (Prentice-Hall 1974, Sphere Books 1977) p. 111 Sphere edn.

Late June 1972 / Base of Mt Jefferson, Cascade Mtns, OR / Thomas E. Smith & friend / Witnesses were fishing from a raft when they saw two Bigfeet, one 6 ft and one 4 ft tall, on shore; they walked away when the witnesses moved nearer the shore / Smith's account of sighting quot. STAAU pp. 417-18 & *Bigfoot* (S&B) pp. 55-6.

June 1972 / Quinalt Reservation, WA / Allen Ebling & others / Saw 8-ft Bigfoot run fast across logging slash / Ebling int. JG, noted TSF p. 54.

June-July 1972 / Peoria, IL / Randy Emert (18) & friends / On 2 occasions saw white, smelly Bigfoot 8-12 ft tall which made a long screeching sound / Peoria, IL, *Journal Star* 26 July 1972, noted Jerome Clark & Loren Coleman, "Anthropoids, Monsters, and UFOs," FSR vol. 19 no. 1 p. 23; COTOE p. 71.

Early July 1972 / Nr Tower, MN / Debby Trucano (13) & friend / Saw white, 4½-ft-tall, 3-ft-wide, Bigfoot in woods near house; later seen by 4 others / "'MO' & Others…," *INFO Journal* vol. III no. 1 p. 51.

Early July 1972 / Springdale, AR / Peter Ragland / Shot at Bigfoot with .22 pistol / Jerome Clark & Loren Coleman, "Anthropoids, Monsters, and UFOS," FSR vol. 19 no. 1 p. 23.

11 July 1972 / Nr Louisiana, MO / Terry Harrison (8), Wally Harrison (5), Doris Harrison (15) / Saw black, 6-7-ft Bigfoot standing by tree in daylight; possibly carried bleeding black dog / Jerome Clark & Loren Coleman, "Anthropoids, Monsters, and UFOS," FSR vol. 19 no. 1 p. 20; Jerome Clark & Loren Coleman, *The Unidentified* (Warner, 1975) pp. 12-14; Brad Steiger, *Mysteries of Time and Space* (Prentice-Hall 1974, Sphere Books 1977) pp. 114-19 Sphere edn; STAAU p. 195.

16 July 1972 / Gering, NE / Two housewives & neighbor / Saw 7-ft Bigfoot; neighbor shot at it; police found tracks / Lincoln, NE, *Journal and Star* 16 July 1972, noted STAAU pp. 172-3.

20 July 1972 / Springdale, AR / Mrs. G.W. Humphrey / Woken by pounding on her trailer home, witness encountered Bigfoot that alternately walked upright and crawled on all fours / Jerome Clark & Loren Coleman, "Anthropoids, Monsters, and UFOS," FSR vol. 19 no. 1 p. 23.

20 July 1972 / Nr New Haven, MO / Daughter of Leonard Strubberg / Driving in the early morning, witness saw huge, silver-gray Bigfoot walking in field / Union, MO, *Franklin County Tribune* 26 July 1972.

20 July 1972 / McKenzie River valley, nr Eugene, OR / Chief surveyor / At the same construction site as 27 June case, witness saw brown, muscular Bigfoot with pointed head and no neck / Investigated by Ron Olson, noted STAAU p. 418.

24 July 1972 / Nr O'Fallon, MO / Two teenage girls / Saw Bigfoot walking at edge of wooded area near sundown / Investigated by John F. Schuessler, noted Brad Steiger, *Mysteries of Time and Space* (Prentice-Hall 1974, Sphere Books 1977), p. 112 Sphere edn.

25 July 1972 / Cairo, IL / Leroy Summers / Saw 10-ft white Bigfoot standing near Ohio River levee / Jerome Clark & Loren Coleman, "Anthropoids, Monsters, and UFOS," FSR vol. 19 no. 1 p. 23.

25 July 1972 / East Peoria, IL / 2 men / 10-ft smelly Bigfoot seen, but 100 searchers found no trace / *Arkansas Gazette* 28 July 1972; also Pekin, IL, *Daily Times* 27 July 1972, noted STAAU p. 203; Jerome Clark & Loren Coleman, "Anthropoids, Monsters, and UFOS," FSR vol. 19 no. 1 p. 23.

Late July 1972 / Springdale, AR / Bill Hurst / Saw Bigfoot in his garden staring at him with "two great big eyes"; when he yelled it ran off / Jerome Clark & Loren Coleman, "Anthropoids, Monsters, and UFOS," FSR vol. 19 no. 1 p. 23.

Late July 1972 / Vineland, NJ / Teenagers / About 2 am saw 8-ft Bigfoot running near sandwash; seen nearby next morning by farmer and wife / Vineland, NJ, *Times Journal* late July 1972, noted STAAU p. 265.

Late July 1972 / Nr Creve Coeur, IL / - / 100 searched woods for Bigfoot after 2 sighting reports in 2 days / *Chicago Tribune* 28 July 1972.

July & Aug. 1972 / Toledo & Defiance, OH / Several / Witnesses said they saw a 6-8-ft creature with wolflike head, elongated nose, red eyes, fangs, and huge feet / COTOE pp. 107-8.

Early Aug. 1972 / Roachdale, IN / Randy Rogers & wife Lou / Bigfoot seen around their property for several weeks (see ch. 7) / Jerome Clark, "On the Trail of Unidentified Furry Objects," *Fate* vol. 26 no. 8 pp. 56-64; see also Jerome Clark & Loren Coleman, *The Unidentified* (Warner, 1975) pp. 14-16 & Jerome Clark, "Anthropoid, and UFO in Indiana," FSR vol. 20 no. 3 p. 17.

Mid-Aug. 1972 / Brookside Park, Cleveland, OH / Wayne E. Lewis & others / Several witnesses independently reported seeing black Bigfoot / Warren, OH, *Tribune Courier* 14 Aug. 1972, noted *INFO Journal* vol. III no. 3 p. 26; Cleveland, OH, *Plain Dealer* 14 Aug. 1972, noted STAAU p. 209.

23 Aug. 1972 / Roachdale, IN / Carter Burdine & Bill Burdine / Found 60 of their chickens had been killed, and shot at Bigfoot they saw (see ch. 7) / Jerome Clark, "On the Trail of Unidentified Furry Objects," *Fate* vol. 26 no. 8 pp. 56-64; see also Jerome Clark & Loren Coleman, *The Unidentified* (Warner, 1975) pp. 17-18 & Jerome Clark, "Anthropoid, and UFO in Indiana," FSR vol. 20 no. 3 p. 18.

Summer 1972 / Nr Rocky Mountain House, Alberta / Three people / Reported seeing head and shoulders of 8-10-ft Bigfoot in bushes / STAAU p. 240, TSF p. 56.

Summer 1972 / Nr Jackson, WY / Woman / Saw Bigfoot crossing field with giant strides / STAAU pp. 177-8.

Summer 1972 / Nr Lander, WY / Tom Hernandez (13) & Kurt Leininger (13) / Boys were riding horses when Bigfoot ran along near them / *Wyoming State Journal* 28 Aug. 1972; Los Angeles *Herald-Examiner* 27 Aug. 1972; *The Sacramento Union* 26 Aug. 1972; Austin, TX, *American* 24 Aug. 1972; Salt Lake City, UT *Tribune* 14 Jan. 1973; see also STAAU p. 178, TSF p. 57.

6 Sept. 1972 / Springdale, AR / Barbara Robinson / Told police that a "prowler" had peered through her window, 7 ft from the ground / Jerome Clark & Loren Coleman, "Anthropoids, Monsters, and UFOs," FSR vol. 19 no. 1 p. 23.

19 Sept. 1972 / Parke County, IN / At least four people / Independently saw a 10-ft Bigfoot with 21-in-long feet / Jerome Clark, "On the Trail of Unidentified Furry Objects," *Fate* vol. 26 no. 8 pp. 63-4; Jerome Clark, "Anthropoid and UFO in Indiana," FSR vol. 20 no. 3 p. 18; COTOE pp. 81-2.

30 Sept. 1972 / Lee Valley, Coos County, OR / Dewey Strong / Saw 7-ft Bigfoot at 4 am, standing in ditch by roadside with arms raised / Myrtle Point, OR, *Herald* 12 Oct. 1972; Barbara Wasson, *Sasquatch Apparitions* (1979) pp. 6-8.

Sept. 1972 / Nr Dixie, ID / Earl Armstrong & another man / While hunting, witnesses saw two Bigfeet, 8 ft tall and covered in reddish-brown hair; 4-toed tracks found / Witnesses int. Russ Gebhart, noted STAAU p. 287 & TSF p. 57.

8 & 9 Oct. 1972 / Placer Street Bridge, Clear Creek, nr Redding, CA / Randy Norton & Steven Gillispie / Saw Bigfoot cross creek at night; next day saw rusty-brown Bigfoot running with knees bent / Redding, CA, *Record Searchlight* 10 Oct. 1972, noted TSF p. 56.

Late Oct. 1972 / Between Carlisle & Germantown, OH / Mr. & Mrs. Ed Miller, three teenagers, & Mr. & Mrs. Gary Moore / At different times witnesses saw black Bigfoot with big glowing eyes running in field; it also snarled and hissed at them / Middletown, OH, *Journal* report, noted COTOE pp. 108-9.

Autumn 1972 / N of Boise, ID / Trapper / Saw Bigfoot / BFN 33 p. 4.

Autumn 1972 / McCall, ID / Man / Drove past 6-ft, light-brown Bigfoot on forest road / Int. Grover Krantz, noted STAAU pp. 286-7.

Autumn 1972 / Nr Seven Persons, Alberta / - / Sightings of Bigfoot with reddish-brown fur moving along Seven Persons Creek / Reports from L. Edvardson, noted STAAU p. 240.

Mid-Nov. 1972 / Nr Orofino, ID / Mr. Harvey / Watched stocky, 8-ft, grayish-white Bigfoot with long, thin arms walk in fields behind house and step over 4-ft fence / Int. Grover Krantz and Russell Gebhart, noted *Bigfoot Bulletin* (Texas) 18.

Nov. 1972 / Ironton, OH / Taxi driver / Saw white Bigfoot dragging a dog or deer / *Plain Dealer* 30 Nov. 1972, noted STAAU p. 209.

c. Nov. 1972 / Dublin, OH / Two security guards / Saw 8-ft Bigfoot at night on golf course / STAAU p. 209.

24 Dec. 1972 / Nr Aloha, WA / Julie Reed & another girl / Saw brown Bigfoot with hanging arms and a stoop cross road at dusk / Ms. Reed int. JG, noted TSF p. 54.

1972 / Nr North Fork of Logy Creek, WA / Rancher / Foul-smelling Bigfoot approached camp fire and stood for several minutes before shuffling away; dogs paralyzed with fear / *Bigfoot* (S&B) p. 146.

Mid Jan. 1973 / On road between Grants Pass, OR, & Eureka / Truck driver / Bigfoot, nearly 7 ft tall, stepped into path of logging truck which was badly damaged (see ch. 7) / Interview with witness repr. STAAU pp. 409-10.

26 Jan. 1973 / Island Lake, Nr Duluth, MN / Bob McGregor (11), Mr. & Mrs. Donald McGregor / Bob saw white furry Bigfoot 8½ ft tall walking across yard and through unfinished house / *Fate* April 1973 p. 40.

14 March 1973 / Lancaster, CA / Three marines / Dark, 8-ft Bigfoot jumped in front of witnesses' car / Lancaster, CA, *Ledger-Gazette* 24 March 1973, noted STAAU p. 313 & TSF p. 73.

21 March 1973 / Bute Inlet, BC / Peter Spika, Luko Burmas, & Nick Pisac / Herring fishermen watched beige, 10-ft Bigfoot walking on beach / Witnesses int. JG & Bob Titmus, noted JG, "Not All Quiet on the Western Front," *Pursuit* vol. 7 no. 4 p. 98; see also *Sasquatch* p. 197.

Late March 1973 / Lancaster, CA / Kim McDonald (19) / 7-ft Bigfoot rose up from the grass in front of witness and ran off / Int. California Bigfoot Organization & her story told in Lancaster, CA, *Ledger-Gazette* 30 March 1973 & quot. STAAU p. 314; see also *Bigfoot* (S&B) p. 70.

5 April 1973 / Nr Estacada, OR / Don Stratton / Saw 5-ft, very broad, Bigfoot digging at rotten tree stump (see ch. 7) / STAAU pp. 408-9.

22 April 1973 / Sycamore Flat campground, Big Rock Canyon, CA / Richard Engels, Brian Goldojarb, William Roemermann / 11-ft Bigfoot ran along road, following witnesses' pick-up truck for about 20 secs / STAAU p. 317, *Bigfoot* (S&B) pp. 71-2.

April 1973 / Lancaster, CA / John Parkhurst / 8-ft black Bigfoot crossed road in front of witness's car / *Bigfoot* (S&B) pp. 68-9.

April 1973 / Easterville, Manitoba / Teacher / Driving, nearly hit broad, 9-ft Bigfoot walking along road; it leapt into woods / Investigated by Brian McAnulty, noted STAAU p. 245.

6 May 1973 / Enfield, IL / Rick Rainbow & three others / Saw 5½-ft, grayish, stooped, ape-like creature near abandoned house; this followed reported sighting of *3-legged* creature nearby / Investigated by Loren Coleman, noted COTOE p. 74.

Mid May 1973 / Palmdale, CA / Ron Bailey / Saw 8-ft Bigfoot standing by telephone pole; large footprints found later / STAAU p. 315, *Bigfoot* (S&B) pp. 89-91.

29 May 1973 / Nr Sykesville, MD / Anthony Dorsey / Made first sighting of Bigfoot with luminous eyes. This was after a UFO was seen to drop an object into a nearby reservoir. Other people reported seeing an 8-ft, black-haired Bigfoot / Investigated by John Lutz, noted STAAU p. 226; also investigated by Dr. Theodore Roth, noted *Bigfoot* (S&B) pp. 119-20; see also "BHM in the NE USA," *INFO Journal* vol. III no. 3 p. 28.

May 1973 / Nr Sitkum, OR / Engaged couple / Met a 10-ft Bigfoot in a mountain park *c.* 1:30 am / JG, "Not All Quiet on the Western Front," *Pursuit* vol. 7 no. 4 p. 98.

Early June 1973 / Jefferson County, AR / Jessie (19), Ricky (17), Sandra (16), Gail (13) / Bigfoot looked in at rear window of witnesses' car when they visited rubbish dump, and was seen several times during following hours (see ch. 7) / Pine Bluff, AR, *Commercial* 14 June 1973.

Early June 1973 / Nr Pine Bluff, Jefferson County, AR / Two boys 12-14 years old / Reported seeing a Bigfoot — "great big ol' shaggy looking thing" — in woods/ Pine Bluff, AR, *Commercial* 12 June 1973.

9 June 1973 / Nr Orofino, ID / Mr. Harvey / Saw 6-ft Bigfoot walking up hillside / Int. Russell Gebhart & Grover Krantz, noted *Bigfoot Bulletin* (Texas) 18.

25 June 1973 / Big Muddy River nr Murphysboro, IL / Randy Needham & Judy Johnson / While parked at night, saw 7-ft white Bigfoot with muddy body hair. As it approached shrieking, they drove off; tracks found later / Investigated by Jerome Clark & Loren Coleman, noted COTOE pp. 54-5; see also New York *Times* 1 Nov. 1973.

26 June 1973 / Murphysboro, IL / Christian Baril (4), Randy Creath, Cheryl Ray / Christian saw "big white ghost" in yard; 10 mins later in neighboring yard Randy & Cheryl saw 7-ft dirty white Bigfoot with glowing pink eyes standing watching them. Went off through trees and left a strong "sewer" odor. Tracked by police and dog; slime found on weeds / Investigated by Jerome Clark & Loren Coleman, noted COTOE pp. 55-7; see also New York *Times* 1 Nov. 1973.

June 1973 / Chapman Creek, Nr Sechelt, BC / Timber worker / Saw Bigfoot jumping up and down; it left "humanlike" footprint / Reported in Sechelt-Peninsula, BC, *Times* & investigated by Joel Hurd, noted STAAU p. 420.

June 1973 / Lancaster, CA / Bret Baylor (12) & younger sister Stefanie / Children saw Bigfoot looking at them "round boulder" / STAAU p. 315, *Bigfoot* (S&B) pp. 92-3.

June 1973 / Collowash River, OR / Man / Witness was sitting by campfire when Bigfoot walked by. When he shot at it, it screamed and ran into the forest / Letter from witness to JG quot. STAAU pp. 419-20.

c. June 1973 / Edwardsville, IL / Several / 3 reports of a red-eyed, smelly Bigfoot seen in woods. It was said to chase people and one man's chest had been clawed / COTOE p. 74.

4 July 1973 / Murphysboro, IL / Carnival workers / Saw Bigfoot watching Shetland ponies / COTOE p. 57.

25 & 26 July 1973 / Nr Durham, ME / Tammy Sairo (12), Lois Huntington (13), George Huntington, Jr. (10), Scott Huntington (8), & Mrs. Neota Huntington / While cycling, children saw 5-ft "chimp" covered with shaggy black fur. It "just stood there and looked." Next day Mrs. Huntington drove quietly to the place and saw "chimp" standing beside road. It ran off on 2 legs and was later seen among trees as neighbors searched / Portland, ME, *Press Herald* 28 July 1973; Brunswick, ME, *Times Record* 27 July 1973; Lewiston, ME, *Daily Sun* 28 July 1973; STAAU pp. 228-9; "BHM in the NE USA," *INFO Journal* vol. III no. 3 p. 28.

29 July 1973 / Kingsbury Grade, SE of Lake Tahoe, NV / Mr. & Mrs. Donald Cowdell, Mr. & Mrs. Charles Searles / Saw 7-8-ft Bigfoot with long shiny black hair and flat leathery face at roadside; it walked into brush / Letter from witnesses in Reno, NV, *Evening Gazette* 11 Aug. 1973, quot. STAAU p. 174 & *Bigfoot* (S&B) pp. 149-50.

July 1973 / Roscoe Inlet, BC / Fisheries patrolman / Watched 6-ft gray Bigfoot rooting in vegetation on beach in daylight / Int. JG & Bob Titmus, noted JG, "Not All Quiet on the Western Front," *Pursuit* vol. 7 no. 4 p. 98.

July 1973 / Castle Craggie Mtns, CA / Naturalist / Watched 8-ft Bigfoot with humanlike face for 45 mins / JG, "Not All Quiet on the Western Front," *Pursuit* vol. 7 no. 4 p. 99.

July 1973 / New Sewickly Township, PA / Man / Saw 8-ft Bigfoot with glowing red eyes staring at him through window; 18-in footprint found / UIRTCSIP p. 136.

July 1973 / Greensburg, PA / Doctor / Fired several shots at a Bigfoot after it had tried to enter his trailer home, but it walked away / Pat Morrison, "UFOs and Bigfoot Creatures: An Adventure into the Unexplained," *Bigfoot* (PRL) p. 29; UIRTCSIP p. 141.

July 1973 / Greensburg, PA / Man / Saw Bigfoot's head pass his bedroom window, 9 ft off the ground, several times. When he looked out he saw Bigfoot running towards woods / Pat Morrison, "UFOs and Bigfoot Creatures: An Adventure into the Unexplained," *Bigfoot* (PRL) p. 31.

July 1973 / Nr Bonneville, WA / Woman & daughter / Saw 6-ft Bigfoot on road / JG, "Not All Quiet on the Western Front," *Pursuit* vol. 7 no. 4 p. 99.

Early Aug. 1973 / Greensburg, PA / Four adults, one child / Witnesses were on golf course when they saw two Bigfeet, one 4 ft tall, the other 6 ft tall. Witnesses went closer, but ran when they saw a third Bigfoot, over 9 ft tall and with glowing red eyes, heading their way / UIRTCSIP p. 141.

14 Aug. 1973 / Greensburg, PA / Two men / Saw huge Bigfoot run across railway tracks 40 ft away; also noted strong smell / UIRTCSIP p. 136.

21 Aug. 1973 / Nr Derry, PA / Woman / Awoke to see Bigfoot staring through bedroom window which was 9 ft above ground level / Investigated by Pennsylvania Center for UFO Research, noted Pat Morrison, "UFOs and Bigfoot Creatures: An Adventure into the Unexplained," *Bigfoot* (PRL) pp. 26-8; see also UIRTCSIP pp. 136-7.

24 Aug. 1973 / Herminie, PA / Man / Saw 7-ft Bigfoot 30 ft away in his garden, it smelled like "rotten eggs." He went to get a gun but it had gone when he returned / Investigated by Westmoreland County UFO Study Group, noted UIRTCSIP p. 137 & *Bigfoot* (S&B) pp. 123-4.

26 Aug. 1973 / Luxor, PA / - / Bigfoot with human-like face seen / Allen V. Noe, "ABSMal Affairs in Pennsylvania and Elsewhere," *Pursuit* vol. 6 no. 4 p. 86.

Aug. 1973 / Antelope Valley, CA / Margaret Bailey & Joyce Baylor / Witnesses sitting in car saw silhouette of creature 12 ft tall; giant footprints found / *Bigfoot* (S&B) pp. 97-9.

Aug. 1973 / Nr Bovil, ID / Man & wife / Saw 10-ft Bigfoot in thick brush while they were camping / Report from Russ Gebhart, noted STAAU p. 289.

Aug. 1973 / Nr Mansfield, OH / Man / Saw 8-ft Bigfoot with very long arms standing by barn; ran away when he shot at it / Investigated by Albert Hartman, noted STAAU pp. 209-10.

Aug. 1973 / New London, OH / - / 7-ft Bigfoot with glowing red eyes seen / Jim Brandon, *Weird America* (Dutton, 1978) p. 179.

Aug. 1973 / Oberlin, OH / Rudy Reinhold & five others / Coon hunters saw 8-ft smelly Bigfoot with glowing red eyes; it chased them / *Cleveland Magazine* Oct. 1973, noted STAAU p. 210.

Aug. 1973 / Beech Hills nr Jeannette, PA / - / Bigfoot with protruding fangs seen / Allen V. Noe, "ABSMal Affairs in Pennsylvania and Elsewhere," *Pursuit* vol. 6 no. 4 p. 86.

Summer 1973 / Bay City, MI / 2 men / Saw Bigfoot while camping in the woods / STAAU p. 201.

Summer 1973 / Mojave Desert nr Lancaster, CA / Mike Pense / Black Bigfoot threw rock at witness's motorcycle / STAAU p. 315, *Bigfoot* (S&B) pp. 91-2.

1 Sept. 1973 / Youngstown Cemetery, PA / Woman & baby, woman's brother & sister / Woman saw Bigfoot walking out of wood towards baby; later Bigfoot seen near house to which she had gone / Investigated by Westmoreland County UFO Study Group, noted UIRTCSIP p. 138; see also Allen V. Noe, "ABSMal Affairs in Pennsylvania and Elsewhere," *Pursuit* vol. 6 no. 4 p. 87.

2 or 3 Sept. 1973 / Whitney, PA / Mr. & Mrs. Chester Yothers / Saw 8-ft Bigfoot standing outside their trailer home; phoned police who came and found tracks / UIRTCSIP p. 138; see also Allen V. Noe, "ABSMal Affairs in Pennsylvania and Elsewhere," *Pursuit* vol. 6 no. 4 p. 87.

Early Sept. 1973 / South Sulphur River bottoms, nr Peerless, TX / - / 2 separate sightings of Bigfoot / Letter from editor of Commerce, TX, *Journal* to SITU, quot. STAAU p. 187; see also Mark Jones & Teresa Ann Smith, "Has Bigfoot Moved to Texas?", *Fate* vol. 32 no. 7 pp. 30-6.

17 Sept. 1973 / Quartz Hill, CA / Two young people / Witnesses' car headlights showed Bigfoot with matted hair standing at edge of driveway; footprints found / Investigated by California Bigfoot Organization, noted STAAU p. 315.

21 Sept. 1973 / Greensburg, PA / Ten boys / Told police they had seen tan-colored Bigfoot in woods; hair samples and footprints found, and the boys saw creature again during the search / Investigated by Westmoreland County UFO Study Group, including Stan Gordon & Allen Noe, noted Allen V. Noe, "ABSMal Affairs in Pennsylvania and Elsewhere," *Pursuit* vol. 6 no. 4 p. 88.

24 Sept. 1973 / Greensburg, PA / Two boys / Found Bigfoot asleep on pile of grass clippings; when they returned with adults the creature had gone / Investigated by Westmoreland County UFO Study Group, noted Allen V. Noe, "ABSMal Affairs in Pennsylvania and Elsewhere," *Pursuit* vol. 6 no. 4 p. 88.

24 Sept. 1973 / Greensburg, PA / Boy / Boy delivering papers saw tall, tan-colored Bigfoot walking with stooped posture "like it was drunk" / Investigated by Westmoreland County UFO Study Group, noted Allen V. Noe, "ABSMal Affairs in Pennsylvania and Elsewhere," *Pursuit* vol. 6 no. 4 p. 88.

27 Sept. 1973 / Beaver County, PA / Two teenage girls / Saw 7-8-ft white Bigfoot with red eyes run into woods. It held a luminous sphere in its hand (see ch. 7) / Investigated by Westmoreland County UFO Study Group, noted UIRTCSIP p. 142 & Allen V. Noe, "ABSMal Affairs in Pennsylvania and Elsewhere," *Pursuit* vol. 6 no. 4 p. 88.

Sept. 1973 / Nr Latrobe, PA / Woman / Woke at 2 am and saw dog attacking Bigfoot, which then broke clear and ran away with tremendous leaps / Allen V. Noe, "ABSMal Affairs in Pennsylvania and Elsewhere," *Pursuit* vol. 6 no. 4 p. 88.

Sept. 1973 / Nr Woodinville, WA / Man / Met 6-7-ft Bigfoot running down the road towards him with its arms up in the air / JG, "Not All Quiet on the Western Front," *Pursuit* vol. 7 no. 4 p. 99.

1 Oct. 1973 / Doctor Rock area nr Big Flat, OR / Rick Blagden / Hunter saw 6-ft-plus, dark, "barrel like" Bigfoot standing near him; after looking at him it slowly walked away / Brookings, OR, *Harbor Pilot* 4 Oct. 1973, quot. STAAU p. 385.

Early Oct. 1973 / Nr Galveston, IN / Jeff Martin or Jim Mays (one name is probably a pseudonym, as the initials are the same) / Saw Bigfoot on 2 occasions, also lights or UFOs in the same area (see ch. 7) / COTOE pp. 82-3; STAAU pp. 206-8 includes verbatim report by Don Worley.

16 Oct. 1973 / Nr St. Joseph, IL / Bill Duncan, Bob Summers, Daryl Mowry, Craig Flenniken / Stopped car to investigate campfire; saw 5-ft Bigfoot close by / Champaign-Urbana, IL, *Courier* 17 Oct. 1973, repr. COTOE pp. 74-5.

22 Oct. 1973 / Middletown, NJ / Girl (16) / Saw Bigfoot with two young, standing in front garden / Investigated by Robert C. Warth, noted Robert C. Warth, "A UFO-ABSM Link?", *Pursuit* vol. 8 no. 2 p. 31.

25 Oct. 1973 / Nr Uniontown, PA / Young man & twin boys / Witnesses were in field watching glowing sphere when they saw two Bigfeet walking by fence (see ch. 7) / Investigated by Stan Gordon & Berthold Eric Schwarz, see UIRTCSIP pp. 142-4 & Berthold Eric Schwarz, M.D., "Berserk: A UFO-Creature Encounter," FSR vol. 20 no. 1 pp. 3-11; see also COTOE pp. 98-106.

Oct. 1973 / Massillon, OH / Several / Witnesses reported a 7-ft Bigfoot with strong smell / Akron, OH, *Beacon-Journal* 27 Oct. 1973, noted STAAU p. 210.

Autumn 1973 / New Buffalo, MI / - / Bigfoot sightings / STAAU p. 201.

Autumn 1973 / Nr Midland, PA / Several / Woman saw Bigfoot with glowing green eyes; other reports of "strange animal"; UFO seen and possible landing site found with 3-toed footprints nearby / UIRTCSIP p. 144.

Autumn 1973 / Albany, KY / - / Dark, 6-ft creature with bushy black tail, "ape/human" face and 3-toed tracks seen by many. Killed livestock but was itself unaffected by gunfire until wounded by farmer Charlie Stern; sightings of this, another, and a youngster then ceased / Investigated by Loren Coleman, noted COTOE pp. 114-16.

Nov. 1973 / Nr Johnson Siding, SD / Three men / 10-ft, shaggy, dirty-white Bigfoot seen in headlights. It picked up a dead deer and ran into undergrowth / Investigated by Tim Church, noted STAAU p. 172.

Nov. 1973 / Nr Uniontown, PA / Man / Saw Bigfoot at night and fired at it with revolver, whereupon it disappeared. Later shot at it again with rifle and it screamed (see ch. 7) / UIRTCSIP p. 146; Stan Gordon, "Pennsylvania Creatures Busy," *Skylook* 77 pp. 15-16.

Nov. 1973 / Fort Norman, Northwest Territories / - / Bigfoot seen / STAAU p. 242.

Late Nov. 1973 / Nr Fouke, AR / Orville Scoggins, his son & grandson / Saw 4-ft Bigfoot with black hair, walking slowly / Little Rock, AR, *Arkansas Gazette* 27 Nov. 1973, noted STAAU p. 192; Texarkana, TX/AR, *Gazette* report noted *Pursuit* vol. 7 no. 1 p. 18.

27 Dec. 1973 / Palmdale, CA / Young woman & her brother / Saw Bigfoot, about twice as tall as a man, walking across desert; it then ran off very fast / STAAU p. 315.

Oct. & Dec. 1973 / Nr Seven Persons, Alberta / - / Sightings of Bigfoot with reddish-brown fur moving along Sevens Persons Creek / Reports from L. Edvardson, noted STAAU p. 240.

1973 / The Buttes, Mojave Desert, CA / Kent Lacy & others / Research team saw hair-covered figure at night; strong "rank odor" was smelled / *Bigfoot* (S&B) pp. 99-100.

1973 / Nr Dublin, OH / Two security guards / Large Bigfoot seen on golf course; 12-in footprint later found / Ron Schaffner, "A Report on Ohio Anthropoids and Other Strange Creatures," *Bigfoot* (PRL) p. 43.

1973 / Lancaster, PA / Two brothers / While bringing in load of hay, saw gray Bigfoot with white mane, "tigerlike fangs," curved horns, and "long grizzly claws"; their horses bolted / Allen V. Noe, "And Still the Reports Roll In," *Pursuit* vol. 7 no. 1 p. 17.

1973 / Lancaster, PA / Farmer / Evening after previous sighting, witness was scything when a similar Bigfoot charged him and tore the scythe from his hands as he fled. Next day the scythe was found with all the wood eaten away / Allen V. Noe, "And Still the Reports Roll In," *Pursuit* vol. 7 no. 1 p. 17.

1973 / Lancaster, PA / Woman / Witness was feeding hens when Bigfoot came and made off with a goose in each hand. She chased it and the Bigfoot threw a goose at her which knocked her down / Allen V. Noe, "And Still the Reports Roll In," *Pursuit* vol. 7 no. 1 p. 17.

1973 / Nr Beacon Park, WA / Louis Awhile & young daughter / Saw Bigfoot cross the road / TSFBF p. 86.

9 Jan. 1974 / Hollywood Boulevard nr Fort Lauderdale, FL / Richard Lee Smith / 7-8-ft, dark Bigfoot ran off limping after witness ran into it in his car at night; others saw it in the area (see ch. 7) / Miami, FL, *Herald* 10 Jan. 1974, noted STAAU p. 278; Duane Bostick, "Florida's Incredible Manhunt for a Supernatural Suspect," *Startling Detective* March 1976 p. 5.

9 Jan. 1974 / Highway 27 nr Fort Lauderdale, FL / Patrolman Robert Hollemeyal / Bigfoot survived gunshot wound and ran off at around 20 m.p.h. (see ch. 7) / Duane Bostick, "Florida's Incredible Manhunt for a Supernatural Suspect," *Startling Detective* March 1976 p. 5.

Mid Jan. 1974 / Rowena, OR / Deputy Sheriff Harry Gilpin / At 4 am on a freezing morning, saw 7-ft Bigfoot on road / TSFBF p. 34.

Jan. 1974 / Aurora, IL / Several / "Big Mo," huge and dirty white, seen around, and large footprints found / Elgin, IL, *Daily Courier-News* 26 Jan. 1974, noted *Shadows* vol. 3 no. 1.

6 Feb. 1974 / Uniontown, PA / Woman & son-in-law / Bigfoot disappeared when shot at; others seen close by, plus a UFO (see ch. 7) / Stan Gordon, "Pennsylvania Creatures Busy," *Skylook* 77 pp. 14-17; see also UIRTCSIP pp. 144-6 & Leonard H. Stringfield, *Situation Red, The UFO Siege!* (Doubleday & Company, 1977) p. 63.

8 March 1974 / Florence, OR / Nick Wells (9) / On his way to school, saw 6-ft Bigfoot in scrub beside road. It growled at him but did not chase him / Int. Peter Byrne, noted TSFBF pp. 34-5.

March 1974 / Nr Nemo, SD / Two small boys / Saw huge Bigfoot with orange-brown fur on a hill / STAAU p. 172.

11 May 1974 / Nr Big Horn Dam, Alberta / Ronald C. Gummow or Gummell / Came upon two 12-ft Bigfeet standing in road. He stopped and they watched him for a few seconds before they "jogged" away / *The Albertan* 14 May 1974; see also STAAU p. 240.

9 June 1974 / Nr Maple Valley, WA / Tony McLennan / Stopped by "injured dog" at roadside. When it stood up he saw a 6-8-ft Bigfoot with glowing red eyes. He drove away and fetched police, but the Bigfoot had gone / Seattle, WA, *Times* 10 June 1974; see also COTOE pp. 46-7.

4 July 1974 / Oakland, NE / Emory Wickstrom & sons Nick & Tom / In the early morning an animal like a "medium size dog with a monkey face" and curved tail, ran, or leapt, across road at speed / Jerome Clark, "Are 'Manimals' Space Beings?", *UFO Report* vol. 2 no. 4 p. 51.

5 July 1974 / Nr Oakland, NE / Dale Jones / Saw 6-ft Bigfoot in cornfield; it ran away / Jerome Clark, "Are 'Manimals' Space Beings?", *UFO Report* vol. 2 no. 4 p. 51.

18 July 1974 / Nr the head of Harrison Lake, BC / Wayne Jones / Sitting by campfire at night, watched 7-8-ft Bigfoot for 5 mins before other people disturbed it; it was licking mud off fingers / *Sasquatch* p. 196.

Late July 1974 / Nr Oakland, NE / Connie Johnson, Sheryl Rupert, & two brothers / Saw Bigfoot coming towards them when out walking. It screeched, and fled when one boy threw a firecracker at it / Jerome Clark, "Are 'Manimals' Space Beings?" *UFO Report* vol. 2 no. 4 p. 51.

July 1974 / Murphysboro, IL / - / "The Big Muddy Monster" seen again / Centralia, IL, *Sentinel* 9 July 1975, noted STAAU p. 204.

July 1974 / Nr Pointe du Bois, Manitoba / Man / Saw "overgrown ape or monkey" about 6 ft 6 in at night on the road / *Manitoba Beaver*, report noted STAAU p. 246.

July 1974 / Nr Freeport, NH / 2 people / In car lights saw 6-7-ft Bigfoot at close range. It had a triangular face, pointed chin, prominent nose, large shoulders, and dark fur / Witnesses int. John Oswald, noted STAAU pp. 229-30.

July 1974 / Fir Mtn, Hood River National Forest, OR / Jack Cochran, Fermin Osborne, J.C. Rourke / Cochran saw Bigfoot watching crane worked by three loggers. Next day all three saw it at same time; 6-ft Bigfoot walked quickly away from them / Investigated by Bigfoot Information Center, noted TSFBF pp. 42-7.

July 1974 / Nr Rutland, VT / Couple / Saw 8-10-ft Bigfoot in meadow at night; later ran across road in front of police / STAAU p. 231.

July-Aug. 1974 / Watova settlement nr Nowata, OK / Mrs. Margie Lee, Deputy Gilbert Gilmore, & Deputy Buck Field / Many sightings at the Lees' home over 2 weeks; Bigfoot uninjured when shot at by deputies (see ch. 7) / COTOE pp. 91-3.

Mid Aug. 1974 / Nr Oklahoma campground, nr Willard, WA / Fisherman / Saw Bigfoot sitting on roadway where it ended at stream; ran for his car and drove away / Investigated by Bigfoot Information Center, noted TSFBF p. 39.

Late Aug. 1974 / Big Rock, CA / Bruce Morgan / Saw shaggy, white-haired Bigfoot with long arms on hands and knees and 6 ft tall in that position, near group sitting with a psychic / *Bigfoot* (S&B) pp. 76-7 & STAAU p. 319.

End Aug. 1974 / Sioux City, IA / Man / Saw Bigfoot outside his house / Jerome Clark, "Are 'Manimals' Space Beings?," *UFO Report* vol. 2 no. 4 p. 58; int. Dr. Laurence Lacey for MUFON & noted Sioux City, IA, *Journal* 31 Aug. 1974 & STAAU p. 179.

Aug. 1974 / Sioux City, IA / Woman / Saw Bigfoot only 3½ ft tall eating tomatoes in her garden; footprints found / Jerome Clark, "Are 'Manimals' Space Beings?," *UFO Report* vol. 2 no. 4 p. 58.

Aug. 1974 / Cascade Mtns, OR / Steve & Jean Fitzgerald & children Dan (16) & Gloria (9) / While holidaying on remote campground, saw Bigfeet several times. They were apparently curious, and watched the family, often coming around at night. Once when gathering wood, Jean found herself face to face with a Bigfoot and fainted / BAOTC pp. 59-62.

Summer 1974 / Columbia River nr Stevenson, WA / Indian boy / Twice, while fishing, saw Bigfoot at first light standing still in shallow water; went into bushes when spotted / TSFBF p. 36.

Summer 1974 / Big Rock, CA / Terry Albright / Almost hit 7-ft black Bigfoot while driving down mountain road / *Bigfoot* (S&B) p. 78.

2 Sept. 1974 / Blackburn State Park nr Dahlongea, GA / Les Alexander, Bob Martin, & Chris Stevens / 8-ft Bigfoot seen eating out of rubbish bins in the early morning. The "Billy Holler Bugger" had been seen before by local residents / Reported in *The Yeti Newsletter* & noted STAAU p. 217.

6 Sept. 1974 / Nr Jefferson, SD / Jim Douglas / Saw very tall, sandy Bigfoot dragging red furry object through alfalfa field. It stood and watched Douglas / Int. Dr. Laurence Lacey, noted Jerome Clark, "Are 'Manimals' Space Beings?," *UFO Report* vol. 2 no. 4 p. 58.

Sept. 1974 / Palm Beach County, FL / Security guard / Fired at and hit Bigfoot, which fled / *The Palm Beach Post News* 11 Feb. 1977.

Sept. 1974 / St. Mary's Peak in the Bitterroot Mtns, MT / Chris Tobias, Diane Stringen, Kathy Mudd, & two other university students / While hiking, saw two black-haired Bigfeet walking along ridge / BAOTC pp. 83-4.

Sept. 1974 / Antelope Valley, CA / Neil Forn & Rich Engels / At night saw 7-ft black-haired Bigfoot standing on rocky crag; 3-toed, 15-in footprints later found / *Bigfoot* (S&B) p. 79.

Mid Oct. 1974 / Nr Holly Springs, AR / - / Several sightings; one man shot at and hit Bigfoot / *Arkansas Gazette* 2 Nov. 1974; Fordyce, AR, *News-Advocate* 6 Nov. 1974, repr. BSIS vol. 2 no. 5 p. 4.

31 Oct. 1974 / Nr Fordyce, AR / Myzell Thompson / Heard dogs barking, saw something outside, and went out to see 7-ft Bigfoot in flashlight. Shot at it; it walked slowly away / *Arkansas Gazette* 2 Nov. 1974; Fordyce, AR, *News-Advocate* 6 Nov. 1974, repr. BSIS vol. 2 no. 5 p. 4.

Autumn 1974 / Carol Stream, IL / Several / Bigfoot with glowing red eyes and gray-tipped head seen and footprints found / Chicago *Tribune* 6 Oct. 1974, noted STAAU p. 204; see also *Shadows* no. 3 p. 1.

Nov. 1974 / Nr San Antonio, TX / John Martinez & friend Rick / While hunting rabbits, saw 6-7-ft Bigfoot with long matted hair on head; dog snarled at it / Report from Rich Grumley, noted *Bigfoot Co-op* Apr. 1981 p. 4.

7 Dec. 1974 / Richmondtown, Staten Is., NY / Frank Pizzolato (11) & Philip Vivolo (12) / In woods saw 6-ft, black, upright "bear" which roared at them / Jerome Clark, "Are 'Manimals' Space Beings?," *UFO Report* vol. 2 no. 4 p. 62; children int. Robert C. Warth, noted Robert C. Warth, "A UFO-ABSM Link?", *Pursuit* vol. 8 no. 2 pp. 33-4.

31 Dec. 1974 / Newhall-Saugus area, nr Canyon High School, CA / 5 children aged 5-14 / Dark-colored, 9-ft Bigfoot raised its arms and jumped off rock into canyon / STAAU pp. 319-20.

Dec. 1974 / McCall, ID / Two boys (10) / When out playing, saw 7-8-ft upright animal "flopping its arms and screeching" at them / Mother int. Russ Gebhart, noted STAAU p. 287; see also Boise, ID, *Idaho Statesman* 13 March 1977.

Dec. 1974 / Bootlegger Trail, MT / Coyote hunter / Fired 3 times with .30-30 at 7-8-ft Bigfoot, and escaped in car when it kept coming / Roberta Donovan & Keith Wolverton, *Mystery Stalks the Prairie* (T.H.A.R. Institute, 1976) p. 90.

Dec. 1974 / Nr Port Angeles, WA / Richard Taylor & Larry Followell / Driving at night, swerved to avoid Bigfoot in road; car wrecked and men injured / TSFBF p. 42.

Dec. 1974 / County Road W, nr Frederic, WI / William Bosak / Saw human-shaped, fur-covered creature inside a UFO (see ch. 7) / Jerome Clark, "The Frightened Creature on County Road W," FSR vol. 21 no. 1 pp. 20-1.

1974 / Nr Castlegar, BC / Young couple / Driving at night, saw Bigfoot standing beside road / Witnesses to Bigfoot Information Center, noted TSFBF pp. 40-1.

1974 / Nr Stone State Park, Sioux City, IA / Man / Wounded Bigfoot with deer rifle / Des Moines, IA, *Sunday Register* 12 Nov. 1978, repr. FN Jan. 1979 p. 18.

1974 / South Mountain, NC / Man / While camping, had fourth sighting of Bigfoot in 20 yrs. 7-ft Bigfoot stood up by camp fire, but went away when fired at / Phone report to JG, investigated by Gordon Strasenburgh, noted STAAU pp. 219-20.

1974 / Jamonville Summit, PA / 13 people / Chased Bigfoot in car; it looked in at them, then hid behind a large stone. It seemed to move almost instantaneously from one side of them to the other / UIRTCSIP p. 146.

21 Jan. 1975 / Richmondtown, Staten Is., NY / Mrs. D. Daly / Driving late at night, had to brake to avoid Bigfoot under 6 ft tall crossing road from church car park and heading for rubbish dump and swamp behind church / Investigated by "Slim" Zumwalt, noted Robert C. Warth, "A UFO-ABSM Link?", *Pursuit* vol. 8 no. 2 p. 34.

21 Jan. 1975 / Richmondtown, Staten Is., NY / Young couple / Saw Bigfoot on church car park in early morning / Investigated by "Slim" Zumwalt, noted Robert C. Warth, "A UFO-ABSM Link?", *Pursuit,* vol. 8 no. 2 p. 34.

23 Jan. 1975 / Miramar, FL / Kim Dunn (rookie policeman) / Saw Bigfoot loping across road / Duane Bostick, "Florida's Incredible Manhunt for a Supernatural Suspect," *Startling Detective* March 1976.

Jan. 1975 / Watertown, NY / Steve Rich (11), Jerry Emerson (11), & another boy / Saw Bigfoot about 5 ft tall walking along edge of forest / BAOTC pp. 161-2; int. Milton LaSalle; Watertown, NY, *Daily Times* 2 Aug. 1977, noted STAAU pp. 233-4.

2 Feb. 1975 / Cape Coral, FL / Richard Davis / Shot once at 9-ft Bigfoot but could not shoot again (see ch. 7) / Marty Wolf, "An Interview with Bob Morgan," *Pursuit* vol. 8 no. 3 pp. 70-1.

Feb. 1975 / Nr Gainesville, FL / - / Bigfoot hit by car / STAAU p. 278.

Feb. 1975 / Bear Swamp, NJ / Motorist / Twice saw Bigfoot cross road; other similar sightings / Investigated by Robert E. Jones, noted Robert E. Jones, "Bigfoot in New Jersey?", *Pursuit* vol. 8 no. 3 p. 68.

6 March 1975 / Nr Lake Okeechobee, Martin County, FL / Steve & Mrs. Humphreys / At night, collided with Bigfoot running fast across road. Much damage to car, but no victim could be found / Marty Wolf, "An Interview with Bob Morgan," *Pursuit* vol. 8 no. 3 p. 71.

24 March 1975 / Black Point — Goulds Canal, Dade County, FL / Michael Bennett & Lawrence Groom / Watched 8-9-ft Bigfoot, rocking blue car with hysterical man inside (see ch. 7) / Report in files of Dade County Public Safety Department, quot. STAAU p. 279.

March 1975 / Camden, AR / - / 7-8-ft Bigfoot seen / Camden, AR, *News* March 1975, noted STAAU p. 192.

28 April 1975 / Rocks, MD / Peter Hureuk / Driving home at 3 am he hit Bigfoot, which ran off clutching its side / Investigated by Robert Chance & reported in York, PA, *Daily Record* 23 Feb. 1978, repr. *INFO Journal* vol. VI no. 6 p. 9; see also STAAU p. 227.

19 May 1975 / Nr Jeannette, PA / Male driver / At dusk saw ape-like creature running on all fours. It stood on 2 legs and ran into woods. It was 7-8 ft tall with thick black hair. UFO seen previous evening not far away / Stan Gordon, "UFO and Creature Observed in Same Area in Pennsylvania," *Skylook* June 1975, p. 13.

May 1975 / Cascade Mtns, OR / Camper / Bigfoot watched for almost an hour as witness cooked and ate dinner / Reported to Bigfoot Information Center, noted TSFBF pp. 231-2.

7 June 1975 / Nr Venice, FL / Ronnie Steves (12) / Was alerted at night by his ducks and went out to see a 6-ft Bigfoot with shaggy hair leaning on post looking down at ducks; tracks found later / *The Sun Coast Times* 17 Jan. 1976, quot. STAAU pp. 276-8.

June 1975 / Nr Beausejour, Manitoba / Youth / Bigfoot banged on car boot as he turned on the road around 4 am / Int. Brian McAnulty, noted STAAU p. 246.

June 1975 / Route 3 nr Saranac Lake, NY / 2 men in car / Saw Bigfoot squatting beside road; walked away on 2 legs as they approached / One witness int. Milton LaSalle, noted STAAU p. 234.

c. 10 July 1975 / Preble County or Drake County, OH / Two 10-yr-old children and one aged 12 / While playing on farm, saw brown-haired creature watching over 6-ft-high corn. They watched from a roof as it ran off very fast. Seen again 2 days later, watching child play with football / Investigated by Don Worley, noted STAAU p. 210; see also Ron Schaffner, "A Report on Ohio Anthropoids and Other Strange Creatures," *Bigfoot* (PRL) p. 43.

July 1975 / Murphysboro, IL / - / Return of "The Big Muddy Monster," reported in the area in 1973 and 1974 / STAAU p. 204.

July 1975 / Turkey Creek area nr Lockridge, IA / Gloria & Wendell Olson / Saw large bushy-tailed animal with monkey face near deserted farmyard / Fairfield, IA, *Ledger* 17 Oct. 1975, repr. Phenomena Research Special Report No. 1 (Nov. 1975) p. 5; see also Brad Steiger, "1975's Unreported UFO-Monster Flap," *Saga* May 1976, p. 54.

July 1975 / Long Plains Reserve nr Portage La Prairie, Manitoba / Two teenage boys / Saw dark, 8-ft Bigfoot near house at night; 5-toed, 20-in footprints found next day / Int. Brian McAnulty, noted STAAU p. 246.

July 1975 / Nr Long Plains Reserve, nr Portage La Prairie, Manitoba / Farmer / A few days later, saw Bigfoot in field 8 miles from boys' sighting, but tracks found only 15 in long / Int. Brian McAnulty, noted STAAU p. 246.

14 Aug. 1975 / Corona, CA / Irene P. Rambo / 10-ft Bigfoot with black hair and human-like teeth looked over her fence in the afternoon. There had been other sightings in Corona / Corona, CA, *Independent* 15 Aug. 1975, quot. *Bigfoot* (S&B) p. 131.

17 Aug. 1975 / Corona, CA / James Mihalko, Ernest Palmeira, & two teenagers / Saw 10-ft Bigfoot with red eyes and black shaggy hair in citrus grove in powerful spotlight / Corona, CA, *Enterprise* 19 Aug. 1975, noted *Bigfoot* (S&B) pp. 132-7.

Late Aug. 1975 / Tygh valley area, north-central OR / Robert Bellamy, Jr., Mrs. Bellamy, another couple, & two children / Stopped car to watch Bigfoot standing on hill / Reported to Bigfoot Information Center, noted TSFBF p. 232.

Summer 1975 / Sequoia National Park, CA / John Clark / While camping saw a 9-ft Bigfoot either covered with long blond hair or wearing something that gave such an appearance / *World Weekly News* 29 Sept. 1981.

Summer 1975 / Colorado Springs, CO / Boy / Heard screeching and saw dark-brown 7- or 8-ft Bigfoot walking across park / Letter from witness to JG, noted STAAU p. 173.

Summer 1975 / Nr Rutherford, NJ / Two boy cyclists / At dusk near lake saw Bigfoot nearly 9 ft tall on trail ahead of them / STAAU p. 268.

Summer 1975 / North Fort Myers, FL / - / Bigfoot seen / STAAU p. 278.

3 Sept. 1975 / Oroville, CA / Mark Karr / Saw 6-7-ft Bigfoot with long arms in early morning while driving; sighting caused him to run into tree / Chico, CA, *Chico Enterprise Record* 3 Sept. 1975, repr. BSIS vol. 2 no. 5 p. 5.

Mid Sept. 1975 / Nr Waterloo, IN / Farmer / At 3 am saw UFO in field, and a large two-legged "animal" walking towards it. It vanished when the light changed color and went out / COTOE p. 84.

Mid Sept. 1975 / Nr Indianola, OK / Three people / Had close sightings of Bigfoot / STAAU p. 182.

22 Sept. 1975 / Manchester, ME / Girl (15) & younger sister / Saw Bigfoot watching man chopping wood. It had long brown hair with a white patch on chest, and ran away when they screamed / Int. Brent Raynes, noted STAAU p. 229.

Sept. 1975 / Nr Kelly Lake, S of Golden, ID / Several youths / Watched Bigfoot for more than an hour, as it moved about ¾ mile below them / Int. Russ Gebhart, noted STAAU p. 287.

1 Oct. 1975 / Section 3 Lake, Pinegrass Ridge, nr Rimrock Lake, WA / Tom V. Gerstmar (17), Earl Thomas (18), Jerry Lazzar (16) / While camping, saw 8-10-ft Bigfoot with black hair and long arms; noticed a bad smell when they left / Yakima, WA, *Herald-Republic* 3 Oct. 1975, & transcript of interview with Thomas by Dick Grover of Project Discovery; both repr. Phenomena Research Special Report No. 1 (Nov. 1975); see also COTOE pp. 47-8.

2 Oct. 1975 / Nr Sexsmith, Alberta / Bob Moody / Saw 7-8-ft Bigfoot beside road, with two others, *c.* 3 and 4 ft tall / Grande Prairie, Alberta, *Daily Herald* Oct. 1975, noted STAAU pp. 240-1.

3 Oct. 1975 / Turkey Creek area nr Lockridge, IA / Herbert Peiffer / Driving tractor late at night, saw 5-ft shaggy black creature on all fours get on hind legs and walk towards him. He left the area quickly. A hunt was unsuccessful, but partially eaten turkeys were found / Fairfield, IA, *Ledger* 17 Oct. 1975 & 28 Oct. 1975, repr. Phenomena Research Special Report No. 1 (Nov. 1975), pp. 5-6.

4 Oct. 1975 / Nr Jake's Corners, Yukon Territory / Ben Able / After passing figure on road, backed to offer a lift, but it didn't answer. It was 5½ ft tall, gray-faced, and with bluish fur, as seen in car headlights / Atlin, BC, *News Miner* 17 Dec. 1975, noted STAAU p. 242.

Early Oct. 1975 / Lummi Indian Reserve nr Bellingham, WA / Captain of the police force / Shot at Bigfoot over 6 ft tall / STAAU p. 17.

24 Oct. 1975 / Lummi Indian Reserve nr Bellingham, WA / Sergeant Ken Cooper & others / Sgt. Cooper saw Bigfoot at close range for several minutes (see ch. 7) / *Daily Mail* 15 Nov. 1975, noted *Fortean Times* no. 15 p. 11; *Fate* vol. 30 no. 9 p. 52; STAAU p. 17.

24 Oct. 1975 / Nr Orofino, ID / Elk hunter / During a snowstorm, saw Bigfoot and took movie film, but quality poor due to distance, weather, and bad light / Film seen by JG, see STAAU p. 290.

Oct. 1975 / Agassiz Provincial Forest, Manitoba / Man looking for mushrooms / Saw Bigfoot running through pine trees; less than 6 ft tall / Int. Brian McAnulty, noted STAAU p. 247.

Oct. 1975 / Pacific, MO / Woman / Saw Bigfoot, known in area as "Brush Ape" / Union, MO, *Franklin County Tribune* 25 May 1977, noted STAAU p. 195.

Oct. 1975 / Giles County, TN / Farmer / Watched Bigfoot in barn kill calf by throwing it on ground / Article by Don Worley in *Argosy UFO* July 1977, noted STAAU pp. 221-2.

Oct. 1975 / Lummi Indian Reserve, nr Bellingham, WA / Sergeant Ken Cooper / Bigfoot yelled as it ran alongside his car at 10 m.p.h. / *Fate* vol. 30 no. 9 p. 52.

Sept. & Oct. 1975 / Noxie, OK / Several, including Kenneth Tosh, Marion Parret, Clifford Bentson, Gerald Bullock / Many sightings of, and futile attempts to kill, Bigfoot (see ch. 7) / Investigated by Jerome Clark & Hayden Hewes, see COTOE pp. 93-7, STAAU p. 180, BAOTC pp. 111-12.

Autumn 1975 / 35 miles N of San Antonio, TX / Man / Watched gray/white-haired Bigfoot 8-9 ft tall through riflescope as it moved tree limbs around at lonely lakeside / Witness wrote to Dr. Grover Krantz, quot. STAAU pp. 182-3.

1 Nov. 1975 / Nr Mount Hood, OR / Leroy Lucas / Saw 7-ft Bigfoot, a dirty-gray color, cross mountain road / Reported to Bigfoot Information Center, noted TSFBF pp. 232-3.

Nov. 1975 / Pine Grove, CA / Rick van Dell (14) & Joe Coughlin (13) / Saw Bigfoot twice within weeks / Sacramento, CA, *Bee* report, noted BFN 15 p. 1 & 16 p. 1.

Nov. 1975 / Citrus County, FL / Seven young men including John Sohl (18) / All saw 3 Bigfeet near their campfire. Sohl was later tossed by one when he tried to photograph it (see ch. 7) / BAOTC pp. 167-8.

Nov. 1975 / Big Days Swamp, Harewood Park, MD / Three boys (16 & 17) / On 3 nights saw 7½-8-ft Bigfoot with bad smell / Investigated by S. Stover & Bernard Brown, see S. Stover, "Does Maryland Have a Sasquatch?", *INFO Journal* vol. VII no. 6 p. 4.

Nov. 1975 / Manchester, ME / Woman / From parked car, saw 6-7-ft Bigfoot by tree. She hooted lightly to attract her husband, but Bigfoot came towards car, so she hooted loudly and it went away / Int. Brent Raynes, noted STAAU p. 229.

26 Dec. 1975 / Vaughn, MT / Two teenage girls / Fired into air above Bigfoot, which dropped to ground and was helped into thicket by others (see ch. 7) / Investigated by Captain Keith Wolverton, see Roberta Donovan & Keith Wolverton, *Mystery Stalks the Prairie* (T.H.A.R. Institute, 1976) pp. 87-9.

Dec. 1975 / Between Lac Du Bonnet & Beausejour, Manitoba / Youth / Saw 7-8-ft Bigfoot approaching his parked car; next day found 15-in prints in snow / Int. Brian McAnulty, noted STAAU p. 246.

Late 1975 / Spottsville, KY / - / Bigfoot seen / Owensburg *Messenger-Inquirer* 9 Feb. 1977, noted STAAU p. 223.

1975 / Yarnell, AZ / Motorist / Saw Bigfoot running behind car; it ran away when he stopped and got out. Saw it again next day on mountainside. It had long arms which swung as it lumbered along / STAAU p. 176.

1975 / Nr Saugus, CA / Man / Top half of Bigfoot holding small animal seen briefly in flashing light of advertising sign / STAAU p. 321.

1975 / Nr mouth of Yashau Creek, Little River, OK / Hunter / Saw long-armed, 8-ft Bigfoot with grayish-black hair which ran off when it became aware of witness / McCurtain, OK, *Sunday Gazette* 9 July 1978, repr. FN Sept. 1978 p. 16.

Jan. 1976 / Sycamore Flats campground, CA / Willie Roemermann / Saw 8-ft creature by flashlight; 5-toed, 16½-in-long tracks found next day / STAAU p. 319.

Early 1976 / Nr The Dalles, OR / Woman & two sons / Saw large dark creature climbing up rock on steep hillside / BFN 18 p. 1.

21 Feb. 1976 / Ulm, MT / Two boys / One saw a hairy arm, the other saw a tall creature with glowing whitish-yellow eyes and covered in dark brown hair / STAAU p. 298.

22 Feb. 1976 / Nr Great Falls Airport, MT / Motorist / Saw 9-ft Bigfoot in field, and UFO hovering in same area (see ch. 8) / Tim Church, "Funny Doin's in Montana 1975-1976," *Bigfoot* (PRL) p. 22; see also STAAU p. 299.

22 Feb. 1976 / Nr Sun River, MT / Man / Saw Bigfoot on a back road / STAAU p. 299.

29 Feb. 1976 / Nr The Settlers Park area, Oakdale, PA / Two people / Saw tall, dark Bigfoot in area where UFO seen the night before (see ch. 8) / Stan Gordon, "UFO/Creature Sightings Continue," *Skylook* 102 p. 10.

Feb. 1976 / Woodlawn area, OH / Two policemen / Both men had separate sightings of Bigfoot / Leonard H. Stringfield, *Situation Red, The UFO Siege!* (Doubleday & Company, 1977) p. 66.

7 March 1976 / Nr Vaughn, MT / Woman / Saw reddish-brown Bigfoot, holding one arm forward, standing in ditch beside road / STAAU p. 299.

23 March 1976 / Mill Valley, CA / Police patrolmen Dan Murphy & Edward Johnson / Heard screaming and growling noises in the brush, and by flashlight saw "large, dark-colored thing" walking upright. It climbed an 8-ft wall. Next day a dead deer was found / Los Angeles, CA, *Times* 26 April 1976, noted *Fortean Times* 17 p. 22; also Washington *Star* 23 April 1976 & Fontana, CA, *The Herald News* report, noted *INFO Journal* vol. V no. 4 p. 13.

March 1976 / Harford County, MD / Woman / Saw in car headlights a huge, black hairy creature standing near her garage; she screamed and it fled, leaving a foul odor / York, PA, *Daily Record* 23 Feb. 1978, repr. *INFO Journal* vol. VI no. 6 p. 7.

March 1976 / Dempsey Road, Great Falls, MT / Boy / Saw Bigfoot standing in middle of road about 9 pm; it went through hedge into house yard / STAAU p. 299.

4 April 1976 / Milford, OH / Group of fishermen / Saw "large baboon" near the Little Miami River; other local people heard strange cries in the woods / Ron Schaffner, "A Report on Ohio Anthropoids and Other Strange Creatures," *Bigfoot* (PRL) p. 43.

4 April 1976 / East Helena, MT / Robert Lea (16) / Saw two Bigfeet in field near house; one picked something up (see ch. 8) / Int. Capt Keith Wolverton & Deputy Ken Anderson, see Roberta Donovan & Keith Wolverton, *Mystery Stalks the Prairie* (T.H.A.R. Institute, 1976) pp. 91-4; *National Enquirer* 3 Aug. 1976; BAOTC pp. 85-6; STAAU p. 300.

23 April 1976 / Nr Flintville, TN / Two teenagers / Bigfoot seen climbing bank at night / *National Enquirer* 1976 (date unknown).

26 April 1976 / Nr Flintville, TN / Gary Robertson (4), mother Mrs. Jennie Robertson, & six men including Deputy Sheriff Homer Davis, Melvin Robertson, & Stan Moore / Bigfoot tried to abduct Gary; 6-man posse chased and shot at it (see ch. 8) / *National Enquirer* 1976 (date unknown) & Jim Brandon, *Weird America* (Dutton, 1978) p. 205; see also STAAU p. 222.

April 1976 / Nr Flintville, TN / Woman / Bigfoot jumped on car roof and stole radio aerial (see ch. 8) / BAOTC pp. 146-7.

Spring 1976 / Nr Pembroke, KY / Five witnesses to 3 sightings / Around 6-ft-tall creature with big shoulders and glowing green eyes seen near lonely houses at night / Investigated by James Moorhatch, noted STAAU p. 223.

Spring 1976 / Chatham, NC / Brody Parker / Farmer watched 7-8-ft Bigfoot for 20 mins. It had black fur and was "sort of hunched over and looking back at me" / *The Denton Record-Chronicle* 17 Sept. 1976.

23 May 1976 / Old Taylor Road, Dothan, AL / Baptist Minister / Dark-haired Bigfoot with red eyes ran beside car for a mile, up to 70 m.p.h. / Don Worley to JG, noted STAAU p. 215.

May 1976 / Harewood Park, MD / Mr. & Mrs. Richard Steward / While clearing brush saw 8-ft Bigfoot with large red eyes / Baltimore, MD, *News American* 27 May 1976, noted S. Stover, "Does Maryland Have a Sasquatch?", *INFO Journal* vol. VII no. 6 p. 4.

Mid-June 1976 / Nr Grove City, FL / Three youths / Had 2 sightings of "skunk ape" on one night. It was 7 ft tall with long, reddish-brown hair and growled at them / Punta Gorda, FL, *Daily Herald News* 18 June 1976, noted *INFO Journal* vol. V no. 4 p. 13.

Mid June 1976 / Nr Grove City, FL / Deputy Carl Williams / Just after midnight, shone car light around pond and saw "big animal ... hunched over," possibly drinking. It had long brown hair and lumbered off into woods / Punta Gorda, FL, *Daily Herald News* 18 June 1976, noted *INFO Journal* vol. V no. 4 p. 13.

June 1976 / Nr North Fort Myers, FL / John Holley, Bill Holley, & friend / Saw Everglades "skunk ape," 6 ft tall, with long black hair, standing in clump of pine trees / Atlanta, GA, *Constitution* 11 June 1976, noted *Fortean Times* 17 p. 22.

4 & 5 July 1976 / Nr Ouray, CO / Heinz Fritz Goedde of West Germany / Holidaymaker hiking in mountains saw Bigfoot which walked away. Next day saw one while trout fishing and tried to photograph it, but it left / Ouray, CO, *Plain Dealer* 3 Feb. 1977, noted STAAU p. 173.

21 July 1976 / Nr Rainbow Dam, MT / Four men / Two Bigfeet seen walking along hill towards river / Great Falls, MT, *Tribune* 31 July 1976, quot. *INFO Journal* vol. V no. 5 p. 14; Minneapolis, MN, *Star* 2 Aug. 1976.

28 July 1976 / Nr Great Falls, MT / Woman / At 5:30 am saw 7-8-ft Bigfoot at site of 22 Feb. 1976 sighting; as she stopped, it walked away / Jim Brandon, *Weird America* (Dutton, 1978) p. 128; Great Falls, MT, *Tribune* 31 July 1976, quot. *INFO Journal* vol. V no. 5 p. 14.

30 July 1976 / Mount Holly, NC / Roger Hoffman / Saw 7-ft hairy Bigfoot in woods at night as he sat on porch; shot at it / Durham, NC, *Morning Herald* 6 Aug. 1976, noted STAAU p. 219.

July 1976 / Santa Ana River bottoms, nr Riverside, CA / Two young boys / Saw tall, hairy "big ape" / STAAU p. 321.

July 1976 / Seigel Creek, ID / Woman / 7-ft Bigfoot with short, dark-brown hair seen with arms around tree. As witness hurried away, it walked with her on a parallel path up the hill / Investigated by Russell Gebhart, noted STAAU p. 287.

July 1976 / Pfeiling Gulch, MT / Mother & daughter / Watched Bigfoot for ½ hour. It was about 8 ft tall, dark brown except for straw-colored hair on head and shoulders. It watched them picking berries / Hamilton, MT, *Bitterroot Journal* May 1977, noted STAAU pp. 296-7.

1 Aug. 1976 / White Meadow Lake, NJ / Two boys (7 & 13) / Saw 8-ft hairy monster while berry picking. Red eyes and hands, not paws, were seen as it walked into foliage / C. Louis Wiedemann, "Mysteries Breaking Out All Over," *Fate* vol. 30 no. 9 p. 38.

10 Aug. 1976 / Watertown, NY / Dennis Smith & Jimmy Slate / Boys saw 8-ft, black hair-covered creature at sunrise; minutes later they saw it again, walking through field. 15-in tracks found / Milton LaSalle, "Bigfoot Sighting," *Pursuit* vol. 10 no. 4 pp. 120-1.

17 Aug. 1976 / Weston, WV / Two teenagers / Saw 8-ft black ape-like creature crouched in the road; it stood up and walked into woods / *UFO Report* Dec. 1976, noted STAAU pp. 224-5.

22 Aug. 1976 / Ocheyedan River, nr Ocheyedan, IA / Dan Radunz (13) / Saw Bigfoot drinking from river / Osceola County, IA, *Gazette Tribune* late Aug. 1976, noted BAOTC pp. 113-14; Sibley, IA, *Tribune* 26 Aug. 1976, noted STAAU p. 196 (the 2 newspaper reports *may* be one and the same!).

24 Aug. 1976 / Whitehall, NY / Marty Paddock & Paul Gosselin / Saw Bigfoot 3 times in same area (see ch. 8) / Glen Falls, NY, *Post-Star* 30 Aug. 1976, quot. STAAU pp. 234-5.

25 Aug. 1976 / Whitehall, NY / Brian Gosselin, police patrolman / Bigfoot came within 25 ft of his squad car (see ch. 8) / Glen Falls, NY, *Post-Star* 30 Aug. 1976, quot. STAAU pp. 234-5.

Aug. 1976 / Nr Kelly Air Force Base, TX / Ed Olivarri / 7-ft brown Bigfoot ran out of his back yard / San Antonio, TX, *Light* 1 Sept. 1976, noted STAAU pp. 187-8.

Aug. 1976 / Nr Kelly Air Force Base, TX / Mrs. Rose Medina / Next-door neighbor to Ed Olivarri, a few days after his sighting, saw 3-ft brown creature sitting on her back step; it ran off on 2 legs / San Antonio, TX, *Light* 1 Sept. 1976, noted STAAU p. 188.

Summer 1976 / Nr Hallsville, TX / - / 12-ft silver-haired Bigfoot seen shucking corn; accompanied by smaller red-tinged female / Longview, TX, *Journal* 28 Nov. 1976, noted STAAU p. 188.

Summer 1976 / Nr Ferrante's Quarry, Bernardsville, NJ / Lisa Farrell (13) & two friends / Caught a glimpse of Bigfoot while playing in the woods; found 3-toed prints/ Bridgewater, NJ, *Courier News* 19 Feb. 1979, repr. FN April 1976 p. 16.

Summer 1976 / Nr Cold Lake, Alberta / - / Bigfoot seen / STAAU p. 241.

Summer 1976 / Brooksville area, FL / - / Many sightings of Bigfoot / STAAU p. 278.

Summer 1976 / White Meadow Lake, NJ / Woman / Saw "large dark form" in back yard at dusk; 5-toed 17-in footprints found / C. Louis Wiedemann, "Mysteries Breaking Out All Over," *Fate* vol. 30 no. 9 p. 41.

Summer 1976 / White Meadow Lake, NJ / Quarry worker / Saw Bigfoot near quarry in daytime; it seemed to have hair longer than shoulder length / C. Louis Wiedemann, "Mysteries Breaking Out All Over," *Fate* vol. 30 no. 9 p. 42.

1 Sept. 1976 / Nr Caroline, Alberta / Hunter / Saw 8-9-ft Bigfoot standing in river. It climbed out and went into bush when he went towards it / Witness wrote to JG, noted STAAU p. 241.

c. 1 Sept. 1976 / Nr Cashton, WI / Farmer / His dog bit 7-ft hairy creature on the leg (see ch. 8) / La Crosse, WI, *Tribune* 28 Oct. 1976; Cashton, WI, *Record* 27 Oct. 1976, both noted *INFO Journal* vol. V no. 6 p. 15.

Sept. 1976 / East Kootenay-Kimberly area, BC / Mickey McLelland / Tall, tan-colored, long-armed Bigfoot seen 125 yds away and followed in car along road / Toronto *Globe and Mail* 10 Sept. 1976, noted *Res Bureaux Bulletin* 6 p. 6.

Sept. 1976 / East Kootenay-Kimberly area, BC / Barbara Pratula / Saw black Bigfoot with light stomach, 6-7 ft tall, behind their store. Took blurred photograph before creature left. Six other people have seen Bigfoot in this area / Unnamed newspaper report repr. BFN 24 p. 1.

3 Oct. 1976 / Nr Glide, on edge of Umpqua National Forest, OR / Rodney Boder / While driving in the evening, stopped to watch 6½-7-ft Bigfoot on hill 150 yds away; after a few seconds it walked away / BFN 26 p. 1.

31 Oct. 1976 / Nr Rochester, Alberta / Daryl Lange (11) & Paul Schleier / Saw 7-ft dark "animal" walking along a road / Athabasca, Alberta, *Echo* 3 Nov. 1976, noted STAAU p. 241.

Oct. 1976 / NW Wasco County, OR / Husband & wife / While arc-welding on 2 occasions, saw large, humanoid, dark creature on boulder about ¼ mile away / BFN 28 p. 1.

Autumn 1976 / Nr Oxbow, NY / Coon-hunter / Saw 7-ft Bigfoot, very heavy, with dark-brown hair, run across clearing in the moonlight / STAAU p. 235.

Nov. 1976 / Goat Rocks Wilderness, WA / Hunter/woodsman / Alone hunting, heard footsteps and took aim at "deer." Saw instead a "large dark form, standing upright." It had lighter palms and face, and watched him for a moment before going into brush / BFN 27 p. 1.

Early Dec. 1976 / Nr McCall, ID / Mrs. Virgil Donica & son (15) / Saw tall dark Bigfoot near house / Hamilton, MT, *Bitterroot Journal* May 1977, noted STAAU pp. 287-8; int. Russell Gebhart, noted *Bigfoot Bulletin* (Texas) 20 p. 2.

1976 / Poplar River, Manitoba / Many / Indians often saw 7-8-ft, broad-shouldered creature which left 3-toed tracks, 16 in by 5 in. It had gray fur with white on its head, and would look in at doors and windows / Report from Royal Canadian Mounted Police at Norway House, quot. STAAU p. 247.

1976 / Cape Fear River area, Chatham County, NC / Numerous / 7-ft ape-like creature with black hair, "a slumping gait," and a deathly scream seen in the area; also 3-toed, 18-in footprints found / The same report was carried in several newspapers, e.g. *The Denton Record-Chronicle* 17 Sept. 1976, Chicago *Sunday Sun-Times* 19 Sept. 1976, Newport News, VA, *Daily Press* 14 Sept. 1976, San Antonio, TX, *Light* 17 Sept. 1976 (repr. *Anomaly Research Bulletin* 3 p. 8), Chapel Hill, NC, *Regional News* 14 Sept. 1976 (repr. *INFO Journal* vol. V no. 4 p. 14); see also STAAU p. 219.

1976 / Central Cascades, OR / Youth (17) / On forest road with dog, saw Bigfoot in brush. Had long, heavily built legs, black hair, and walked with swinging arms / BFN 23 p. 1.

1976 / Tanner Creek, N OR / Young couple / Bigfoot seen crossing creek / BFN 21 p. 1.

1976 / Nr Claysville, PA / Man / While hunting, saw huge figure moving in shadows of wood. It was 7-7½-ft tall. On calling out, it stopped and then slipped away into the fog / Ron Anjard, "Bigfoot in Western Pennsylvania?", *Fate* vol. 30 no. 12 p. 71.

1976 / Port Angeles area, WA / Logging truck driver / Almost ran Bigfoot down as it stood in road when he drove load of logs down mountain road / BFN 26 p. 1.

17 Jan. 1977 / Natchez, MS / Several / "Almost human," huge, hairy, creature over 6 ft tall growled at dog. Walked with a limp and appeared curious. Large footprints and other traces found / Reported widely, including *The States-Item* 19 Jan. 1977, *Arkansas Gazette* 20 Jan. 1977, Natchez, MS, *Democrat* 20 Jan. 1977, all noted *Anomaly Research Bulletin* 5 p. 14; Jackson, MS, *Daily News* 19 Jan. 1977, noted *INFO Journal* vol. V no. 6 p. 15.

23 Jan. 1977 / Blewett Pass nr Ingalic Creek, WA / David Kernoul & Dean DeWees or DeWess / Saw and shot at Bigfoot by chicken pen / Wenatchee, WA, *World* 26 Jan. 1977, quot. *Fate* vol. 30 no. 6 p. 32; Yakima, WA, *Republic* 25 Jan. 1977, noted *Anomaly Research Bulletin* 5 p. 14.

Jan. 1977 / Simpson County, KY / Policeman / Saw Bigfoot crossing road at night; other sightings in area / STAAU p. 223.

Early Feb. 1977 / Delray Beach, FL / Golf course superintendent / 7-ft "skunk ape" with shaggy black hair seen drinking from lake (see ch. 8) / FL, *The Palm Beach Post News* 11 Feb. 1977.

Early Feb. 1977 / Delray Beach, FL / Security guard / Saw gorilla-like creature near golf course / FL, *The Palm Beach Post News* 11 Feb. 1977.

Feb. 1977 / Moon Lake, FL / Several / Three Bigfeet, one 10 ft tall, seen in house yard; other sightings in same area / Report from Duane & Ramona Hibner, noted STAAU p. 280.

Early March 1977 / West-central OR / Housewife / Saw Bigfoot under 8 ft tall and about 4 ft wide, standing near barn at twilight. Walked away after several minutes; footprint found / Report from Bill Espesito, noted BFN 30 p. 1.

Early March 1977 / Alliance, OH / Two young men / Driving at night, saw 7-8-ft Bigfoot with big, bright yellow eyes, cross road into woods. Went to look for it, and one of them saw it again, running fast across road; heard noises and found tracks / Mark W. Swift & Jim Rastetter, "A Report on Recent Bigfoot Type Creatures Seen in North-eastern Ohio," *Bigfoot* (PRL) p. 24.

8 March 1977 / Nelson Township, OH / Mrs. Barbara Pistilli & two teenagers / 8-ft Bigfoot walked towards house; but fled after being shot at / Revenna *Record Courier* 10 March 1977, noted STAAU p. 210; Mark W. Swift & Jim Rastetter, "A Report on Recent Bigfoot Type Creatures Seen in North-eastern Ohio," *Bigfoot* (PRL) p. 25.

16 March 1977 / Nr Eatonville, WA / Soldier / While hiking, saw Bigfoot and was later treated for shock / Widely reported in newspapers, and mentioned BFN 31 p. 1, BSIS vol. 1 no. 1, *INFO Journal* vol. VI no. 1*, Res Bureaux Bulletin* 17 p. 2.

17 March 1977 / Alliance, OH / Woman / Van driver saw 7-8-ft Bigfoot step over fence and approach her, unafraid of headlights / Int. Swift & Rastetter, noted Mark W. Swift & Jim Rastetter, "A Report on Recent Bigfoot Type Creatures Seen in North-eastern Ohio," *Bigfoot* (PRL) p. 25.

28 March 1977 / Nr Spuzzum, BC / Richard Mitchell / Saw Bigfoot, 7½ ft tall with peculiar gait, by side of road / Vancouver, BC, *Sun* 2 April 1977, noted *Res Bureaux Bulletin* 17 p. 2.

12 April 1977 / Rising Sun, IN / Tom & Connie Courter / 12-ft Bigfoot with black hair and red eyes bumped against their car and dented it, near their trailer home / Report by Ron Schaffner in *Unusual News* Oct. 1977 p. 4; Cincinnati, OH, *Post* 20 April 1977, noted STAAU p. 208; COTOE p. 209.

13 April 1977 / Rising Sun, IN / Tom & Connie Courter / Bigfoot seen on hill late at night; Tom Courter fired 16 shots at it but no trace could later be found / Report by Ron Schaffner in *Unusual News* Oct. 1977 p. 4; Cincinnati, OH, *Post* 20 April 1977, noted STAAU p. 208; COTOE p. 209.

April 1977 / Moon Lake, FL / Three men in truck / Saw 9-ft black Bigfoot by full moon; it leapt road in one try / Report from Duane & Ramona Hibner, noted STAAU p. 280.

Spring 1977 / Nr Gerber, MT / Three men / Chased 6½-ft Bigfoot covered with black hair 4 in long. It turned to face them so they drove off / STAAU p. 300.

7 May 1977 / Hollis, NH / Gerald St. Louis & two sons Alan (14) & James (12) / At night, Bigfoot shook truck where family were sleeping (see ch. 8) / Reported widely, including Boston *Herald American* 16 May 1977 (noted *Res Bureaux Bulletin* 18 p. 6 & quot. STAAU p. 230) & 17 May 1977; Rutland, VT, *Herald* 16 May 1977 (noted *INFO Journal* vol. VI no. 2 p. 6).

12 & 13 May 1977 / Wantage Township, NJ / Sites family / Bigfoot visited farm and killed rabbits; returned and was shot at by family (see ch. 8) / S.N. Mayne, "The Wantage Event," *Pursuit* vol. 10 no. 4 pp. 124-7; Robert E. Jones, "The Report of a Recent Bigfoot Incident in Wantage Township, New Jersey, with Autopsy Report of Mutilated Rabbits," *Vestigia Newsletter* 3 pp. 1-2.

18 May 1977 / Pacific, MO / Motorist / Saw 8-9-ft Bigfoot cross road / Union, MO, *Franklin County Tribune* 25 May 1977, noted STAAU p. 195.

18 May 1977 / Nr Eaton, OH / Two boys (13) / Chased by Bigfoot (see ch. 8) / Witnesses int. Ron Schaffner & Betty Parks, see Ron Schaffner, "A Report on Ohio Anthropoids and Other Strange Creatures," *Bigfoot* (PRL) pp. 43-4.

21 May 1977 / Nr Eaton, OH / - / More Bigfoot sightings / Eaton, OH, *Register Herald* 25 May 1977.

23 May 1977 / Nr LaBelle, FL / Four people / As they walked from broken-down van, saw 7-8-ft, black "skunk ape" cross road / Belle Glade, FL, *Herald* 26 May 1977, noted STAAU p. 280.

May 1977 / Nobleton, FL / Two men / Saw Bigfoot fighting with dogs / Report from Duane & Ramona Hibner, noted STAAU p. 280.

May 1977 / German Township, PA / Couple & three children / Saw back of 6-ft Bigfoot, with shaggy reddish-brown hair, walking slumped over, beside rural road / Uniontown, PA, *Herald* 20 May 1977, noted STAAU p. 264.

May 1977 / Pittsylvania County, VA / Woman / Saw 7-ft Bigfoot / Danville, VA, *Bee* 17 May 1977, noted STAAU p. 225.

4 June 1977 / Ruthven, Ont. / Boy (15) / Saw tall black upright creature in foliage / Report from Wayne King, noted STAAU p. 251.

11 June 1977 / U.S. 27 in Clare County, MI / Abby Matthews & Nicholas A. Zurawic / Saw three creatures around 7 ft tall, 300-500-lb weight, run across road with big strides / Report by Wayne King of Michigan Bigfoot Information Center following his investigation.

14 June 1977 / Silver City, MT / Two campers / Saw three Bigfeet, 10 ft tall / BSIS vol. 1 no. 5, noted *Anomaly Research Bulletin* 8 p. 12.

14 & 15 June 1977 / Uniontown, PA / Student (20) / Saw Bigfoot near his home / *Anomaly Research Bulletin* 8 p. 12, & BSIS vol. 1 no. 5.

27 June 1977 / Nr Theresa, Jefferson County, NY / Two railway workers / Saw Bigfoot watching them; later found large manlike tracks / BAOTC p. 162; Watertown, NY, *Daily Times* 2 Aug. 1977, noted STAAU p. 235.

28 June 1977 / Nr Theresa, Jefferson County, NY / Two railway workers / Saw Bigfoot watching them; later found large manlike tracks. Different location from their 27 June sighting / BAOTC p. 162; Watertown, NY, *Daily Times* 2 Aug. 1977, noted STAAU p. 235.

June 1977 / Nr Barryton, MI / Robert Kurtz & brother-in-law / Glowing eyes seen at night; men investigated and saw Bigfoot which walked into forest / Report by Wayne King of The Michigan Bigfoot Information Center following his investigation.

6 July 1977 / Abilene Boys' Ranch nr Hawley, TX / Tom Roberts (14), Larry Suggs (15), Renee McFarland / The "Hawley Him" threw rocks at the witnesses / Abilene, TX, *Morning Reporter-News* 7 July 1977, noted BAOTC pp. 140-1 & STAAU p. 188.

7 July 1977 / Little Falls, WA / Three campers / Saw Bigfoot-type creature / BSIS vol. 1 no. 6.

10 July 1977 / Nr Elizabeth Lake, UT / Mr. & Mrs. Robert Melka, Sgt. & Mrs. Fred Rosenberg / Watched three Bigfeet for 10 mins as two played together in meadow or ran around at high speed / Bountiful, UT, *Davis County Clipper* 2 Sept. 1977, quot. STAAU p. 175.

18 July 1977 / Salina, KS / Woman / Gorilla-like creature left 3-toed prints in witness's back yard / Salina, KS, *Journal* 20 July 1977, Kansas City *Star* 21 July 1977, noted *Anomaly Research Bulletin* 8 p. 12.

21 July 1977 / Key Largo, FL / Two men / Saw Bigfoot in field / BSIS vol. 1 no. 6.

July 1977 / Key Largo, FL / Charlie Stoeckman, Charlie Stoeckman Jr. (13), Sawn Tubbs / Stoeckman saw "skunk ape" three times / Marathon, FL, *Florida Keys Keynoter* 28 July 1977, quot. STAAU pp. 280-1; see also BAOTC pp. 168-9.

July 1977 / Harford County, MD / Woman & daughter / Saw Bigfoot sitting on ground leaning against picnic table in their garden; walked into woods when they screamed / York, PA, *Daily Record* 23 Feb. 1978, repr. *INFO Journal* vol. VI no. 6 p. 7.

July 1977 / Shaler, PA / John Tiskus / Saw Bigfoot about 7½ ft tall drinking water from his swimming pool at 2 am / Pittsburgh, PA, *North Hills News Record* 18 July 1977, noted STAAU p. 264.

9 Aug. 1977 / Green Grass, SD / Three policemen / At 3 am saw by spotlight 6-7-ft hairy ape-like creature moving in creek bottom / *Eagle Butte News* 18 Aug. 1977, noted Hall (1) p. 65.

9 Aug. 1977 / On County Road 1100N nr Elwood, IN / Mrs. Melinda Chestnut / Driving alone at 2 am, saw 8-10-ft Bigfoot walking upright. Ran into woods when she directed headlights at it / Anderson, IN, *Herald* 11 Aug. 1977, noted STAAU p. 208; Alexandria, IN, *Times-Tribune* 17 Aug. 1977, noted BAOTC p. 119.

Mid Aug. 1977 / Nr Grand River, nr Little Eagle, SD / Todd Alexander (12), Chad Alexander (9) / Saw "long hairy legs" in bushes / Mobridge, SD, *Tribune*, 3 Nov. 1977, noted Hall (1) p. 65.

Mid Aug. 1977 / Along Grand River at Little Eagle, SD / Craig Two Hearts (16) / Saw Bigfoot / Richard Boeth & Elaine Sciolino, "Bigfoot is Back," *Newsweek* 31 Oct. 1977, noted Hall (1) p. 65.

20 Aug. 1977 / Belt Creek Canyon, MT / Staff Sergeant Fred Wilson & two others / At 2 am saw 15½-ft Bigfoot with tan hair and no neck standing upright in bushes. Fired at it, but drove off when it ran towards them / Great Falls, MT, *Tribune* 20 Aug. 1977, noted STAAU pp. 300-1.

22 Aug. 1977 / Highway 274 nr Trinidad, TX / Three women / Saw Bigfoot on road / A Corsicana newspaper, date unknown, noted STAAU p. 188.

27 Aug. 1977 / Nr Clear Lake, WA / Vernita Frazier (11) / On picnic with family, saw Bigfoot 10 ft away and screamed. It growled and ran into brush / BAOTC p. 51; BSIS vol. 1 no. 6.

Late Aug. 1977 / Cuberant Basin, nr North Ogden, UT / Eight hikers — Jay Barker, Larry Beeson, sons, & teenage friends / Saw *c.* 10-ft, white-haired Bigfoot which walked away; found partly eaten rabbit nearby / *INFO Journal* vol. VI no. 4; BAOTC p. 89; BSIS vol. 1 nos 6 & 7; Ogden, UT, *Standard-Examiner* 25 Aug. 1977, noted STAAU p. 175.

30 Aug. 1977 / Route 258, nr West River, MD / Ronald Jones / Saw Bigfoot on road and chased it into field (see ch. 8) / Annapolis, MD, *Evening Capital* 1 Sept. 1977, noted STAAU p. 227.

Aug. 1977 / Jackson, MS / Donald Bracey / Bigfoot limped across road in front of car / Jackson, MS, *News* 23 Dec. 1977, repr. BSIS vol. 2 no. 2 p. 3.

Aug. 1977 / Stilwell, OK / Brian Jones, two Ritchie boys / Saw red eyes looking in at window; outside Jones met foul-smelling, 8-ft Bigfoot which lifted him off the ground. Dropped him and ran off when others appeared. They shot at Bigfoot, which threw rocks at them. There had been frequent sightings in previous 3 years / Witnesses int. Bigfoot Research Society members, see their *Bigfoot Bulletin* 2, 3, 4, 6.

Summer 1977 / Nr East Baton Rouge, LA / Chris Denaro / Saw 9 ft Bigfoot while parked in woods with girlfriend / STAAU pp. 192-3.

Summer 1977 / Around Spearfish, SD / Betty Johnson & daughters Brenda, Bonnie, & Becky / Saw two Bigfeet in cornfield eating corn, one 7-8 ft tall and black, the other smaller with brownish-red body and black face; whistled / Letter to editor of Eagle Butte, SD, *News* 20 Oct. 1977 from Pauline Johnson, noted Hall (1) p. 65.

Summer 1977 / Red Scaffold, SD / Young girl / While at home alone, was frightened by "foul-smelling, hairy creature" / Eagle Butte, SD, *News* 18 Aug. 1977, noted Hall (1) p. 65.

2 Sept. 1977 / Highway 31 nr Corsicana, TX / Man / Saw 7-ft Bigfoot on road / A Corsicana newspaper, date unknown, noted STAAU p. 188.

5 Sept. 1977 / Caro, MI / Karl Traster (14) & Steven Traster (10) / While playing in yard, saw 8-9-ft smelly Bigfoot with long brown hair, breasts, big teeth, and long fingernails / Saginaw, MI, *News* 28 Nov. 1978, repr. BSIS vol. 3 no. 1 pp. 1-2.

5 Sept. 1977 / Caro, MI / Wayne W. King & friend, Charles J. Roose, Karl Traster (14) / At midnight visited site of Traster boys' sighting and saw long-armed, black Bigfoot with "large glowing eyes about the size of golf balls," about 10 ft tall; another, bent over, was close by / Saginaw, MI, *News* 28 Nov. 1978, repr. BSIS vol. 3 no. 1 p. 2.

9 Sept. 1977 / Barryton, MI / Robert & Becky Kurtz / Saw black Bigfoot crossing road / Report by Wayne King of The Michigan Bigfoot Information Center, following his investigation.

Mid Sept. 1977 / Nr Little Eagle, SD / Chris Howiatow & others / "Big ape" watched them from hillside as they checked cattle; then ran into brush as they approached / McLaughlin, SD, *Messenger* 20 Oct. 1977, noted Hall (1) p. 66; see also Bonnie Lake, "Bigfoot on the Buttes; The Invasion of Little Eagle," *UFO Report* vol. 5 no. 6 p. 28.

Mid Sept. 1977 / Nr Cannonball River, ND / Paul Monzelowsky & son / Chased 8-9-ft Bigfoot in pickup truck. It ran "as fast as a horse" and leapt across creek / Richard Boeth & Elaine Sciolino, "Bigfoot is Back," *Newsweek* 31 Oct. 1977, noted Hall (1) p. 66; see also Bonnie Lake, "Bigfoot on the Buttes; The Invasion of Little Eagle," *UFO Report* vol. 5 no. 6 p. 29.

27 Sept. 1977 / Highway 66 nr Ashland, OR / John C. Martin / Saw 7-8-ft Bigfoot run across road at night / *INFO Journal* vol. VI no. 4 p. 15; BFN 36 p. 1.

28 Sept. 1977 / E of Little Eagle, SD / Nancy Chasing Hawk, Esther Thunder-shield, Myron Fast Horse / After hearing howling outside, turned on truck lights and saw tall, hairy animal with green eyes run into brush / Worthington, MN, *Globe* 4 Oct. 1977 & Pierre, SD, *Capital Journal* 6 Oct. 1977, noted Hall (1) p. 66.

Sept. 1977 / Mount White Chuck, WA / Mrs. Mildred Quinn / Awoke from sleep to see black figure with long arms and big shoulders leaning against rock, watching her. Closed her eyes and prayed; when she opened them it had gone / Int. Jeanne Roush, noted BFN 42 p. 1; see also *INFO Journal* vol. VI no. 6 p. 15 mentioning Portland, OR, *Journal* 12 Jan. 1978, & BSIS vol. 2 no. 2 p. 2.

Sept. 1977 / Little Eagle, SD / LeMar Chasing Hawk / Saw 9-ft Bigfoot in bushes; ran home / Bismarck, ND, *Tribune* 26 Nov. 1977, noted Hall (1) p. 71; see also Bonnie Lake, "Bigfoot on the Buttes; The Invasion of Little Eagle," *UFO Report* vol. 5 no. 6 p. 28.

1 or 2 Oct. 1977 / Nr Bend, OR / Gary Benson (25) & Ronald Kershey (25) / Shot 4 times at 7-ft, black-haired creature with silver hair at shoulders and monkey face which, they claimed, attacked them / Unnamed newspaper report repr. BFN 39 p. 1; also briefly noted *INFO Journal* vol. VI no. 4 p. 15.

1 or 3 Oct. 1977 / Apoka, FL / Security officer / Reportedly attacked and scratched by 10-ft Bigfoot which tried to break down door / Apoka, FL, *Chief* 7 Oct. 1977; BSIS vol. 1 no. 8.

c. 2 Oct. 1977 / Belleview, FL / 22-yr-old welder / While hitchhiking, attacked by black, smelly "skunk ape" 6-ft tall / Orlando, FL, *Sentinel* 5 Oct. 1977.

c. 6 Oct. 1977 / N of Little Eagle, SD / Phoebe Little Dog / Saw Bigfoot / Pierre, SD, *Capital Journal* 17 Oct. 1977, noted Hall (1) p. 66.

11 Oct. 1977 / Ocala National Forest, FL / Revd S. L. Whatley / Baptist minister saw Bigfoot while cutting wood (see ch. 8) / Ocala, FL, *Star-Banner* 16 Nov. 1977, repr. BSIS vol. 2 no. 1 p. 2; San Francisco *Chronicle* 15 Nov. 1977, repr. BSIS vol. 1 no. 9 p. 4.

13 Oct. 1977 / SE of Little Eagle, SD / Cecilia Thundershield, Dan Uses Arrow, Albert Dog / First two witnesses saw Bigfoot come from woods, and they fetched Dog who saw it re-enter woods. It had long arms almost to knees and walked slouched over / Sioux Falls, SD, *Argus-Leader* 15 Oct. 1977 & McLaughlin, SD, *Messenger* 20 Oct. 1977, noted Hall (1) pp. 66-7; see also Bonnie Lake, "Bigfoot on the Buttes; The Invasion of Little Eagle," *UFO Report* vol. 5 no. 6 p. 31.

13 Oct. 1977 / N of Little Eagle, SD / Phoebe Little Dog / Saw Bigfoot in cattle pasture, same place as her *c.* 6 Oct. sighting / Pierre, SD, *Capital Journal* 17 Oct. 1977, noted Hall (1) p. 67; see also Bonnie Lake, "Bigfoot on the Buttes; The Invasion of Little Eagle," *UFO Report* vol. 5 no. 6 p. 31.

Mid-Oct. 1977 / Annapolis, MD / Debbie Carpenter (13), Kevin Epley (5) / Black-haired, black-eyed, 7-ft Bigfoot seen sitting on log in woods / Annapolis, MD, *Evening Capital,* 19 Oct. 1977.

22 Oct. 1977 / Along the Grand River, Corson County, SD / Four men on horseback / Saw Bigfoot basking in sun; it ran away and they could not find it / Timber Lake, SD, *Topic* 27 Oct. 1977 & 10 Nov. 1977, noted Hall (1) p. 67.

25 Oct. 1977 / Nr Grand River Bridge, Little Eagle, SD / Alwin Ducheneaux / Saw Bigfoot in his headlights around midnight / Bonnie Lake, "Bigfoot on the Buttes; The Invasion of Little Eagle," *UFO Report* vol. 5 no. 6 p. 31.

29 Oct. 1977 / Elkhorn Buttes, NE of Little Eagle, SD / Verdell Veo (police officer), Jeff Veo (15), another teenage son, & officers Bobby Gates & Selvin Arlen / Saw Bigfoot by moonlight and men followed it. Pursuit ended as they had no weapons against Bigfeet 8-9 ft tall (see ch. 8) / Timber Lake, SD, *Topic* 3 Nov. 1977, & Worthington, MN, *Globe* 8 Nov. 1977, noted Hall (1) p. 67; see also Bonnie Lake, "Bigfoot on the Buttes; The Invasion of Little Eagle," *UFO Report* vol. 5 no. 6 p. 69.

Late Oct. 1977 / Little Eagle, SD / Irene Village Center / Saw Bigfoot in marshy brush / Bonnie Lake, "Bigfoot on the Buttes; The Invasion of Little Eagle," *UFO Report* vol. 5 no. 6 p. 72.

Autumn 1977 / Nr La Plant, SD / Melvin Garreaux / Saw Bigfoot; tracks found / McLaughlin, SD, *Messenger* 6 Oct. 1977, noted Hall (1) p. 69.

Autumn 1977 / Little Eagle, SD / Hanna Shooting Bear / At night, saw Bigfoot near a mobile home (see ch. 8) / Mobridge, SD, *Tribune* 3 Nov. 1977, noted Hall (1) pp. 69-71; see also BAOTC p. 93.

Autumn 1977 / Standing Rock Reservation, SD / Mr. & Mrs. Walter Chasing Hawk / While driving at night, saw green eyes in lights. Thinking it was a deer, Chasing Hawk got out with rifle, but saw 8-ft Bigfoot. Police found nothing when they searched / Worthington, MN, *Globe* 8 Nov. 1977, noted Hall (1) p. 71.

Autumn 1977 / Grand River, Little Eagle, SD / Mrs. Angus Long Elk / Saw Bigfoot by river / Bismarck, ND, *Tribune* 26 Nov. 1977, noted Hall (1) p. 71.

Oct. or Nov. 1977 / Nr Belville, LA / Leonce Boudreaux / Saw Bigfoot in woods / Roseburg, OR, *News-Review* 5 June 1978, repr. FN June 1978 p. 19; int. Bigfoot Research Society, see their *Bigfoot Bulletin* 10.

5 Nov. 1977 / Nr Little Eagle, SD / Verdell Veo (police officer), Gary Alexander, & others / Surrounded Bigfoot, but it escaped after chase of several hours (see ch. 8) / Timber Lake, SD, *Topic* 10 Nov. 1977, noted Hall (1) p. 67; see also Bonnie Lake "Bigfoot on the Buttes; The Invasion of Little Eagle," *UFO Report* vol. 5 no. 6 p. 71.

13 Nov. 1977 / N of Little Eagle, SD / Male driver / Saw Bigfoot on road and drove into ditch / Timber Lake, SD, *Topic* 10 Nov. 1977, noted Hall (1) p. 69.

Mid Nov. 1977 / Ocala National Forest, FL / Hunter / Fired 6 times at 8-ft "ape-like" creature weighing approx 800 lbs / Ocala, FL, *Star-Banner* 19 Nov. 1977, noted *INFO Journal* vol. VI no. 6 p. 15.

23 Nov. 1977 / Little Eagle, SD / About 12 women & children / Held campfire party to lure Bigfoot; two seen crouching in brush / Bismarck, ND, *Tribune* 26 Nov. 1977, noted Hall (1) p. 69.

3 Dec. 1977 / Elkhorn Buttes, NE of Little Eagle, SD / Gary Alexander, Lowell Olson, Keith Olson / Watched two Bigfeet for 3 mins; one was 8-8½ ft tall and dark, the other a foot shorter / Timber Lake, SD, *Topic* 15 Dec. 1977, noted Hall (1) p. 69.

5 Dec. 1977 / Elkhorn Buttes, NE of Little Eagle, SD / Verdell Veo (police officer) / Saw 2 Bigfeet / Timber Lake, SD, *Topic* 15 Dec. 1977, noted Hall (1) p. 69.

Mid Dec. 1977 / Mich Coal Mine near Oskaloosa, IA / Theresa McGee / 8-10-ft Bigfoot with "bristly-like fur" and arms held out jumped from shadow of tree when witness went to sweep snow / Oskaloosa, IA, *Herald* 20 Dec. 1977, repr. BSIS vol. 2 no. 2 p. 3.

Late Dec. 1977 / Maddox Road area, Jackson, MS / Donald Bracey / 6-ft Bigfoot, eating something, seen by road 5:30 pm / Jackson, MS, *News* 23 Dec. 1977, repr. BSIS vol. 2 no. 2 p. 3.

Late Dec. 1977 / Maddox Road area, Jackson, MS / Robert Trussel / Bigfoot crossed road in front of car, and witness had to swerve. This was at 10 pm, same place and date as previous sighting / Jackson, MS, *News* 23 Dec. 1977, repr. BSIS vol. 2 no. 2 p. 3.

Early Winter 1977 / Williams, IN / William Tharp Jr. & sister Jackie / Bigfoot grabbed Jackie by the arm, but let go when she screamed; 13-in footprints found / Report from JG, noted *Bigfoot Co-op* Feb. 1981 p. 2.

Winter 1977 / NW of Little Eagle, SD / Gary Alexander & others / Saw two Bigfeet while snowmobiling; they looked but did not run / Bismarck, ND, *Tribune* 7 Jan. 1978, noted Hall (1) p. 71.

Early Jan. 1978 / Nr Riceville, LA / Hunter / Saw tall, black Bigfoot with red eyes 3 times in same area. Once it leapt 6-ft fence after growling at him / Crowley, LA, *Post-Signal* 7 Jan. 1978, repr. *INFO Journal* vol. VI no. 6 p. 14.

Early Jan. 1978 / Newberg, OR / - / Same witness saw Bigfoot on 2 nights. It was 6 ft tall, 350-450 lbs, had a flat face and square teeth, and was covered with 4-in hair / McMinnville, OR, *News-Register* 18 Jan. 1978, noted *INFO Journal* vol. VI no. 6 p. 14.

10 Jan. 1978 / Fawn Grove, MD / Man / Saw 10-ft Bigfoot near high school. Its eyes seemed to shine white in the night, and it smelled / York, PA, *Daily Record* 23 Feb. 1978, repr. *INFO Journal* vol. VI no. 6 p. 7.

16 Jan. 1978 / Nr Crowley, LA / Boy / Saw "big ape" eating minnows from stream. Had big shoulders, and was hair-covered except for buttocks and soles of feet. Hopped away on one leg when witness threw stones at it / Lafayette, LA, *Advertiser* 17 Jan. 1978, noted *INFO Journal* vol. VI no. 6 p. 14.

Jan. 1978 / Nr Iliamna & Newhalen, AK / - / Several sightings in the area / Reports in *The Anchorage News* Jan. 1978, noted BAOTC pp. 69-70.

c. 25 Feb. 1978 / Pella Bridge nr Harvey, IA / Boy (10 or 11) / Saw Bigfoot on road near bridge; it looked at him, then went into woods / Des Moines, IA, *Sunday Register* 12 Nov. 1978, repr. FN Jan. 1979 p. 18.

2 March 1978 / Nr Peach Bottom Atomic Power Plant, nr Delta, PA / Norval Thomas / Driver saw Bigfoot over 7 ft tall in truck headlights; large prints found later and squealing noise heard / York, PA, *Record* 7 March 1978, repr. BSIS vol. 2 no. 4 p. 2 & *INFO Journal* vol. VI no. 6 p. 8.

Early March 1978 / Spring Grove, PA / Woman motorist / Saw Bigfoot on the road; police found tracks in snow / York, PA, *Dispatch* 9 March 1978, repr. BSIS vol. 2 no. 5 p. 3.

6 March 1978 / East Brewton, AL / Ruth Mary Gibson, Luke McDaniel, Johnny Gibson (19), Lt Doug McCurdy / Red-eyed Bigfoot visited rural house at night (see ch. 8) / Mobile, AL, *Press Register* 12 March 1978, repr. BSIS vol. 2 no. 6 p. 5; Fort Walton, Beach, FL, *Playground News* 26 Nov. 1978, repr. BSIS vol. 3 no. 1 p. 11.

Late March 1978 / Jay pipeline between Flomaton & Jay, AL / 5 truckloads of men / Saw Bigfoot and ran to fetch guns, but it could not be found later / Fort Walton, Beach, FL, *Playground News* 26 Nov. 1978, repr. BSIS vol. 3 no. 1 p. 11.

Late March 1978 / Conecuh River, AL / Man / Saw Bigfoot standing in river picking something out of water / Fort Walton, Beach, FL, *Playground News* 26 Nov. 1978, repr. BSIS vol. 3 no. 1 p. 11.

30 April 1978 / Rayner Park, Mason, MI / Three men / 8-ft black Bigfoot with green shining eyes seen in car headlights / Lansing, MI, *State Journal* 2 May 1978, repr. BSIS vol. 2 no. 6 p. 5.

30 April 1978 / Logy Creek, WA / Yakima Indian / Frightened by close Bigfoot sighting while fishing / Yakima, WA, *Valley Sun* 8 June 1978, repr. FN July 1978 p. 16.

Late April or early May 1978 / Nr Bel Air, MD / Businessman & son / Saw Bigfoot peering in at them through picture window. Its rusty-colored hair was matted with leaves and it had long chipped teeth / York, PA, *Dispatch* 23 May 1978, repr. BSIS vol. 2 no. 7 p. 3.

April 1978 / Granite, MD / Farmer / Saw "bear" walking upright across field followed by 2 smaller creatures on all fours / S. Stover, "Does Maryland Have a Sasquatch?", *INFO Journal* vol. VII no. 6 p. 5.

April 1978 / North Branch of Patapsco River, MD / Four young boys / While camping saw 7-ft Bigfoot / S. Stover, "Does Maryland Have a Sasquatch?", *INFO Journal* vol. VII no. 6 p. 5.

31 May 1978 / Mason, MI / James Jenks / Watched Bigfoot enter shed / Lansing, MI, *State Journal* 2 July 1978, repr. FN Aug. 1978 p. 16.

Early June 1978 / Central Cascades, OR / Young couple / Saw Bigfoot (possibly 2) walking fast towards forest / BFN 44 p. 1.

4 June 1978 / Nr Krotz Springs, LA / Leonce & Mrs. Boudreaux / Saw 7-8-ft Bigfoot with long, reddish-brown hair walking upright; it made nightly visits to garbage dump / Chattanooga, TN, *News-Free Press* 5 June 1978, repr. *INFO Journal* vol. VII no. 1 p. 1; New Orleans, LA, *Times-Picayune* 7 June 1978, repr. BSIS vol. 2 no. 7 p. 2; int. Bigfoot Research Society, see their *Bigfoot Bulletin* 10.

19 June 1978 / North Tram Road, Vidor, TX / Bobby & Beckie Bussinger / Many sightings around their house, so witnesses moved out (see ch. 8) / Orange, TX, *Leader* 20 June 1978, repr. FN July 1978 p. 17; Orange, TX, *Leader* 21 June 1978, repr. FN Aug. 1978 p. 17; see also *APRO Bulletin* vol. 27 no. 4 p. 4.

26 June 1978 / South Crossett, AR / Mike Lofton (l0) / Saw and shot at 7½-ft Bigfoot (see ch. 8) / Crossett, AR, *News Observer* 29 June 1978, repr. FN July 1978, p. 18.

June 1978 / Ohio 95 nr Richland County Line, OH / Male motorist / Had accident when frightened by seeing Bigfoot on the road / Mt Vernon, OH, *News* 18 July 1978, repr. BSIS vol. 2 no. 9 p. 2.

8, 10, & 12 July 1978 / Butler, OH / Kline family & Ken O'Neil (15) / 3 separate sightings of "Bighead" (see ch. 8) / Report No. 008 by Para-Hominoid Research of OUFOIL; see also *UFO Report* Jan. 1979 pp. 65-6, & Mansfield, OH, *News Journal* 11 July 1978, repr. FN July 1978 p. 19.

13 July 1978 / M-36, Ingham County, MI / Francis Jones & Michael Hacksworth / Saw Bigfoot cross road in early morning / Lansing, MI, *State Journal* 18 Aug. 1978, repr. BSIS vol. 2 no. 10 p. 2.

27 July 1978 / Ottosen, IA / Donette Henkins (9) / Saw "short, hairy, apelike animal with fangs and deep-set eyes" which stood in shadows a few inches away and growled / Omaha, NE, *World-Herald* 2 Aug. 1978, Algona, IA, *Algona Upper Des Moines* 3 Aug. 1978, Algona, IA, *Algona Kossuth County Advance* 7 Aug. 1978, Humboldt, IA, *Independent* 5 Aug. 1978, all noted Hall (2) p. 4.

27 July 1978 / Ottosen, IA / Mrs. Jan Henkins & two others / After Donette's sighting, saw similar creature between 2 buildings while walking downtown / Algona, IA, *Algona Upper Des Moines* 3 Aug. 1978 & Humboldt, IA, *Independent* 5 Aug. 1978, noted Hall (2) p. 4.

30 July 1978 / Ottosen, IA / Dawn Henkins (11), Mrs. Henkins, & neighbor / Apelike creature with wide forehead walked from between buildings on Main Street at night / Omaha, NE, *World-Herald* 2 Aug. 1978 & Algona, IA, *Algona Kossuth County Advance* 7 Aug. 1978, noted Hall (2) p. 4.

31 July 1978 / Ottosen, IA / Three or four boys aged 10-12 / Saw Bigfoot in shed, and again later. It did not attempt to attack (see ch. 8) / Omaha, NE, *World Herald* 2 Aug. 1978, Fort Dodge, IA, *Messenger* 1 & 3 Aug. 1978, Humboldt, IA, *Independent* 5 Aug. 1978, Algona, IA, *Algona Upper Des Moines* 3 Aug. 1978, noted Hall (2) pp. 4-5.

31 July 1978 / Fowlerville, MI / Boy (4) / Told mother he had seen a "gorilla" in front yard. Mother heard thud and scream and saw part of a possible Bigfoot on other occasions / Lansing, MI, *State Journal* 18 Aug. 1978, repr. BSIS vol. 2 no. 10 p. 2.

6 Aug. 1978 / Blue Hole Creek nr Athens, AL / David Conley (17), Stanley Eastep (16), Ronnie Loonie (15) / While fishing at night saw Bigfoot in car lights / Athens, AL, *News Courier* 8 Aug. 1978, repr. FN Oct. 1978 p. 16; see also Culman, AL, *Times* 10 Aug. 1978, repr. BSIS vol. 2 no. 9 p. 5, & *People* 7 Jan. 1979.

14 Aug. 1978 / Oceana, WV / Bill Pruitt / Policeman fired at Bigfoot (see ch. 8) / Charleston, WV, *Gazette* 15 Aug. 1978, repr. BSIS vol. 2 no. 9 p. 2.

16 Aug. 1978 / Fowlerville, MI / Gary Browning / Shot at Bigfoot which ran out of underbrush / Lansing, MI, *State Journal* 18 Aug. 1978, repr. BSIS vol. 2 no. 10 p. 2.

c. 19 Aug. 1978 / South Sulphur, nr Commerce, TX / Wayne Matlock / In daylight, Bigfoot crossed road ahead of witness and went across pasture toward river / Mark Jones & Teresa Ann Smith, "Has Bigfoot Moved to Texas?", *Fate* vol. 32 no. 7 p. 35.

Mid Aug. 1978 / South Sulphur, nr Commerce, TX / Harvey Garrison / Driving at night, saw 7½-ft Bigfoot cross 42-ft road in 3 steps / Int. Dallas Bigfoot Research Society, noted Mark Jones & Teresa Ann Smith, "Has Bigfoot Moved to Texas?", *Fate* vol. 32 no. 7 p. 35.

Mid Aug. 1978 / South Sulphur, nr Commerce, TX / Wayne Matlock, Anthony Wilson, Ray Rutherford / 2 days after Garrison sighting, on same road, three boys saw Bigfoot around midnight / Mark Jones & Teresa Ann Smith, "Has Bigfoot Moved to Texas?", *Fate* vol. 32 no. 7 p. 35.

Mid Aug. 1978 / Nr Owensboro, KY / Several men / Cornered Bigfoot beside pond and shot it with pistol from 10 ft. It fled into woods, leaving no trace of blood / Keith Lawrence, "The Fairview Horror," *UFO Report* May 1979 p. 70.

21 Aug. 1978 / Nr Minerva, OH / Cayton family & six friends / Two large cats seen with Bigfoot near house at night. Other sightings in the area (see ch. 8) / Report No. 009 by Para-Hominoid Research of OUFOIL; see also Canton, OH, *Repository* 30 Aug. 1978, repr. BSIS vol. 2 no. 10 p. 4, & 2 brief newspaper reports repr. FN Sept. 1978 pp. 19 & 20.

24 Aug. 1978 / Concord Township, MI / Mindy Singletary / At night saw Bigfoot drinking from swimming pool / *UFO Report* Jan. 1979 p. 65.

28 Aug. 1978 / Concord Township, MI / Dennis M. Hoath / Saw black, 7½-ft (compared to height of green corn behind it) Bigfoot; non-human tracks found / *UFO Report* Jan. 1979 p. 65.

28 Aug. 1978 / Dean Bottoms nr Moulton, IA / Two students / Saw 7-8-ft Bigfoot on dirt road at night; next day 3-toed prints 14 in long found at the site / Des Moines, IA, *Sunday Register* 12 Nov. 1978, repr. FN Jan. 1979 p. 18.

29 Aug. 1978 / Benton, AR / Mrs. Mildred Wilton / Saw 5-ft dark Bigfoot rattling chain link fence late at night / Benton, AR, *Courier* 31 Aug. 1978, repr. FN Oct. 1978 p. 20.

Aug. 1978 / Nr Owensboro, KY / Larry Nelson, brother, & two friends / Fired 3 .45 bullets into Bigfoot's chest from 45 ft; it ran away into woods apparently unhurt / Keith Lawrence, "The Fairview Horror," *UFO Report* May 1979, p. 30.

11 Sept. 1978 / Ottosen, IA / Anna Dodrill & Elery Lynch / Red-eyed, black-faced Bigfoot stared in at kitchen window / Des Moines, IA, *Sunday Register* 24 Sept. 1978, repr. FN Nov. 1978 p. 18; Fort Dodge, IA, *Messenger* 14 Sept. 1978 & Algona, IA, *Algona Kossuth County Advance* 18 Sept. 1978, noted Hall (2) p. 6.

12 Sept. 1978 / Ottosen, IA / Robert Newell IV (18) / Watched tall, hairy, hunchback Bigfoot exploring farm buildings early in the morning / Des Moines, IA, *Sunday Register* 24 Sept. 1978, repr. FN Nov. 1978 p. 18; Algona, IA, *Algona Kossuth County Advance* 18 Sept. 1978 & Humboldt, IA, *Independent* 16 Sept. 1978, noted Hall (2) pp. 6-7.

25 Sept. 1978 / Southern Curry, OR / Barbara Megli / Investigating when chickens and horses were disturbed, saw Bigfoot standing in a clearing / Brookings, OR, *Brookings-Harbor Pilot* 28 Sept. 1978, repr. FN Nov. 1978 p. 20.

27 Sept. 1978 / Farm S of Renwick, IA / Forty high-school students / Saw two Bigfeet in cornfield, one with red eyes and one with blue eyes / Des Moines, IA, *Register* 1 Oct. 1978, noted Hall (2) p. 7.

27 or 28 Sept. 1978 / NW of Renwick, IA / Mark Thompson (16) / Saw 7-ft, brownish-black-haired Bigfoot in soybean field. Moved away when witness flashed pickup lights and honked horn / Des Moines, IA, *Sunday Register* 1 Oct. 1978, repr. FN Dec. 1978 p. 18; Fort Dodge, IA, *Messenger* 29 & 30 Sept. 1978, noted Hall (2) p. 7.

28 Sept. 1978 / Kansas Turnpike, nr Bonner Springs, KS / Motorist / Saw 8-10-ft, auburn-haired Bigfoot in headlights at 2:30 am. Braked to avoid it, and it was lost in shadows / Topeka, KS, *Capital-Journal* 30 Sept. 1978, repr. FN Dec. 1978 p. 16.

c. 10 Oct. 1978 / Nr Geraldton, Ont. / Randy Corcoran (18) / Hiker badly shaken after sighting of Bigfoot over 6 ft tall in woods / Montreal *Gazette* 23 & 25 Oct. 1978, noted *Res Bureaux Bulletin* 40 p. 8.

12 Oct. 1978 / Evart, MI / Catherine & Robert Cook / Massively built Bigfoot seen briefly as it walked into woods / Report by Wayne King of The Michigan Bigfoot Information Center following his investigation.

21 Oct. 1978 / Millington, MI / Rodney Gouine (19), George A. Proctor, Jr. (19), his father, & sister Tracy (18) / At 1:30 am saw Bigfoot walking across neighbor's lawn / Saginaw, MI, *News* 28 Nov. 1978, repr. BSIS vol. 3 no. 1 p. 1.

5 Nov. 1978 / Krotz Springs, LA / Jack Potter & girlfriend / While driving, saw reddish Bigfoot running fast, and heard growling / Eugene, OR, *Willamette Valley Observer* 22 Dec. 1978.

6 Nov. 1978 / Skamania County, WA / Jack Webb & four other hunters / Saw 7-8-ft Bigfoot, brownish-black, and with long arms and legs, standing near trees; it walked slowly into woods / Stevenson, WA, *Skamania County Pioneer* 17 Nov. 1978, repr. FN Dec. 1978 p. 19 & BSIS vol. 3 no. 1 p. 3.

19 Nov. 1978 / Evart, MI / Norman Lee Nowland & Chris A. Jirrard / While deer hunting, saw heavy Bigfoot about 7 ft tall walking into dense forest / Report by Wayne King of The Michigan Bigfoot Information Center following his investigation.

Nov. 1978 / Nr Margie, MN / Richard Johnson / Saw reddish Bigfoot in swamp / International Falls, MN, *Daily Journal* 13 July 1979, repr. FN Aug. 1979 p. 17.

2 Dec. 1978 / Lansing, MI / Morse Easterling / Saw 7-ft Bigfoot near his apple orchard; it disappeared quickly (see ch. 8) / Report by Wayne King of The Michigan Bigfoot Information Center following his investigation; Bay City, MI, *Times* 16 Feb. 1979, repr. FN April 1979 p. 19 & BSIS vol. 3 no. 3 p. 5.

13 Dec. 1978 / Barnes Road, Millington, MI / Mrs. Diane Meharg / Watched Bigfoot near trees from kitchen window for over 15 mins until it walked into trees. It had heavy arms and legs, no neck, and was dark in color / Millington, MI, *Herald* 2 Jan. 1979, repr. FN March 1979 p. 16.

16 Dec. 1978 / Kansas 126, Cherokee County, KS / Man / 6-ft, bad-smelling Bigfoot tried to run witness's car off road / Pittsburgh, KS, *Morning Sun* 17 Dec. 1978, repr. FN Jan. 1979 p. 16.

21 Dec. 1978 / Toluca, NC / Minnie Cook (88) / Saw "Knobby" outside her house. Tracks found and screams heard in the area of Carpenter's Knob, and other sightings reported / Robert L. Williams, "'Knobby', North Carolina's Bigfoot," *UFO Report* Sept. 1979, pp. 24-7; Durham, NC, *Morning Herald* 4 Jan. 1979, repr. FN Feb. 1979 p. 20; see also other newspaper reports in same issue of FN, & in FN March 1979 & BSIS vol. 3 no. 2.

Late Dec. 1978 / Casar, NC / Sammy Price / While working in backyard, heard high-pitched scream and saw 6-7-ft "tree" which started to walk / Robert L. Williams, "'Knobby', North Carolina's Bigfoot," *UFO Report* Sept. 1979, pp. 24-7.

Late Dec. 1978 / Casar, NC / Kay Price / Day after previous sighting, heard scream and saw "Knobby" eating soybean crop in field / Robert L. Williams, "'Knobby', North Carolina's Bigfoot," *UFO Report* Sept. 1979, pp. 24-7.

15 Jan. 1979 / Casar, NC / Mrs. Kay Price, Gaye (18) & Wanda Smith / Saw "Knobby" by road, Gaye went closer (see ch. 8) / Charlotte, NC, *News* 18 Jan. 1979, repr. FN Feb. 1979 p. 19; Robert L. Williams, "'Knobby', North Carolina's Bigfoot," *UFO Report* Sept. 1979, p. 26.

Jan. 1979 / Polacca, AZ / Hopi Indians / Several sightings around village / Phoenix, AZ, *Arizona Republic* 11 Feb. 1979, repr. FN Apr. 1979 p. 16.

Early March 1979 / Pennyrile Parkway, Christian County, KY / Motorists / Saw 7-8-ft hairy "apeman" on several evenings / Hopkinsville, KY, *Kentucky New Era* 3 Mar. 1979, repr. FN May 1979 p. 16; Madisonville, KY, *Messenger* 8 Mar. 1979, repr. FN May 1979 p. 18.

9-11 March 1979 / Flower Lake nr Tunica, MS / Mr. & Mrs. Tom Goff, Rodney Goff, & friend / After 2 visits by Bigfoot, family lay in wait and shot at it (see ch. 8) / Tunica, MS, *Times-Democrat* 15 Mar. 1979, repr. FN May 1979 p. 18.

28 & 30 April 1979 / Dunn Lake nr Barrière, BC / Tim Meissner (16) / Fishing with friends, saw Bigfoot across lake; returned, saw it again and shot at it (see ch. 8) / Vancouver, WA, *The Columbian* 6, 7, & 9 May 1979; Roseburg, OR, *News Review* 7 May 1979, repr. FN May 1979 p. 20.

April 1979 / Neahkahnie Mountain, Seaside, OR / Monte Kauffman / Saw "great big, man-like ape" about 150 yards away; had dark coat with lighter face and chest / Seaside, OR, *Signal* 5 April 1979.

Late spring 1979 / South Mountain, NC / Fisherman / Saw black shape run into undergrowth; next day shot at same creature / Robert L. Williams, "'Knobby', North Carolina's Bigfoot," *UFO Report* Sept. 1979, p. 27.

8 May 1979 / Arlington, WA / J.J. Senko / Saw 7-9-ft hairy "thing" run fast across Highway 9 / Everett, WA, *Herald* 4 June 1979.

30 May 1979 / US 395 nr Bridgeport, CA / Bill Iffttiger / Truck driver saw 8-ft Bigfoot dash across road / *UFO Report* Nov. 1979, p. 6.

June 1979 / Mayville, MI / Two teenage girls / Saw 7-ft Bigfoot while playing hide-and-seek / Bay City, MI, *Times* 15 June 1979.

June 1979 / Lancaster, CA / Mrs. Shirley DeWolfe & family / Four witnesses saw large hairy creature 7-8 ft tall striding along 140th Street East; similar creature seen in same place a few years earlier / Report from Rich Grumley, noted *Bigfoot Co-op* Oct. 1980 p. 4.

2 July 1979 / Forest Township, Genesee County, MI / Woman / Saw tall, brown creature in swampy area near house / Report by Wayne King of The Michigan Bigfoot Information Center following his investigation.

10 July 1979 / Nr Steinbach, Manitoba / Member of farm family / Saw "11-foot tall" hairy creature outside; next morning found footprints 18 in long / Winnipeg, Manitoba, *Tribune* 12 July 1979, noted *Res Bureaux Bulletin* 49 p. 4.

16 Aug. 1979 / Hoosier National Forest nr Williams, IN / Andy Keith (19) / Saw Bigfoot smelling like strong dead fish cross road; other sightings in area / Indianapolis, IN, *Star* 19 Aug. 1979, repr. FN Sept. 1979 p. 18; report from JG, noted *Bigfoot Co-op* Feb. 1981 p. 2.

Early Sept. 1979 / Nr White House, TN / Bill Cook / Farmer wrestled with slant-eyed Bigfoot which escaped; local reports of animal killings / Milwaukee, WI, *Sentinel* 28 Sept. 1979, repr. FN Nov. 1979 p. 13.

Mid-Sept. 1979 / Big Sioux River nr Bruce, SD / Jeff Anderson (13), Carrie Williams (13), & others / 3-ft, brown creature on 2 legs seen more than once on river bank / Brookings, SD, *Register* 28 Sept. 1979, repr. FN Nov. 1979 p. 14.

Sept. 1979 / Burnt Woods, nr Toledo, OR / Mark Osborne & 4 other hunters / Saw creature with orange-brown hair around camp; found large handprints on truck / Portland, OR, *Oregon Journal* 2 Oct. 1979.

Sept. 1979 / Nr Manchester, IA / Jerry Erwing / Saw 7-8-ft Bigfoot with "topknot" walking bent over / Waterlook, IA, *Courier* 24 Feb. 1980, repr. FN Mar. 1980 p. 18.

12 Oct. 1979 / Nr Webster City, IA / Bryon Davis / At 3:30 am saw 7-ft, reddish-brown Bigfoot in woods. It got up and left, as if disturbed while sleeping / Webster City, IA, *Freeman-Journal* 19 & 30 Oct. 1979, repr. FN Dec. 1979 pp. 18 & 19.

Mid-Oct. 1979 / Little Saskatchewan Indian reserve nr Gypsumville, Manitoba / Clifford & Norman Shorting, Ivor Traverse, David Thompson, & other Indians / Green-eyed, black, 8-ft Bigfoot seen several times on reserve / Winnipeg, Manitoba, *Free Press* 16, 17, & 18 Oct. 1979 & Vancouver, BC, *Province* 18 Oct. 1979, all repr. FN Nov. 1979.

22 Oct. 1979 / Rauville area, nr Watertown, SD / Several / Man and wife saw 5-ft creature with dark red eyes sitting beside Highway 81; other sightings of 4-5-ft, black creature / Norfolk, NE, *Daily News* 24 Oct. 1979, repr. FN Nov. 1979 p. 18; Watertown, SD, *Public Opinion* 22 Oct. 1979, repr. FN Dec. 1979 p. 20.

1 Nov. 1979 / Nr Wheeler, OR / John Parson / Hunter found large footprints; at night saw 7-8-ft Bigfoot with pointed head and no neck standing in moonlight near camper / Report from John Fuhrmann & Peter Guttilla, noted *Bigfoot Co-op* Dec. 1980 p. 3.

15 Nov. 1979 / Minburn, IA / Larry Wilson / Saw dark, hunched Bigfoot in farmyard; officers found prints in grass but no creature / Quincy, IL, *Herald-Whig* 18 Nov. 1979, repr. FN Nov. 1979 p. 18; Des Moines, IA, *Tribune* 16 Nov. 1979, repr. FN Jan. 1980 p. 18; Des Moines, IA, *Register* 17 Nov. 1979, repr. FN Jan. 1980 p. 18.

22 Nov. 1979 / La Grande, WA / - / At least 3 cars stopped on Washington 7 at midnight to watch 9-ft creature on road; had wide shoulders and reddish-brown fur / Tacoma, WA, *News Tribune* 23 Nov. 1979.

14 Dec. 1979 / Nr Rochester, MN / Woman / Saw "ugly" 7-ft Bigfoot in car headlights; it covered its eyes with an arm / Rochester, MN, *Post-Bulletin* 17 Dec. 1979, repr. FN Jan. 1980 p. 18.

Early Jan. 1980 / Adel, IA / Larry Wilson / Farmer went outdoors when dogs barked and saw "hunched over, dark thing" in yard; police found foot-long prints in grass / *Weekly World News* 22 Jan. 1980.

13 Jan. 1980 / Nr Edgewood, IA / Tim BuShaw & friend / Saw 8-ft Bigfoot with "topknot" and long hair within 6 ft of their car / Waterloo, IA, *Courier* 24 Feb. 1980, repr. FN Mar. 1980 p. 18.

15 Jan. 1980 / Nr Manchester, IA / Cyril O'Brien / Railroad engineer on train saw strange creature on all fours eating carcass; 6-toed tracks found in area / Waterloo, IA, *Courier* 24 Feb. 1980, repr. FN Mar. 1980 p. 18.

23 Jan. 1980 / Nevada Test Site, NV / Workman / While driving in desolate nuclear testing ground, saw dark-haired, 6-7-ft Bigfoot walk across road and into sagebrush; no tracks found / Kansas City, MO, *Times* 28 Jan. 1980, repr. FN Feb. 1980 p. 20.

Jan. 1980 / Nashville, TN / Don Roberts / Saw broad-shouldered animal with rubber-like face run through field on two legs / Willow Creek, CA, *Klam-Ity Kourier* 30 Jan. 1980.

3 Feb. 1980 / Nr South Weber, UT / Pauline Markham / Saw black Bigfoot coming down ridge in daylight / Ogden, UT, *Standard-Examiner* 12 Feb. 1980; Salt Lake City, UT, *Deseret News* 12 Feb. 1980, repr. FN Mar. 1980 p. 17.

4 Feb. 1980 / Nr South Weber, UT / Ronald Smith / By moonlight saw Bigfoot in field (see ch. 8) / Ogden, UT, *Standard-Examiner* 12 Feb. 1980; Salt Lake City, UT, *Deseret News* 12 Feb. 1980, repr. FN Mar. 1980 p. 17.

25 Feb. 1980 / Riverdale, UT / Lee Padilla / Tall Bigfoot ran across road (see ch. 8) / Ogden, UT, *Standard-Examiner* 27 Feb. 1980.

1 April 1980 / Boone County, KY / Jackie Jones & David Stulz / Flat-faced, broad-shouldered, 4-ft Bigfoot prowled around mobile home; ran off on 4 legs when Stulz chased it / Covington, KY, *Kentucky Post* 2 April 1980, repr. FN May 1980 p. 18.

Mid-May 1980 / Mount St. Helens, WA / 2 men / While trying to get off mountain after volcanic eruption, saw Bigfoot walk out of forest onto road, look at them, and return to forest / Report from Bob Walls & Peter Guttilla, noted *Bigfoot Co-op* Feb. 1981 p. 7.

9 June 1980 / Scotts Valley, CA / Dave Wilhelm & Ben Lawson / On campsite noticed garbage smell, heard loud footsteps and heavy breathing, saw 12-ft creature in car headlights; next day found footprints / Watsonville, CA, *Register Pajaronian* 17 June 1980, repr. FN Sept. 1980 p. 17.

16 June 1980 / Snow King Mountain, Jackson, WY / Glenn Towner & Robert Goodrich / At 3 am saw 12-ft creature with hunchback, long dark hair, and arms that hung to ground; made a long-drawn-out moan or growl with labored breathing and chased them off the mountain / *Idaho State Journal* 18 June 1980; Idaho Falls, ID, *Post-Register* 18 June 1980, repr. FN Aug. 1980 p. 15.

17 June 1980 / Union County, OH / Patrick Poling / Working in cornfield, saw 7-ft creature walking with bent knees along fence-line (see ch. 8) / Akron, OH, *Beacon Journal* 29 June 1980, repr. FN July 1980 p. 19.

19 June 1980 / Russells Point, OH / Ray Quay / Part-time police officer saw "big and hairy" creature near barn, smelling like "limburger cheese on a hot muffler" / Waukegan, IL, *The News Sun* 26 June 1980.

24 June 1980 / Union County, OH / Mrs. Donna Riegler / Saw Bigfoot lying in road (see ch. 8) / Akron, OH, *Beacon Journal* 29 June 1980, repr. FN July 1980 p. 19.

26 June 1980 / Logan County, OH / Larry Hamey / Working on tractor at night, saw Bigfoot come out of woods towards tractor, then return / Akron, OH, *Beacon Journal* 29 June 1980, repr. FN July 1980 p. 19.

6 July 1980 / Rainier, OR / Bill Leon Buol / Saw dark Bigfoot behind barn at dusk / St. Helens, OR, *The Chronicle* 10 July 1980, repr. FN Aug. 1980 p. 15.

18 July 1980 / Scotch Run Valley, nr Mainville, PA / Rick Knovich / Saw Bigfoot with long black hair in railroad bed by road; it walked towards him and Knovich grabbed gun, forgetting about his camera; creature went into bush as Knovich got out of car / Berwick, PA, *Press-Enterprise* 16 Aug. 1980, repr. FN Oct. 1980 p. 19.

27 July 1980 / Nr Granite Falls, WA / Car passenger / Driving in woods, saw giant gray figure with glowing eyes / Report from Peter Guttilla, noted *Bigfoot Co-op* Oct. 1980 p. 3.

18 Aug. 1980 / Jonestown Mountain nr Berwick, PA / Bill & Tom Talanca / Driving down mountain, saw husky black hairy creature standing in road / Berwick, PA, *Press-Enterprise* 26 Aug. 1980, repr. FN Oct. 1980 p. 19; *Anthropology Newsletter*, Bloomsburg State College, Bloomsburg, PA, vol. 5 no. 3 (Nov.-Dec. 1980) p. 2; investigated by Gary S. Mangiacopra.

28 Aug. 1980 / Nr Grants Pass, OR / Scott Ericson (13) / Saw creature looking like Bigfoot when he went to post letter / Report from John Green/Peter Guttilla, noted *Bigfoot Co-op* Apr. 1981 p. 3.

30 Aug. 1980 / Mine Creek, nr Malad, ID / Clynn Josephson & Brian Belnap / While panning for gold, saw 9-10-ft, long-haired, black Bigfoot / Pocatello, ID, *Idaho State Journal* 11 Sept. 1980, repr. FN Nov. 1980 p. 15.

3 Sept. 1980 / Lake Hughes, nr Palmdale, CA / Clyde Williams / Driver saw black, hairy Bigfoot with whitish hair around shoulders and human-like face; it ran in front of car, then up mountainside / Lancaster, CA, *Ledger-Gazette* 10 Sept. 1980.

4 Oct. 1980 / Maysville, KY / Charles Fulton & Anna Mae Saunders / Saw white Bigfoot in porch (see ch. 8) / Lexington, KY, *Leader* 14 Oct. 1980, & West Palm Beach, FL, *Post* 10 Oct. 1980, both repr. FN Dec. 1980 p. 15.

10 Oct. 1980 / Nr Maysville, KY / Woman / Bigfoot chased her round her car at Central Shopping Center / Lexington, KY, *Leader* 14 Oct. 1980, repr. FN Dec. 1980 p. 15.

10 Oct. 1980 / Fleming County, KY / J.L. Tumey / Bigfoot raided freezer; chased and shot at by Tumey (see ch. 8) / Flemingsburg, KY, *Times-Democrat* 15 Oct. 1980, repr. FN Dec. 1980 p. 18.

Oct. 1980 / Dabney State Park, Sandy, OR / Kay Martin, David Brown, & Claudia Herholz / Teenagers in car saw tall Bigfoot cross road and climb bank / Portland, OR, *Oregon Journal* 7 Oct. 1980, repr. FN Nov. 1980 p. 20.

Oct. 1980 / Sitting Bull Falls, NM / Gene Bryan & Mike Waldrop / While camping with families, heard "loud and horrifying" scream and saw creature standing by tree / Carlsbad, NM, *Current-Argus* 28 Oct. 1980, repr. FN Jan. 1981 p. 20.

Oct. 1980 / Artesia, NM / Marion Dean / Saw black 7-ft Bigfoot with white eyes standing in alley near her apartment / Carlsbad, NM, *Current-Argus* 2 Nov. 1980, repr. FN Mar. 1981 p. 17.

7 Nov. 1980 / Battle Creek, MI / John Pelfrey / Saw three Bigfeet which ran off grunting / Battle Creek, MI, *Enquirer & News* 7 Nov. 1980, repr. FN Jan. 1981 p. 15.

22 Nov. 1980 / Snohomish County, WA / Steve Moro / Saw dark Bigfoot standing by pipeline near creek, then walked away hunched over; had long arms below knees / Report from Linda Williford, noted *Bigfoot Co-op* Feb. 1981 p. 9.

Bibliography

Books

Alley, J. Robert, *Raincoast Sasquatch: The Bigfoot/Sasquatch Records of South-East Alaska, Coastal British Columbia & Northwest Washington from Puget Sound to Yakutat*, Surrey, BC, and Blaine, WA: Hancock House Publishers, 2003

Bayanov, Dmitri, *America's Bigfoot: Fact, Not Fiction*, Moscow, Russia: Crypto-Logos Publishers, 1997

Beck, Fred, *I Fought the Apemen of Mt. St. Helens*, 1967; New Westminster, BC: Pyramid Publications, second printing 1996

Berry, Rick, *Bigfoot on the East Coast*, Stuarts Draft, VA: Rick Berry, 1993

Bindernagel, Dr. John, *North America's Great Ape: The Sasquatch*, Courtenay, BC: Beachcomber Books, 2002

Bord, Janet & Colin, *Alien Animals*, London: Paul Elek, 1980; Harrisburg, PA: Stackpole Books, 1981

—*The Evidence for Bigfoot and Other Man-Beasts*, Wellingborough: Aquarian Press, 1984

Byrne, Peter, *The Search for Big Foot: Monster, Myth or Man?*, Washington: Acropolis Books, 1975; New York: Pocket Books, 1976

311

Clark, Jerome, and Loren Coleman, *Creatures of the Outer Edge*, New York: Warner Books, 1978

Coleman, Loren, *Bigfoot! The True Story of Apes in America*, New York: Paraview Pocket Books, 2003

Coleman, Loren, and Patrick Huyghe, *The Field Guide to Bigfoot, Yeti, and Other Mystery Primates Worldwide*, New York: Avon Books, 1999

Daegling, David J., *Bigfoot Exposed: An Anthropologist Examines America's Enduring Legend*, Lanham, MD: AltaMira Press, 2004

Gordon, David George, *Field Guide to the Sasquatch*, Seattle, WA: Sasquatch Books, 1992

Green, John, *The Sasquatch File*, Victoria, BC: Cheam Publishing, 1973

—*On the Track of the Sasquatch* (incorporating *On the Track of the Sasquatch* and *Year of the Sasquatch*), New York: Ballantine Books, 1973; published individually by Cheam Publishing, BC, 1968 & 1970, and revised editions published 1980 as *On the Track of Sasquatch, Books I and II.*

—*Sasquatch: The Apes Among Us*, Victoria, BC: Cheam Publishing, 1978; Seattle: Hancock House Publishers, 1978

—*The Best of Sasquatch Bigfoot*, Surrey, BC, and Blaine, WA: Hancock House Publishers, 2004

Guttilla, Peter, *The Bigfoot Files*, Timeless Voyager, 2003

Halpin, Marjorie M., and Michael M. Ames (Eds), *Manlike Monsters on Trial: Early Records and Modern Evidence*, Vancouver, BC: University of British Columbia Press, 1980

Hunter, Don, with René Dahinden, *Sasquatch*, Toronto, Ont: McClelland & Stewart, 1973; Scarborough, Ont: New American Library of Canada, 1975; revised edition, McClelland and Stewart, 1993

Johnson, Stan, *Bigfoot Memoirs: My Life with the Sasquatch*, Newberg, OR: Blue Water Press, 1995

Keel, John A., *Strange Creatures from Time and Space*, Greenwich, CT: Fawcett Publications, 1970; London: Neville Spearman, 1975; London: Sphere Books, 1976

Krantz, Grover S., *Big Footprints: A Scientific Inquiry into the Reality of Sasquatch*, Boulder, CO: Johnson Books, 1992

—*Bigfoot Sasquatch Evidence*, Hancock House Publishers, 1999

Long, Greg, *The Making of Bigfoot: The Inside Story*, New York: Prometheus

Books, 2004

Markotić, Vladimir and Grover Krantz (Eds), *The Sasquatch and other Unknown Hominids*, Calgary, Alberta: Western Publishers, 1984

Murphy, Christopher L. (with Joedy Cook and George Clappison), *Bigfoot in Ohio: Encounters with the Grassman*, New Westminster, BC: Pyramid Publications, 1997; revised and updated edition re-titled *Quest for the Grassman, Bigfoot in Ohio*, Surrey, BC, and Blaine, WA: Hancock House Publishers, 2005

Murphy, Christopher L. (in association with John Green and Thomas Steenburg), *Meet the Sasquatch*, Surrey, BC and Blaine, WA: Hancock House Publishers, 2004

Murphy, Daniel W., *Bigfoot in the News* (photocopied press reports), New Westminster, BC: Progressive Research, 1995

Napier, John, Bigfoot: The *Yeti and Sasquatch in Myth and Reality*, London: Jonathan Cape, 1972; London: Abacus Books, 1976; New York: Dutton, 1973

Orchard, Vance, *Bigfoot of the Blues*, Walla Walla, WA: Vance Orchard, 1993

Patterson, Roger, *Do Abominable Snowmen of America Really Exist?*, Yakima, WA: Franklin Press, 1966; revised and updated edition: Roger Patterson and Chris Murphy, *The Bigfoot Film Controversy*, Surrey, BC, and Blaine, WA: Hancock House Publishers, 2005

Perez, Danny, *Big Footnotes: A Comprehensive Bibliography Concerning Bigfoot, the Abominable Snowman, and Related Beings*, Norwalk, CA: D. Perez Publishing, 1988

—*Bigfoot at Bluff Creek*, Norwalk, CA: D. Perez Publishing, 1994; revised edition 2003

Place, Marion T., *Bigfoot All Over the Country*, New York: Dodd, Mead & Company, 1978

Powell, Thom, *The Locals: A Contemporary Investigation of the Bigfoot/Sasquatch Phenomenon*, Surrey, BC and Blaine, WA: Hancock House Publishers, 2003

Pyle, Robert Michael, *Where Bigfoot Walks*, New York: Houghton Mifflin, 1995

Rife, Philip, *Bigfoot Across America*, Writers Club Press, 2000

Sanderson, Ivan T., *Abominable Snowmen: Legend Come to Life*, Philadelphia: Chilton Book Co., 1961; New York: Jove Publications, revised abridgement, 1977

Slate, B. Ann, and Alan Berry, *Bigfoot*, New York: Bantam Books, 1976

Sprague, Roderick, and Grover S. Krantz (Eds), *The Scientist Looks at the Sasquatch*, Moscow, ID: The University Press of Idaho, 1977 (new edition with three new articles published 1979)

Steenburg, Thomas N., *Sasquatch: Bigfoot: The Continuing Mystery* (new edition of *The Sasquatch in Alberta*), Surrey, BC, and Blaine, WA: Hancock House Publishers, 1993

—*In Search of Giants*, Surrey, BC, and Blaine, WA: Hancock House Publishers, 2000

Wasson, Barbara, *Sasquatch Apparitions: A Critique on the Pacific Northwest Hominoid*, Bend, OR: Barbara Wasson, 1979

Wylie, Kenneth, *Bigfoot: A Personal Inquiry into a Phenomenon*, New York: Viking Penguin, 1980

Magazines and Newsletters

Printed magazines are now rare, with all new material being posted onto websites. One newsletter that is still published in printed form, and issued monthly by Daniel Perez, is *Bigfoot Times*. This is available from him at 10926 Milano Avenue, Norwalk, CA 90650. The web address is www.bigfoottimes.net and the e-mail address is perez@worldnet.att.net.

Another surviving newsletter is *Bigfoot Co-op*, which has been published for 25 years, and its editor Constance Cameron still publishes six issues a year. Contact her at 14602 Montevideo Drive, Whittier, CA 90605 – e-mail CCCameron50@aol.com.

Bigfoot/Sasquatch reports can also be found in the monthly *Forteana News*, available from Lucius Farish at 2 Caney Valley Drive, Plumerville, AR 72127-8725 – e-mail ufons@webtv.net.

The Ohio Bigfoot Research Team's *Bigfoot Newsletter* is issued monthly by e-mail. Information at www.geocities.com/squatch_45694/news.html.

Bigfoot Sources Online

A large number of websites provide information on all aspects of Bigfoot research, together with up-to-date sightings, photographs, and other illustrations, and commentary from a variety of viewpoints. Rather than providing a long list of web addresses, which in any case may become outdated quickly, we are giving details of just a few websites which are useful jumping-off points:

www.bigfootencounters.com or www.n2.net/prey/bigfoot: Both these addresses reach Bigfoot Encounters which gives links to more than 70 other sites, and also has "videos, images, and sounds."

www.bfro.net: The Bigfoot Field Researchers Organization.

www.internationalbigfootsociety.com: The International Bigfoot Society site lists over 50 links.

www.lorencoleman.com: Cryptozoologist Loren Coleman's website includes Bigfoot information.

www.oregonbigfoot.com: Oregon Bigfoot with sighting reports and links to other sites.

www.pibburns.com/cryptozo.htm: Philip R. "Pib" Burns' Cryptozoology Web Ring has links to more than 50 Bigfoot sites.

www.rfthomas.clara.net/bigfoot.html: Bigfoot: Fact or Fantasy?

www.texasbigfoot.com: Texas Bigfoot Research Center has over 70 links to other Bigfoot sites.

Index

Easterville, Manitoba, 250, 254, 260,
269
Eaton, OH, 151, 292
Eatonville, WA, 291
Ebling, Allan, 259, 265
Edgewood, IA, 307
Edison, GA, 232
Edwards, Red, 229
Edwardsville, IL, 271
Eel River, CA, 56, 231
Effingham, IL, 224
Elfers, FL, 245, 246, 247
Elizabeth Lake, UT, 293
Elizabeth, IL, 227
Elkhorn Buttes, SD, 156, 297, 298
Ellington farm, 176
Ellisburgh, NY, 5, 218
Elsie, OR, 242
Elwood, IN, 294
Emerson, Jerry, 280
Emert, Randy, 265
Enfield Horror, xii
Enfield, IL, 269
Engels, Richard, 269, 278
Engen, Floyd, 112, 254
Ennis, Don, 259
Epley, Kevin, 297
Ericson, Scott, 309
Erlinger, Willie, 226
Erwing. Jerry, 306
Estacada, OR, 72, 102, *103*, 129, 240,
248, 249, 251, 269
Eugene, OR, 265, 266
Eureka, CA, 56, 128, 231
Eureka, NV, 236
Eureka, OR, 269
Evans, Stanley, 149
Evans, WA, 252
Evart, MI, 303, 304
Everett, Bob, 232
Ewalt, Joseph, 22, 221
Exeter Watchman, 5
Faircloth, Larry, 259
Fall River Mills, CA, 230
Farmer City, IL, xi, 259
Farrell, George, 221
Farrell, Lisa, 288
Fast Horse, Myron, 296

Faulkner, Charles, 184, 185
Fawn Grove, MD, 299
Fayette County, PA, xi
Feather River. CA, 255
Fergeson, Mr. and Mrs., 237
Ferral, Jack, 220
Ferrante's Quarry, NJ, 288
Ferrier, Gordon, 253
Ferry County, WA, 265
Field, Buck, 139, 277
Fife Heights, WA, 255
Figg, Becky, 258
Figg, James, 265
Fillmore, CA, 241
film, 90–102, 176, 186, 190, 196, 247,
283
Fish Lake, CA, 249
Fish Lake, IN, 6, 218
Fishermen, Tim, 265
Fishermen, V.M., 265
Fitzgerald, Mr., 18, 220
Fitzgerald, Steve and Jean, 278
Flagstaff, AZ, 47, 226, 262
Flanders, Gorden, 178, 179
Fleetwood, Roy, 251
Fleming County, KY, 169, 309
Flenniken, Craig, 274
Fletcher, Albert, 37, 225
Flintville, TN, 147, 286
Flomaton, AL, 300
Flood, BC, 232
Flood, Charles, 225
Floodwood, MN, 251
Florence, OR, 276
Florida, xv, 136, 140, 141, 142, 149,
153, 196, 202, 203, 210, 230, 233,
240, 244, 245, 246, 247, 256, 257,
262, 263, 264, 276, 278, 280, 281,
282, 284, 287, 288, 290, 291, 292,
293, 296, 298
Flower Lake, MS, 164, 305
Flowers, Edward, 260
Fluorescent Freddie, 242
Followell, Larry, 279
Fontana, CA, 87, 244, 245
Footedale, PA, 258
footprints, 7, 8, 14, 21, 26, 28, 31, 34,
35, 36, 41, 52, 67, 69, 73, 77, 80, 82,

Janet & Colin Bord

Janet & Colin Bord met and married early in the 1970s. Colin was a freelance photographer at that time, Janet was a freelance publishing editor, and they lived in London, England. They pooled their skills and began writing books together, their earliest success being *Mysterious Britain*, which was followed by several more exploring the mysteries, folklore, and antiquities of the British landscape. During this time they moved from the city into the peaceful countryside of the Welsh borderlands. Also in the 1970s, they began to collect photographs and illustrations of mysteries such as ghosts, monsters, and UFOs, and the Fortean Picture Library came into existence, supplying illustrations for use in magazines, books, and TV programs around the world. During the 1980s, now living in a large remote house in the hills of North Wales, they wrote several books on a wide range of Fortean topics, including *Alien Animals, Bigfoot Casebook, Modern Mysteries of Britain, Modern Mysteries of the World* (published in the USA as *Unexplained Mysteries of the 20th Century*), *Life Beyond Planet Earth?,* and *The World of the Unexplained* (showcasing the most interesting photographs in their pictorial archive). In more recent years Janet Bord has written several books including *Footprints in Stone: Imprints of Giants, Heroes, Holy People, Devils, Monsters and Supernatural Beings, Fairies: Real Encounters with Little People,* and *The Traveller's Guide to Fairy Sites,* and is currently writing two books on the holy wells of Britain and Ireland.